STAINFORTH
TEL: 841239

11/07

- 9 APR 2

EDLINGTON
01302 73

8/05
2 9 AUG

0 1 AUG 2

15 OCT 20

- 7 MAY 2

DONCAS

DONCASTER LIBRARY SERVICE

30122 03125516 5

DRIBBLE!

Also by Harry Pearson

The Far Corner
Racing Pigs and Giant Marrows
A Tall Man in a Low Land
Around the World by Mouse
Achtung Schweinehund!

DRIBBLE!

The Unbelievable
Football Encyclopaedia

Harry Pearson

Little, Brown

LITTLE, BROWN

First published in Great Britain in 2007 by Little, Brown

Copyright © Harry Pearson 2007

The moral right of the author has been asserted.

All rights reserved.
No part of this publication may be reproduced, stored in a
retrieval system, or transmitted, in any form or by any means,
without the prior permission in writing of the publisher, nor be
otherwise circulated in any form of binding or cover other
than that in which it is published and without a similar
condition including this condition being imposed
on the subsequent purchaser.

A CIP catalogue record for this book
is available from the British Library.

ISBN 978-0-316-02794-6

Typeset in Baskerville by M Rules
Printed and bound in Great Britain by
Clays Ltd, St Ives plc

Little, Brown
An imprint of
Little, Brown Book Group
100 Victoria Embankment
London EC4Y 0DY

An Hachette Livre UK Company

www.littlebrown.co.uk

ACKNOWLEDGEMENTS

The unbelievable material in these pages previously appeared in different form in the *Guardian* and *When Saturday Comes*; my thanks to both publications for allowing it to be reproduced here. I would also like to thank Andy Lyons at WSC and Ben Clissitt at the *Guardian* for giving me a platform to witter from for so many years, and all the editors and sub-editors who have laboured to turn my work into something recognisable as English.

HARRY PEARSON

DONCASTER LIBRARY AND INFORMATION SERVICE	
30122031255165	
Bertrams	28.10.07
B	£9.99
796.334 PEA	

- A -

Acting Managers

We live in a TV age and so it is hardly surprising that more and more football managers are tailoring their performances during games for the benefit of the cameras.

It all began with Sir Alex Ferguson. The Manchester United manager's grim touchline behaviour was widely blamed for his team's failure to win the title in 1991–92, the prevailing view being that his clearly visible tension transmitted itself to his players. Since then the Scot has rarely been seen on television without a benign smile on his purple face. Many viewers think this is even scarier than the tortured grimace he used to wear, seeing it as the most sinister display of jollity since the child catcher turned up offering free sweets in *Chitty Chitty Bang Bang*. The results speak against them, however.

Ferguson's success has led other coaches to follow in his footsteps. Nowadays they seem increasingly to be acting on a cue from the producer. They give us pensive, elated, stoic and determined-man-of-vision-staring-at-destiny-while-sucking-on-a-pen-top. Not once are they caught looking bewildered, or staring serenely into space with the happy expression of a bloke who has just remembered the names of the key personnel in *Goober and the Ghost Chasers*. Never do they sit, as poor old Don Revie used to, with their hands stuffed deep in their pockets, knees pressed firmly together and the pained, shifty look of someone who is deeply regretting having that extra cup of tea before coming to the memorial service. They have abandoned Ron Saunders in favour of Robert De Niro.

Acting Players

Footballers have generally rejected attempts to lure them into making feature films. This is not through any shyness, but because they have great artistic integrity and are rarely offered the sort of challenging parts they crave. Jimmy Greaves, for instance, infamously turned down the part of Jimmy Greaves in *Goal*, the official film of the 1966 World Cup, because he had his heart set on playing the Geoff Hurst role. Similarly when John Huston was casting *Escape to Victory* Glenn Hoddle stubbornly insisted that he would not play Glenn Hoddle because he 'didn't want it turning into a typecasting situation'.

'Glenn was really interested in exploring his craft, pushing the envelope, challenging himself,' the theatrical agent Theo Cravat explained later. 'He had identified the role he wanted in the movie but unfortunately the producer was adamant that the part of Pelé was earmarked for Pelé. It was typical Hollywood – a safety-first choice.

'They offered us the part of John Wark instead, but we thought it was totally underwritten. The scriptwriters had never really got past the "no front teeth, totally incomprehensible accent" aspect of the character. Glenn suggested a few changes: putting the teeth back, and giving John Wark a smart yet modern haircut, a set of strong personal beliefs based on the lyrics of Supertramp and a light, pleasant singing voice, but the director said that would make him too much like the Russell Osman character (a role which, incidentally, was originally promised to Jeremy Irons), and besides, by that time Glenn had got his Pelé head on and there was no chance of him getting it off in time. Could Glenn Hoddle have played John Wark as

Pelé? Yes, I believe he could, but it was too dangerous artistically and so they didn't give him the chance.

'I saw the film when it came out and, yes, Pelé did a decent job as Pelé, but I still feel that Glenn would have made it more believable, given it more dimensions. Later, Jean Luc Godard told Glenn that if he had been French they'd have built a movie around him – *Pauline at the Beach* in all probability.'

Animals

Alnwick Town chairman John Common had a peculiar sense of humour. His idea of a practical joke was to leave an animal carcass ('The smallest a mole, the largest a sheep') in the visitors' dressing room.

In any other walk of life this might have marked John Common out as being as mad as a bag of cheese, but in the world of football his antics are frankly not that unusual, even leaving aside Barcelona fans' attempt to pelt Luis Figo with a boar's head, or those El Salvador supporters who take it as their patriotic duty to bombard visiting goalkeepers with dead cats.

Ten years ago, for example, Eastbourne United officials were shocked to find a pig's head nailed to the front of their dug-out before a Unijet Sussex County League clash with Worthing United. It turned out to be the handiwork of Worthing defender Dave Clarke. Clarke, a part-time butcher, explained, 'It is something I have been doing as a laugh for some years. Unfortunately on this occasion people didn't see the funny side.' Miserable buggers, eh?

Dave Clarke would undoubtedly have found more sympathy for his hilarious offal-related japes in Norway. In 2003 Tromsø were battling desperately against relegation when a supporter, Jarle Johansen, offered to kill a goat in the centre circle before the team's final game of the season against Lyn. 'Can you imagine how much fun it would be,' Johansen said, 'if I was allowed to slaughter the goat, then Tromsø crushed Lyn?' Whether he followed this statement with a burst of maniacal laughter is not recorded. Amazingly instead of phoning the local funny farm and alerting them to the presence of a man who was himself clearly several points short of safety, Tromsø's directors said they would 'consider the proposal'. Eventually, after careful deliberation, they rejected it. The goat was spared and, happily, Tromsø stayed up.

Football's animal magic comes in many forms. In the heady days of the 1970s Carlisle United used to place a stuffed fox (perhaps female, possibly called 'Olga' – debate still rages from Longtown to Penrith) in the centre circle before home games. As prematch entertainment this may seem somewhat dull, but it sufficed in Cumbria, a place once summed up by former Carlisle star Stan Bowles with the immortal words, 'Freezing cold and sheep shit in the garden.'

Luckily the animal doesn't have to be dead to take part in the fun of match day. Few who have visited Edgar Street will forget the sight of the Hereford bull being paraded around at half-time. It certainly is a magnificent beast; powerful, muscular and considerably lighter on its feet than Michael Ricketts.

In a variation on the bull idea, a few years back a Bolivian club side took to parading a vicuña around the pitch before games. After a while the fans got the idea into their heads that this relative of the llama was psychic and communicated news of forthcoming victories by smiling. A long-faced vicuña signalled certain defeat and inevitably sparked a stampede for the exits. Eventually the club, mindful of the effects this grumpy beast was having on gate receipts, got rid of it. Nobody knows what became of the animal, though suspicion remains that it is probably sitting on the pools panel.

Arturo Anteater

In the late 1990s Israeli super-agent **Pini Colada** attempted to persuade clubs that due to the escalating cost of indigenous players they would be better advised spending their money on foreign imports. 'Here is your choice,' he told interviewer Frank Gutt in 1998, 'you can have Robbie Fowler for £12 million and £50,000 a week in wages, or you can have Arturo the Giant Anteater on a free transfer from the Argentinian pampas, and all he wants is clean straw, a warm burrow and his own termite mound.' Asked if the anteater was any good, Colada replied, 'He unnerves defences.' Pressed on whether he believed Arturo would unnerve tough British defenders such as Neil Ruddock, he responded, 'I don't care if you are Neil Ruddock, Vinnie Jones, Julian Dicks or whoever. If you have got a shaggy South American with a three-foot-long sticky tongue stood behind you, you are going to be unnerved.' Colada also represented a number of other top animals, though he refused to deal with herbivores, believing that they 'lacked heart'. This opinion was proved conclusively when Bon Bon, a red squirrel Colada had sent on trial to Leeds United (claiming that 'with his size, agility, speed and ginger hair he is the obvious successor to Gordon Strachan'), ran up a floodlight pylon during a reserve match at Barnsley and refused to come down until the crowd had gone home.

Antocliché

The antocliché is football punditry's equivalent of the antonym. Sadly even masters of English such as Lee Dixon rarely employ it. This is a pity since it would be nice to hear every once in a while of an unnatural goalscorer, or to listen as a studio expert reacts to a sliced volley that sailed over the bar like a helium-filled balloon by saying, 'Oh dear, and this boy certainly has got a savoury right foot.' It would be gratifying to hear a pundit rubbish a Kaka tap-in with the words 'And if he hadn't been Brazilian we'd have stopped talking about that long before the pub shut', and explain the revival in fortunes of a previously floundering club with a quick 'In the past fortnight the word coming out of the club is that the manager finally found the dressing room.' This latter comment would, of course, be followed swiftly by a reminder of what had gone on over the previous six months, an arched eyebrow and the words 'But what the supporters have to remember, Gabby, is that a bad manager doesn't become a good manager overnight. Though, to be fair, in this game you're only as poor as your last result.'

Aqsaqtuk

A type of football played by the indigenous Inuit of Baffin Island, Aqsaqtuk utilises a caribou-hide ball stuffed with moss and is played on a pitch that can be anything up to ten miles in length. The most singular feature of the game, however, is that it is played between mixed-sex teams divided along marital lines: couples play singletons. The effects of this are easy to imagine. The married team argue among themselves about who last cleaned the toilet while the singles worry that passing the ball too often to one particular team-mate might be construed as an invitation to intimacy. As a result most moves break down in a wave of paranoia, bitterness and cries of 'Admit it, you've always resented my creativity', and a dull 0–0 stalemate is the usual outcome.

Arithmetic

In 2006 the G-14 group of clubs announced a compromise proposal to Fifa's rules limiting the number of teams in Europe's top divisions. 'The Group of fourteen has eighteen members, so why shouldn't a sixteen-club top flight consist of twenty teams?' asked G-14's general manager Thomas Kurth rhetorically. 'We believe that if football operated according to this new 14–18 numerical system in which one unit represents 1.285, it would solve many problems. For example, Sepp Blatter could impose his limit of a maximum of forty-five games per season and still leave us free to play fifty-eight. Of course, people will say it flies in the face of logic, but you must remember: football is bigger than the laws of mathematics.'

Arts

In 2004 Tony Adams was made patron of the Young Writers Festival at the Royal Court Theatre. Doubters questioned the former Arsenal centre-half's qualifications for the post, but given most young playwrights' obsession with savagery, lunacy and dysfunction, spending your formative years in close proximity to Bob Wilson was surely preparation aplenty.

At the time many within the game hoped that Adams's appointment would be the first of many in the arts for retired British defenders. Our nation's artists have always been eager to acknowledge the inspiration they draw from a well-drilled and coldly brutal defensive unit. Unfortunately arts administrators have tended steadfastly to ignore the contribution that full-backs and stoppers can make to the cultural life of the nation. Instead of seeking direction from strapping, raw-boned men with so much scar tissue their faces look like they're made of cooked pasta, administrators have become mesmerised by flair players such as Pat Nevin, Chris Waddle and Nicolas Serota.

It is testament to the durability of this remarkable prejudice in artistic circles that Adams was the first robust English clogger to scale such heights since another Highbury man, Peter Storey, briefly took charge at Glyndebourne Opera House during the 1974–75 season.

Storey was a fellow of rugged virtues who spent his spare time working for a North Sea oil company. As a drill bit. His other off-the-field activities included a brush with the Obscene Publications Squad over some creative Continental material that was alleged to have wormed its way mysteriously into the tyre of a lorry that was attempting to enter Britain.

Critics are still divided over the exact worth of Storey's theatrical legacy, though few would disagree that his decision to mix the classics with more modern works such as Benjamin Britten's *Billy Budd* and Jens Bumpsen's *Danish Farm Girls Go Dutch III* was a challenging, at times almost cathartic, experience for the picnicking opera-goers.

Those observers who always felt that having a burly centre-back pacing up and down the galleries and rehearsal rooms of Britain barking out encouraging words ('Let's get up their arses', 'Channels, channels', 'Funnel him', 'Let's not let the feeling of alienation drift into the comfort zone of simple loneliness'), or sticking the occasional elbow in to prevent the sort of costly loss of context that can lead to a slide into self-referential kitsch, were convinced that Adams's appointment would mark a sea change in policy among the arts establishment when it comes to 'the big lads at the back'.

Glenn Hoddle once said that 'it is easier to destroy a work of art than to create one' (proof positive that he has never tried to set light to a Pink Floyd album), but destruction and creation are two sides of the same mattress. 'If the Royal Court had room for Tony Adams, surely,' one columnist asked, 'there must be space at the Tate Modern for Steve Bould?' The call went unanswered, alas.

In Europe things have generally been handled differently. On the Continent cultural institutions seeking reinvigoration traditionally look to the earthy, combative skills of uncompromising central defenders and obdurate man-markers. One thinks of Andoni 'The Butcher of Bilbao' Goicoechea's successful spell as curator at the Prado in Madrid (a post for which he was selected, incidentally, after it was revealed that in a glass case in his sitting room he keeps the boots he was wearing when he snapped Diego Maradona's ankle – a witty echo of the work of Marcel Duchamps and Mike Doyle); or German hardman Jürgen Kohler's magical period at Bayreuth during which he proved conclusively that lack of pace is no handicap when it comes to directing Wagner. Although his decision to have Siegfried's cloak of obscurity made in the colours of Manchester United did lead to an unsavoury row with Sir Alex Ferguson.

Of course things have not always worked out. The appointment of Juventus's Claudio Gentile as artistic director of La Scala is the example usually cited by those who feel that the creative arts and the back four should never mix.

Gentile was noted for his gritty style (though he also had his sensitive side: he once sued a newspaper in Rome for describing him as 'a barbarian' and received a large financial settlement plus the right to burn down the Colosseum and carry off as many local women as he could lift) and it was believed that the Milan opera house would benefit from a few clattering challenges, the odd bit of shirt-ripping and the occasional grabbing of a star performer's vitals during set pieces.

Alas, things went wrong when Claudio insisted on rewriting *La Bohème*, replacing 'Your Tiny Hand is Frozen' with an aria of his own composition, 'Your Weedy Shin is Broken.' The

Milanese audience, who had wanted Giuseppe Bergomi and his quizzical eyebrows all along, was not impressed. As one critic noted, 'Gentile's roughness is nowhere near ironic enough for clever people like me to enjoy.'

– B –

Backing

In football backing comes in a variety of forms, but generally it is something a manager awards a current player because he has no money to buy anyone better.

fearing a Backlash

When a team meets Manchester United or Arsenal after they have been knocked out of Europe or been beaten at home by Portsmouth the underdogs unsurprisingly fear a backlash. This thunderous force is generated by the powerful defence mechanisms of these giant clubs, which absorb any attack, multiply it and then turn it back on the enemy like the force-field of a spaceship piloted by hyper-intelligent creatures with massive brains that throb like toads. Usually this backlash simply results in the destruction of lesser vessels such as West Brom, but what if Arsenal were to meet Manchester United after both sides had suffered humiliating early exits from the Champions League at the hands of opposition from Eastern Europe? Some scientists believe that the combined force of both backlashes coming together at the Emirates or Old Trafford could produce an explosion similar to that of a hundred-megaton nuclear bomb. However, other experts believe that if two backlashes of equal force meet they will simply cancel one another out, leading to football's equivalent of the bursting of a damp paper bag – a dull 0–0 draw.

Backside

Top strikers such as Michael Owen or Peter Crouch may go through a period when they are unable to score, but the experts assure us that all they need is for one to go in off their backsides and the goals will flow again. It is, of course, a confidence thing. A forward's goals arrive down a complicated series of tubes buried deep in his subconscious. These pipelines can easily become furred up or clogged, especially if he has been forced to feed off scraps. The only way to clear the obstruction is to force a strike through via the backside, the blockages are cleared and the goals come whooshing out again in a big rush.

Ball Factor

During the opening round of matches at every World Cup since time immemorial one question has been raised more than any other: 'How big a factor will the ball be?' From kick-off until midway through the group stage people ask this over and over again, usually with the furrowed brow and earnest intonation of Garth Crooks approaching a carefully prepared pun. Many newcomers to what Pelé once memorably dubbed 'A big load of hype over some sweaty men running around to no good purpose' will think that in a game called foot*ball* the ball will always be of considerable importance. But that is only because they have never played in a Sunday-morning pub match, or watched Blackburn Rovers.

According to England's Paul Robinson, the +Teamgeist ball

used in Germany 2006 was 'goalkeeper unfriendly'. People would have been more likely to take the Spurs keeper's complaint seriously were it not for the fact that goalkeepers say the same thing about every ball in every World Cup tournament. This is because as far as goalkeepers are concerned the ball is always unfriendly. It is the enemy, the source of all his or her woes and fears. When an outfield player looks at a football he sees a football. When a goalkeeper looks at a football he sees humiliation, Danny Baker clips videos and his team-mates standing with their hands on their hips staring at him and slowly shaking their heads as the opposition jubilantly pile on top of one another over by the corner flag.

As far as goalkeepers are concerned the ball is too small, too light and too fast. For goalkeepers the ideal ball would be one of those great big red ones they encourage women to use as part of natural childbirth. Preferably filled with cement and pinioned to the centre circle by ten yards of steel cable.

The goalkeepers' complaints about the exciting new marketing opportunity – sorry, World Cup match ball – appear a clear case of what experts term the Trueman Paradox. This old philosophical gambit is named after the great Yorkshire grumbler F.S. Trueman, who regularly claimed on *Test Match Special* that due to changes in the laws of cricket, batting and bowling were now far, far easier than they were 'in my day'. Yet since cricket is a contest between bowler and batsman it would surely follow that winning it could not possibly be easier for both of them. Or could it?

In the case of the World Cup ball, if it is impossible to predict its flight it is surely just as difficult for the outfield player to aim his shot accurately as it is for the goalkeeper to save it. After all, a bullet that veers randomly must be a hindrance to the marksman.

That at least would have appeared a reasonable assumption. But when the contest got underway in Germany the

+Teamgeist proved to be a very different beast from previous problem balls such as the Questra, Tricolore and Fevernova. When Germany's Philipp Lahm struck the opening goal of the competition the prevailing view among the pundits in the BBC studio was that 'He didn't put any curl on it, but it curled into the goal.'

This suggested something truly impressive from the designers of the fourteen-panel rounder-than-ever-before orb, a ball that not only swung both ways unbidden, but swung both ways unbidden *towards the back of the net!* This, in other words, was a smart ball, one that homed in on the old onion bag like a racing pigeon seeking its roost. No wonder the custodians loathed it so. Oddly, though, while the ball seemed smart when struck by Germans, Italians, Argentinians or Brazilians it remained resolutely stupid when kicked by Frank Lampard.

Banksy's Law

Named in honour of the late Minister for Sport, Culture and Self-Publicity, Tony Banks. In 2004 Mr Banks announced that he would press for legislation to stop football falling into the hands of the wrong sort of people. Under 'Banksy's Law' the honesty, integrity and probity of anyone wishing to take over a football club would be thoroughly investigated and if they were found to have any they'd immediately be barred from buying it.

Banners

A feature of football, particularly FA Cup Finals, in the 1970s and 1980s, banners were traditionally painted on a bed sheet and held above their heads by two men in tank tops. They usually came in three forms: celebratory ('Norman Bites Yer Legs'), humorous ('Currie Gives Tottenham The Runs') and rude about Jimmy Hill.

Banter

Speaking on his retirement, Neil 'Razor' Ruddock voiced an opinion often heard from footballers: 'After all the years I've been coming into a football ground and sharing a lot of laughs and banter with thirty or forty lads, I can't see me staying home with the old lady and going shopping at Lakeside every day.'

At the time some felt that Mrs 'Razor' Ruddock (or 'Ladyshave' as she is known) might help her man a bit by gradually weaning the burly hoofer off the life he once knew. Before one of those feared shopping trips, for example, she might pace about the front room, head-butt the sideboard a few times and yell, 'You know what those other people who are going to be at Lakeside this afternoon are doing now, Neil? They're laughing at you. They're saying you've lost it. They're saying you're old and fat and couldn't find your way across the car park and into the soft furnishings department of BHS even if me and Robbie Savage were pushing you in a wheelbarrow. Are you going to let them go on laughing? Or are you going to ram it so far down their throats they'll have to sit on the khazi if they want to giggle?'

Using role-play techniques she might encourage Razor to treat the queue at Sainsbury's cold-meat counter as if it was a crowded penalty area, knock over a couple of sales staff in Diesel to 'let them know he was there', and engage in a quick bit of 'handbags' with one of the women who spray you with scent whenever you walk through the cosmetics section of a department store.

Experts, however, suggested that even such tough love would not be enough. Nor, they said, would using the PFA's special new range of products designed to help retired players – banter patches and bit-of-stick-from-the-lads inhalers – be much help. Because the atmosphere in a football dressing room has been scientifically proven to be one of the most addictive substances known to man. One whiff of it and most players are hooked for life.

This was not always the case, of course. Half a century ago the dressing rooms at British football grounds were very different. The maximum wage, brutal tackling and the fact that manly pranks such as putting a pound of chopped liver in a team-mate's jock-strap had been taken away and melted down as part of the war effort created an environment few men relished. As a result players were happy to retire and enter the altogether merrier world of the tobacconists shop, the news-agents, or, in the case of England full-back Ray Wilson, the funeral parlour.

In the late-sixties, though, football was drawn in by the swinging style of the times. Players started hanging out with pop stars such as Eric Clapton and Esther and Abi Ofarim at fashionable nitespots like Mansfield's Club Rum-Baba. Inevitably many of them began to experiment with mood-altering substances.

'I don't know who it was,' one observer of the scene during those heady days recalled later, 'Hendrix or the bloke from The Barron Knights who looked like he was wearing a stocking mask, but at some point one Saturday night at the Twisting Blister in Seven Sisters I remember somebody turned Big Terry Hennessey on to the idea of having a laugh. I could see Terry, who was very much a straight-down-the-line eight-pints-and-a-quick-exchange-of-blows-with-Alan-Gilzean sort of guy, was nervous about the notion. But once he got into it he was soon chuckling away like a maniac at anybody who did a Norman Wisdom impression.'

While some scientists still express concern about the long-term psychological effects having a laugh can have on footballers, most people now accept that in moderation it is relatively harmless. The real problem is that it can, and so very often does, lead users to experiment with more dangerous substances.

Such was the case in the 1980s when a new powerful form of having a laugh began to appear in British dressing rooms. Craic was brought into the country from Dublin using mules (or sling-back sandals, if no mules were available).

Today much of the craic that finds its way into dressing rooms comes not direct from the well-organised cartels of Galway and Kilkenny, but is bought 'on the street' from people in Burberry baseball caps. 'It's not the craic itself, but the stuff the dealers mix it with that does the damage,' one expert told BBC's *Football Fracas*. 'They're unscrupulous. They'll cut the craic with anything that looks a bit like it in order to increase their profit margins.'

The effects on users can be traumatic. Last year several players at a leading Second Division side suffered severe psychological damage after using street craic. When the substance was analysed it proved to contain just 25 per cent pure craic, the rest being a potentially lethal cocktail of *6–0–6* and *Parliamentary Question Time*. 'It was horrible,' recalled a teammate. 'One minute the lads were the life and soul of the dressing room, putting rude words to "Simply the Best" and wee-ing into the tea urn and the next one of them started talking in this terrible nasal whine and saying, "The referee at today's match, Alan, I've gotta say he was taking the Michael." Then the others all jumped to their feet, waving their shin-pads in the air and shouting, "Resign! Resign!" It fair made my hair stand on end.'

Keith Beast

Keith Beast burst like a blister on to the football scene in the late 1950s. Long-haired, scruffy and prone to sitting cross-legged on the edge of the penalty area banging his bongos and swaying about self-consciously, he was dubbed 'the fifth Beat' by the press because he shared the same aims, philosophy and cavalier attitude to personal hygiene as Ginsberg, Corso, Kerouac and Tommy Lawrence.

Ingmar Bergman

Swedish film director. His masterpiece *The Seventh Shirt* featured a famous scene in which Denis Law plays a game of three-and-in against Death, the contest ending anticlimactically when the Grim Reaper is sent for an early bath after quite literally scything down the Manchester United forward.

Bigness

Sam Allardyce is known throughout the game as Big Sam. England boss Steve McClaren on the other hand is never referred to as Big Steve. Yet keen observers will have noticed that in terms of height and build there is not much to choose between the pair. The fact is that while the former Middlesbrough manager is big he is not Big in a football sense. In football, Bigness is more than just size.

Arsène Wenger is taller than Allardyce, indeed he is also taller than those two other football Biggies Joe Jordan and Ron Atkinson, but even if the Arsenal manager ballooned up to twenty stone he would still never be Big Arsène. Part of that is down to his character, part to his place of birth. Some believe it is almost impossible for anybody who speaks a romance language ever to be Big in the British sense (That Felipe Scolari has managed it is testimony to the hours the Brazilian has spent eradicating even the faintest physical or emotional trace of his native land from his person. As a result when you look at the Portugal manager you don't think, Samba, you think, Punch-up at a Durham wedding).

Those who communicate in more robust northern tongues can manage it, but they have to work extra hard. Peter Schmeichel is big, as the late Ron Pickering would doubtless have put it, 'in every sense of the word'. But then as the BBC pundit never tires of telling Gary Lineker, part of the art of goalkeeping is 'making yourself big', so he has an advantage over other candidates. The Dane has also shied away from the ultimate test of Bigness. It is all very easy being Big up in the commentary box or the stands. Being Big in the dug-out is a different matter. Of European coaches possibly only Guus Hiddink has the necessary blend of stature and down-to-earth belligerence to achieve that.

The Blunderkind

The Blunderkind is an intriguing variation on **The Robbo**. He is a player who is picked not for his ability, but for his lack of it. Why? Because these days the game is all about psychology and what could be more uplifting to your average footballer than the certain knowledge that no matter how bad a game he is having there is someone on his team who is guaranteed to be playing far worse than him? If you want to feel tall stand next to a midget.

The importance of The Blunderkind to the mental balance of the side first became apparent in Argentina in 1978 when César Luis Menotti took the pressure off key players such as

Ossie Ardiles and Mario Kempes by picking Alberto Tarantini. Tarantini was a rock at the heart of the Argentinian defence, though only in the sense that he was large, immobile and it hurt if you kicked him. Yet his hairy, hapless barbarism gave his team-mates the confidence and freedom to go out and play.

Despite Tarantini's success The Blunderkind did not really establish himself until twenty years later. In France 1998 we had a final in which Mario Zagalo of Brazil attempted to lighten the weight of expectation on his players by employing centre-half Júnior Baiano. Watching Baiano try to trap the ball was to be put in mind of a pantomime cow attempting to free its foot from a bucket. He was blessed with the sense of balance of a *Daily Mail* editorial on asylum seekers. He had a trial with Hansa Rostock and they rejected him. Yet what a job he did for his team! Because with him beside them Rivaldo and Co. could express themselves without fear, knowing that whatever sort of a mess they made everybody would be too busy marvelling at Baiano's ineptitude to notice it.

Júnior might have won the World Cup for Brazil, had not Aimé Jacquet responded brilliantly to the threat with a twin-pronged crap attack of his own. Not content with Christian Karembeu – nicknamed 'Mad Dog', though during his time at Middlesbrough the only sort of insane hound he resembled was one that had just been shot with a tranquilliser gun – Jacquet also fielded Stephane Guivarc'h up front. The striker's name means 'swift stallion' but he played more like a knackered donkey. Between them the pair smothered Baiano's naive haplessness beneath a blanket of carefully prepared lead-booted idiocy. Guivarc'h's contribution in particular was priceless. The French have never truly replaced him. Proof is to be found in the fact that since the banana-footed Breton departed, Thierry Henry has never again played quite so well for Les Bleus.

Boasting

In 2005 tabloid newspapers revealed that many top young stars of the Premiership liked to engage in 'the disgusting practice' known as 'boasting'. 'Basically they pick on a girl in a nightclub and then two or more players swank away in either ear until she faints from boredom', a source was quoted as saying. Called upon to comment, George Best confessed, 'I was a serial bragger who showed off in front of three Miss Worlds,' but added that 'when it came to swaggering I never needed help from anyone. Though if any of my Northern Ireland team-mates wanted to hide in a cupboard and watch the maestro in action then that was a different matter, obviously.'

Bollocks

Testicles play an important part in determining success in football. At the start of the 2003–04 season, for example, Sunderland's captain Jason McAteer observed, 'We're going to have to grow an extra pair of bollocks if we're going to get promoted this year.' The Irishman plainly didn't regard such orchital generation as beyond the capabilities of his team-mates and it must therefore be concluded that footballers can sprout a fresh set of testicles with the same facility as a lizard does a new tail.

Frankly it is as well they can. Because later in the same season Alan Shearer noted of Newcastle's lowly Premiership position, 'We've got to work our bollocks off to get out of this.'

One can glean from these statements that while you need four testicles to get into the top flight, you need to shake them off as quickly as possible if you want to stay there.

To understand why it might be so we must look to the Ancients. A Greek philosopher likened the male libido to being chained to a lunatic. This clearly explains why being drained of testosterone is an advantage in the Premiership. For it is plainly difficult enough to keep pace with Thierry Henry without having to drag some Peruvian goalkeeper along with you.

This is why teams find it so hard to make the transition from Championship to Premiership. Watford, who battled through the play-offs in 2006, failed to shed the appendages they sprouted for the purpose and kindly coach Adie Boothroyd hadn't the heart to pick up a pair of game shears and take the drastic measures necessary. As a result the Hornets were, quite literally, dragged down by their bollocks.

McAteer gave no details, but it is reasonable to assume that the number of extra pairs of bollocks necessary for promotion increases exponentially as you drop down the league ladder – one extra pair in the first, two in the second and so on until by the time you get to the bottom of the pyramid, teams seeking promotion need to grow them by the barrow load. Unfortunately scientists were unable to confirm this thesis as numerous phone-calls to clubs in the Wearside League went unanswered, the staff in all probability too busy sewing extra material into the shorts to come to the phone.

Bonding

Ancient ritual by which the English team ethic is formed. Refined over the centuries it generally involves spending £5000 on Louis Roederer Crystal and then all having sex with the same woman. When the story appears in the *News of the World* strong ties of comradeship are formed between the participants that often last almost until the end of the next contract.

Kyran Braddle

Early in his reign as Chelsea owner Roman Abramovich stunned football when he launched a shock swoop on Old Trafford to pick up United's teenage catering sensation Kyran Braddle. According to those who had watched him in action, Braddle was 'very much the spotty-faced, slack-jawed burger-bar lad's spotty-faced, slack-jawed burger-bar lad'. Chelsea signed the sixteen-year-old for a seven-figure sum believed to be in the region of £7. Braddle put pen to paper at Stamford Bridge and was promptly loaned to a hot dog concession out-side the Valley, Charlton. 'We feel this will be of greater benefit to his football catering education than standing round in the background at Chelsea leaning on a mop and fantasising list-lessly about Christina Aguilera,' said a spokesman for the Blues. Asked for his views on the deal that could have made him a millionaire by the time he turned 857, Braddle stared blankly at the questioner for several minutes before saying, 'Y'wha'?' He was later released without charge.

Bring Back Bullying Campaign

Rod Rugg was not a name normally associated with radical educational campaigns. The maverick midfield dreadnought from Dronfield had a career that was played out in a blizzard of headlines and dandruff, birds, booze and the occasional bazooka.

'When I was playing, "role model" was something you did if you got lucky down Rope-a-Blokes disco with a Page Three stunner,' Rugg confessed in September 2006. 'But recently I've found myself really wanting to put something back in. Unfortunately, due to what Pelé memorably dubbed "a bit of trouble in the trouser department", that hasn't been possible for some while, so I've had to get involved in this charity lark instead. Hurgh hurgh! Only joking. Some mornings you could hang a side of bacon off of it, I can tell you. Not that I've done that for a while. I mean, no point now my team-mates aren't watching, is there?'

Rugg had just launched a campaign that he believed could put an end to childhood obesity and improve the football skills of a generation of youngsters. 'Basically I am calling for the return of compulsory bullying in our schools,' Rugg said.

Rugg was moved to act when he realised that his two sons by wife number-five ('or vice versa, it's hard to keep track without consulting the CSA') were getting absolutely no bullying at school whatsoever. 'Neither of those lads even knows what a Chinese burn is,' he said in disgust, 'and if you ask them if anyone has flushed their head down the toilet lately they just look at you as if you are mental. No wonder kids these days are so fat. There's nobody at school they have to run away from in terror any more.'

According to Rugg the rot set in in the 1980s when local councils started selling off the crucial areas behind the bike sheds and a new generation of well-meaning but misguided teachers refused to countenance compass-jabbing, head-knuckling and armlocks on the grounds that they were, in some nebulous and unexplained way, cruel and divisive. He says the effect of this is only now truly being felt.

'If you look at the skills of a generation of young footballers you can see that they have definitely been undermined by the lack of bullying,' Rugg says. 'Take my old team-mate at the Thrushes, "Jinking" Billy Pillock. When Billy was in his pomp there was no finer winger in football. We used to call him "the wizard of dribble" though actually that was more on account of an infection he picked up during a preseason trip to Hamburg. Hurgh hurgh! But anyway, if you asked Billy where he learned his devastating body swerve and his lightning change of pace he'd tell you it was from dodging the big lads in the boys' toilets at playtime. They used to smoke in there, like, and if they caught you they'd make you lie on your back next to the urinals and use your mouth as an ashtray. Cruel? Maybe. But it gave Billy a great career in the game of football. At the time a lot of us felt that he should have played for England and I still think he would have done if it hadn't been for the bed-wetting and the suicide attempts.'

Rugg's campaign to bring back bullying quickly gained political momentum and Conservative leader David Cameron, a public schoolboy to his stoner marrow, pledged to reintroduce the once popular gauntlet run of wet-towel flicking to the national curriculum.

'My worry is that even a full-on return of traditional bullying could be too late to save British football,' Rugg said at the time. 'I watched the Carling Cup Final on Sunday and I was appalled by what I saw from those Chelsea and Arsenal players. That fight disgusted me. There's surely no more proof needed of the effect that decades of do-gooders have had on our kids than the fact that a collection of twenty-two of the nation's fittest and healthiest so-called footballers cannot produce a single decent right-hander between them.

'People have been saying it's all the influence of the foreigners. But I don't hold with that. You didn't have to play against Ari Haan for more than a couple of minutes to find out that abroad isn't all Danish pastries and lingerie, I can tell you.' The campaign is ongoing at the time of publication.

British Players Abroad

When David Beckham joined Real Madrid there was much speculation over whether he had the skills necessary to succeed for Los Galacticos. Was his technique as polished as his famously glistering gonads, or would he be shown up by Raul and Co. as so much nutty slack?

To some the portents did not look promising. After all, when Ian Rush left Liverpool for Juventus he appeared the very embodiment of the penalty-area predator, stealthy, spare and deadly – a Welsh Paolo Rossi. In the unforgiving surroundings of Serie A, however, he looked clumsy, gauche and all shin from hip to toe. Rush went out an assassin and came back an ass.

Might the same happen to Beckham? people asked. To seasoned observers that always seemed unlikely. Because to be blunt foreign clubs no longer buy British players for their artistry. They have had their fingers burned too often. Nowadays when the Spanish or Italians want what they endearingly term 'fantasy', they look to their fellow Latins, or the French, or the Dutch. When they buy British it is gritty realism they are after.

They find it in some unlikely quarters, too. Steve McManaman is a case in point. In England he was regarded as a creative force, a player to unlock defences with a mazy run. Not so in Spain. Real Madrid fans praised the Liverpudlian for his team ethic, commitment and no-frills approach. If anyone mentioned his flair and dribbling ability, they would study his or her face with narrowed eyes desperately looking for signs of irony or madness. What appeared extraordinary about McManaman in the Premiership – his ball skills – seemed ordinary when set against those of Luis Figo and Zinedine Zidane. Conversely what was commonplace in England is noteworthy in Spain.

The best example of this role reversal is Vinnie Samways. The former Spurs and Everton midfielder played nearly two hundred games in La Liga. In England 'Mr Vin' was regarded as incisive, intelligent, but lightweight, the epitome of the Continental schemer. In Spain with Las Palmas by contrast he earned plaudits as a marauding bulldog, seeing red more often than a fighting bull and cementing his reputation as a tough guy after a training ground scrap with Oktay Derelioğlu saw the Turkish international scurrying back to Istanbul.

The British players that have done best in the major European leagues – Spain, Italy and Germany – have generally embodied virtues typical of the football of these islands. They have been tenacious battlers, or strong, courageous centre forwards. Men, in short, who tended to regard being able to walk upstairs unaided as a sign of cowardice. There have been exceptions, of course: Lawrie Cunningham had enough wizardry to impress even the Bernabéu and nobody has ever accused Trevor Francis of being combative (well, apart from Alex Kolinko, obviously), but by and large even the most successful British exports such as Kevin Keegan have won fans with their industry and bravery rather than their style and grace.

John Charles, Gerry Hitchens, Mark Hateley, John Aldridge, Ray Wilkins, Steve Archibald, Sammy Lee. All of them did well in Serie A or the Primera Liga and whatever their other fine qualities none of them was known for their mesmerising close control or breathtaking range of passes. Meanwhile those who apparently did have one or both of those gifts foundered.

Paul Ince was hardly a rip-roaring success at Internazionale, but the Guv'nor did better in Milan than a far more talented Londoner who'd tried his hand there in the early 1960s. At Milan the mercurial Jimmy Greaves quickly fell foul of coach Nereo Rocco, a man he would later categorise as being 'so tough he made Frank Bruno look like Wayne Sleep'. Treated 'like a prisoner', Greaves found it impossible to settle away from Blighty. He was not alone. The feelings of many British players who tried their luck overseas were best summed up by Neil Franklin after his brief (he played just six matches) spell in Colombia in 1950. Abroad, the England international concluded, was maybe wonderful for a holiday, 'but a holiday and living there are two vastly different matters'.

In Turin the hard-working David Platt impressed more than the brilliant Denis Law. The Scots forward joined Torino along with England's Joe Baker in 1961. The pair didn't stay long. Law was sent off for retaliation and Baker punched a photographer in Venice and tossed his camera into the Grand Canal. Forbidden from drinking alcohol in public by the club management, they both ended up in hospital after the future Arsenal forward crashed his Alfa Romeo.

The battlers and the targetmen seem better able to keep themselves out of this sort of bother than their more admired brethren. That was an ability Beckham shared. He also had the work rate, the selflessness and the devotion to duty to follow in the considerable footsteps of Osasuna's Sammy Lee or even his colleague in Pamplona, the mighty Ashley Grimes. In fact by the time he left the Bernabéu many Spanish fans were calling him 'the new Vinnie Samways'.

Brothers

The arrival of Wayne Rooney's brother Graham on the football scene called to mind one of football's immutable laws. According to insiders at Everton, Rooney Junior had the potential to be even better than his elder brother. These words will fill the hearts of Goodison fans with regret. Because it is a law of football that if an elder brother is a great player, the younger one won't be.

The reason for this state of affairs was revealed by psychologist Oliver James who argues that elder children try to please their parents by following conventional paths to success and are anxious about their status, while their younger siblings rebel by going off back-packing. Something that anyone who saw Joel Cantona play will empathise with.

Giuseppe Buffoon

In Italy in 2006 Paolo Di Canio found himself once again at the centre of a controversy when he confessed that since his teenage years he had hero-worshipped the infamous 1930s Italian leader Giuseppe 'Big Trousers' Buffoon. 'The ideas of the great Buffoon still speak to me,' the former West Ham forward told *Corriere della Sera*. 'He believed that a man must strut about with his chin in the air and draw attention to himself by any means possible, whether it was by wearing tight **short shorts**, growing outmoded Midge Ure-style sideburns, or making provocative hand gestures. I believe passionately in that, and in tattoos and big motorbikes, too.' However, Di Canio denied that his views were an insult to people of different cultures and ethnic backgrounds: 'I am a moron not a racist,' he declared proudly.

Bung

Traditional sweetener served to English managers in the restaurant of a motorway service station. Usually made from brown paper with some sort of green filling, it is a bit like a cinema hot dog – everyone knows they are there, but no one will admit to ever having had one.

– C –

Cabbies

Cabbies are poorly paid men driving ropey motors who help footballers relieve stress and tension by allowing themselves to be beaten up by them late at night.

Card School

An adult education establishment, usually located at the back of the team bus, at which senior players teach the younger ones how to lose large sums of cash.

Cartoon Characters

Manchester United's very public attempt to secure the services of Mickey Mouse in December 2002 sparked an immense amount of interest in animated players throughout the Premiership.

'Buying Mickey Mouse made great sense both in football terms and in business terms,' the then Old Trafford chief director of money, Peter Kenyon, would later explain. 'There are only two ways to crack the massive Chinese market, three if you include getting the whole population addicted to opium, but we at Manchester United would never consider doing that because it is totally and utterly unethical and far too expensive.

'It therefore boiled down to a straight choice, Mao or mouse. We have enquired about Mao, but our offer to the Chinese Government was rebuffed. It was pointed out to us subsequently that Mao is clinically dead. And while that didn't prevent Middlesbrough signing Alen Boksic, we felt it a risk too far. We therefore began monitoring the situation in Hollywood closely. There were reports that Mickey was unhappy about no longer being guaranteed a place in the starting line-up and had fallen out with Roy Disney because he believed he did not offer him enough support when he was briefly addicted to bacon rind. We were confident we could secure his paw print during the transfer window.'

United's bullishness hid inner anxiety. Other clubs were also in the hunt for the mouse. Aston Villa for one, though the possibility of a deal being struck was always unlikely. 'The Disney crowd are very tight-knit,' said one LA insider at the time, 'and are likely to take their lead on this issue from Donald Duck. His attitude to David O'Leary's team is very hostile following the recent tabloid speculation about the relationship between Lee Hendrie and Don's wife Daisy.'

It was also well known at that time that Mickey's wife Minnie favoured a move to Arsenal or Chelsea. 'No disrespect to Manchestershire,' said a close friend in Beverly Hills, ' but Minnie is a very Metropolitan gal. She worries that a five-foot-high rodent in a rah-rah skirt would struggle to find acceptance in a provincial English city. She has never forgotten that time in the 1970s when her husband played in a testimonial match for Mick Bates at Elland Road and the crowd threw cheese at him.'

Arsenal confirmed an interest in the big-eared, squeaky-voiced mouse – who they saw as an ideal replacement for Tony Adams – but Arsène Wenger knew that, as always at Highbury, money would be an issue. Instead the Frenchman concentrated on cartoon youth, with his scouts scouring the globe for talent. Already he was said to be on the trail of Chuckie from *Rugrats* and Arthur the Aardvark's best buddy Buster Baxter. Potentially more far-reaching was the deal with the Japanese anime studio that produced *Princess Mononoke* and *Spirited Away*.

'The great thing with the cartoon characters is that there is no language problem,' explained the head of Arsenal's youth development programme, Liam Brady. 'When we bring them over we can simply have them dubbed into English by stalwart Gunners fan Alan Davies.'

'Injuries are also a factor in their favour,' advised Chris Coleman of Fulham who was reported to be having talks with the agent of Belgian star Tintin. 'These guys are incredibly resilient. How many real footballers could be knocked pancake flat by a steamroller and bounce back to their feet thirty seconds later as if nothing had happened? Well, OK, apart from Terry Butcher, then?'

The sudden interest in signing cartoons had not come out of the blue. 'Footballers have increasingly become two-dimensional characters and so it is inevitable that two-dimensional characters will increasingly become footballers,' said Fiscal Tripp of London trend analysts Maple, Tubular, Steel and Glass. 'In the next twelve months we will probably see computer-generated characters such as Donkey from *Shrek* and *Toy Story*'s Mr Potatohead playing at Old Trafford. And no jokes about Ruud Van Nistelrooy and Wayne Rooney, puh-lease!'

One man who was not happy with the wave of transfer speculation was PFA chief Gordon Taylor. 'Instead of importing over-the-hill foreign cartoons the clubs should concentrate on drawing their own,' he said.

'They should be investing in pencils, crayons and paper instead of giving one last big pay day to the likes of Asterix the Gaul. The way things are going soon popular British cartoon characters such as Captain Pugwash, The Lampies and Harry Redknapp will have disappeared from the Premiership altogether.'

Chelsea boss José Mourinho was unimpressed by Taylor's comments. 'The British cartoon is not as technically accomplished as his foreign counterpart,' he said. 'Sure, Sir Prancelot, Roobarb and Custard, even Bod, are tenacious and full of energy, but they are also very, very crude. If you ask any fan what he would like to see most, it is a winning team and you are not going to win with a back four built around Cut-Throat Jake or Nelly and Noah.'

Mourinho may have had a point but there are other areas of animation in which Britain leads the world. Unsurprisingly it was wily Big Sam Allardyce who was first to try and exploit our nation's expertise at stop-frame filming. 'Obviously Wallace and Gromit are beyond the pocket of a club like this,' Big Sam said at the time. 'So that is why I am considering tabling a bid for the Fat Controller. OK, he is old and overweight, but he still has a great engine. In fact he has several.'

Strangely despite all the speculation nothing ever came of it.

Cash Culture

On the eve of the glamorous 2005 Carling Cup semi-finals football was rocked by scandal as the tabloids revealed that a number of top Premiership footballers had become addicted to the stars' drug of choice – money. According to reports one Manchester United player was under investigation by police after he was found in possession of cash with a street value of £30,000. 'There is no doubt that there is a currency culture within the modern game,' said one detective. However, the PFA's Gordon Taylor was quick to support his members, saying, 'You will find money in all areas of modern society. I myself am not averse to Hoovering up the odd half-million or so, just to freshen myself up of a morning. There is nothing wrong with that.'

'It is true that taken in small doses cash is perfectly harmless,' admitted one money counsellor whose private clinic attempts to wean addicts off cash by charging them £12,000 a day for a monastic cell and meals of bread and water. 'But taken in large quantities it can have hideous side-effects. For example, designer velour tracksuits, elaborate jewellery and huge neo-Georgian houses in Cheshire with Burberry stair carpets.'

Thane of Cawdor

The winter of 2006 saw much unrest at Manchester City as troublesome Scottish midfielder the Thane of Cawdor joined Joey Barton in criticising the club for 'lack of ambition'. Cawdor's agent, Lady Macbeth, was widely blamed for being behind the unrest, but she was unrepentant, claiming that her client has been treated with disrespect by the club and was far more than just an ordinary member of the team. 'This even-handed justice commends the ingredients of our poison'd chalice to our lips,' she told the *News of the World*, adding that City seemed content with mid-table mediocrity. Addressing manager Stuart Pearce, she asked: 'Wouldst thou have that which thou esteem'st the ornament of life (i.e. the Premiership), And live a coward in thine own esteem, Letting "I dare not" wait upon "I would", Like the poor cat i' the adage?' Pearce professed himself nonplussed by the question: 'To be honest I haven't a clue what Lady Macbeth is going on about,' he told the BBC. 'But what I will say is that we stood by Thaney during the occult revelations and the visions of bloody ghosts incidents, and it seems our reward is to be stabbed in the back. Literally.'

Celebrity Alan Swap

In the winter of 2006 Channel Four revealed that Alan Curbishley's move from Charlton to West Ham and Alan Pardew's trip in the opposite direction were part of a new reality TV show, *Celebrity Alan Swap*, in which 'well known Alans exchange places with consequences, which as well as providing hours of entertaining television, serve to tell us an awful lot about what it means to be called Alan in postmodern Britain'. Despite predictable moans that Alan Pardew wasn't actually a celebrity, the series proved such a hit that a second series in which Sky pundit Alan Mullery changes places with wacky Canadian songstress Alanis Morissette is being filmed even now. According to reports, Mullery has already penned a number of pained laments reflecting the angst of being the first man to be sent off in an England shirt, while Morissette is said to be proving a football pundit on a par with the legendary Clive Allen, despite never having seen a game in her entire life. Asked how she has found exchanging the world of introverted singer-songwriting for sitting next to Chris Kamara and Frank McLintock, Morissette said, 'It's ironic. Er, or do I mean moronic?'

Celebrity Signings

In 1999 Manchester United's reported interest in bringing Hidetoshi Nakata to Old Trafford seemed to revolve less around his playing abilities than the fact that since he signed for Perugia the Italian club have sold half a million shirts with his name on the back in Japan. In the brave new commercial world of football this is, of course, a major consideration. Faced with a choice between a sturdy centre-half who will strengthen the team and a sexy but erratic Latin forward who will strengthen the club's merchandising arm, most managers these days are encouraged to take the latter option.

It therefore came as no surprise, then, when reporters learned that Alex Ferguson was hoping to clinch an audacious £25 million deal that would change the face of English football. Leonardo DiCaprio, it seemed, was on his way to United. DiCaprio was such a well-proven shirt-shifter that the United board reputedly saw his total lack of footballing skill as more or less irrelevant when set beside the financial benefits he would bring to the team, or 'core activity production unit' as they preferred to call them.

According to DiCaprio's agent, the handsome young actor was very excited by the prospect of donning the famous red shirt. 'Leo knows that in England United is even more massive than Kate Winslet,' he told me. 'He has played substance-abusers, he has played wealthy psychopaths, now he will be playing Aston Villa. In many ways it is the culmination of this phase of his career.'

How exactly DiCaprio would fit in to the team was not explained, but his agent's assertion that 'Leo will be preparing for his new role in his usual intelligent, instinctual and thorough manner, i.e. by drinking a lot and hanging around in nightclubs with loads of blonde women' suggested that he may have been viewed as a direct replacement for Teddy Sheringham.

Early indications were that as far as the Premiership was concerned United's signing of the star of *Titanic* would be just the tip of a very large iceberg. For as Thomas Carlyle so wisely observed, 'When Manchester sneezes the rest of England wipes spittle from its cheeks.'

The Red Devils' interest in DiCaprio set in motion a similar frenzied hunt for cash-generating glamour among their rivals. Chelsea made noises about snapping up Christian Slater, Brad Pitt, Tom Cruise and as many other internationally known names as manager Gianluca Vialli could write on the back of a beermat while chairman Ken Bates counted to sixty. On Merseyside, meanwhile, Liverpool were linked with Jerry Seinfeld, a man once described by Glenn Hoddle as 'a little bit special in a situation-comedy situation'.

At Arsenal the wily Arsène Wenger had taken a slightly different tack, opening discussions with blockbusting thriller writer John Grisham. 'You know, if you are going into an airport bookshop,' the Frenchman observed of his potential new signing, 'you will see that anything with Grisham's name across it is selling fantastically. I do not see that a shirt will be so different from a book in this respect.' The cunning Alsatian will also see a chance to recuperate some of his investment by selling Hollywood the rights to make a film of the Grisham shirt, in all probability starring Susan Sarandon.

Not everyone was happy with the new developments, however. The chairman of Spurs at the time Alan Sugar voiced concerns about the influx of what he termed 'Carlos Characterparts' into the Premiership and his views were echoed by PFA head honcho Gordon Taylor. 'We are not arguing', Taylor said, 'about your DiCaprios, your Depardieus or your Inglesiases. Their presence can only benefit the English game. My concern is with the less well-known and far cheaper celebrities who are bound to follow and the has-beens just coming over here for one last big pay-check. It's one thing to bring over Harrison Ford, but do we really want to see that big Yank bloke with the moustache who was in the detective show back in the seventies with the woman who played the sultry alien princess in *Buck Rogers in the 25th Century*, or the little bald fellow who ran the record shop in *Mork and Mindy*, or Jim-Bob Walton? If something is not done, though, they will come, mark my words. I've already had a rep on to me from Chester. Apparently the chairman there has just bought the butler from the Ferrero Rocher advert. You have to ask, when will this craziness end?'

Now.

Chairmen Coaching

'Technique is very important, pace is important and you have to be physically strong. But you also have to be mentally educated', so said England coach Sven-Göran Eriksson. The Swede was talking about young English footballers, but some in the game wondered if his words shouldn't be applied more widely. 'We coach youngsters, we coach pros, we coach refs, we even coach coaches,' says the FA's Dave Pigment, 'but the guy with the most important position in any football club receives no coaching whatsoever, the chairman.'

The situation abroad is very different. In Amsterdam the famous Ajax system brings in self-satisfied and hard-hearted boys as young as eight and begins the process of grooming them for the task of launching a new heritage replica kit while withdrawing concessionary season tickets for the unwaged.

At the superb Clairefontaine facility just outside Paris, meanwhile, the French are already bringing through the next generation of the country's club presidents. Visit on a weekday afternoon and you will see the cream of the Gallic crop – sleekly fat, immaculately manicured, prematurely balding adolescents, their skins glowing with wealth – being put through their paces. One group is sensuously slurping the aspic from canapés without spilling a morsel down the front of their ostentatious calf-length cashmere overcoats; another sits stern-faced next to a platoon of pneumatic yet dead-eyed blondes; a third smiles uncomprehendingly at remarks whispered in their ear by a team of distinguished ex-players led by Michel Platini; and all this under the watchful eye of the maestro himself, Bernard Tapie.

In France genetics play a part in identifying the potential chairman of the future. 'Because of financial DNA we find that children with parents who are rich make the best chairmen,' says Tapie. 'They have what our sports scientists have identified as a higher percentage of the type of green tissue that helps them when it comes to developing the muscular bank balances needed to succeed in the boardroom.'

England was lagging behind, which was something Pigment, the Football Association's new Director of Director Development, had been brought in to address. It is not before time. With the likes of Roman Abramovich, the Glazer boys and Mohamed Al Fayed filling up positions traditionally occupied by British scrap offal merchants many fear that the opportunities for English chairmen these days are severely limited.

'I sometimes wonder if the Ken Bateses, Robert Maxwellses and Peter Swaleses would make it through today,' whimpered Peter Ridsdale, a man who lived the dream and reaped the whirlwind. 'If these foreigners are allowed to keep coming over here and taking our seats, a whole generation of English directors may be flushed down the toilet without ever getting a chance to run up massive debts, make portentous speeches and sell the stadium to a supermarket chain. In the long-term that's going to be disastrous for our national game.'

'We got complacent,' says Pigment in response. 'We believed we had a production line for chairmen and could turn out Louis Edwardses, Bob Lordses and Michael Knightonses indefinitely. Times change. The days of the old street chairmanship in which groups of grubby-faced lads with scabs on their knees would kick a ball made from old potato peelings held together by twine up and down an alley, while one pitiful outcast with a weak chest and a dad who owned the local pickled onion factory peered out through the gap under an outside toilet door, imagining it was the directors' box and vowing that one day he would be in a position suddenly to sell the best of them to Stockport County just because they forgot to say "good morning, sir", no longer exist,' says Pigment. 'It's sad, but it's fact.'

Some doubted that it was possible to coach the sort of skills displayed by recent top English chairmen such as Freddy Shepherd.

Pigment disagrees: 'Clearly when it comes to self-awareness and human insight you can't take out what God put in,' he says. 'Freddy was an incredibly talented chairman. But he didn't get where he is today without honing his God-given gifts. After all, there are thousands of smug middle-aged men in Britain with pomposity to burn and absolutely no sense of their own ridiculousness, but you don't find many of them saying, "We're not going to be anybody's mugs any more", to groups of journalists. And the reason for that is hard work. I know for a fact, for instance, that during his younger days Freddy was handicapped by a hint of irony that often prevented him keeping a straight face during some of his pronouncements. He spent hours on the training ground getting rid of it. Not many young lads are prepared to make that type of sacrifice. If we want to see the Freddys of the future, we have to encourage the ones that will.'

Channel Footy

Satellite channel that lasted for just four years at the end of the twentieth century but during that time produced some of the greatest football shows ever seen. The highlights from a typical week's broadcasting in September 1999 give a taste of the riches that were on offer.

FRENCHIE & JOCK

Classic odd-couple cop drama starring Arsène Wenger as the fastidious Frenchie and Alex Ferguson as bluff, gruff Jock. This week the bickering, ill-matched, crusty but benign detective duo find themselves on the trail of a Russian Mr Big. They need to work out a way to catch him, but instead spend most of their time throwing soup and insults at one another. With special guest star Bela Lugosi as Peter Kenyon.

ONE FOOT IN THE GRAVY

Welcome rerun of the classic sitcom about grumpy old agent **Pini Colada**. This week Pini receives an unexpectedly large cheque from an Australian client and ends up in court with predictably hilarious consequences. As the man himself would say, 'I do not believe my percentage!'

FOOTBALLERS' HIVES

Glossy drama serial set among football's glamorous apiarist community. In episode one Bazza worries the permissive behaviour of his queen may be giving wife Shazza ideas when he finds her being smothered in royal jelly by a group of workers who are supposed to be putting in a jacuzzi. Meanwhile, Wazza's attempt to take his swarm up to the moor top to gather heather nectar is thwarted by the lack of suitable bootspace in his Lamborghini. And Nozza's dream move to Brentford ('Don't you see, Chezza, I was born to play for the Bees!') is put on hold when a group of nomadic African hunter-gatherers who had been hoping to spend a few days living like Ian Wright get into his garden and eat all the honey.

THE KUMAS AT NO. 42

Spoof chatshow featuring the hapless host, West Brom winger Jason, and his zany Welsh family, Mum, Dad and Grandpa Tosh. This week's guests include Luis Figo who unexpectedly reveals that he has always dreamed of playing for Albion – 'West Bromwich, Brighton and Hove, Burton or Rovers, I don't mind really, it's the romantic cadence of the name that has captured my heart.'

WALKING WITH FOOTBALLERS

Brilliant series in which top palaeontologists reconstruct the extraordinary world that existed fifty years before the dawn of Sky using state-of-the-art computer animation techniques. Whisked back into this dark and primitive era, viewers are able to watch as ferocious half-backs with thighs the size of coal bunkers stalk their prey, a group of agile inside forwards, and when they spot the one who 'doesn't really fancy it' ruthlessly separate him from the herd and kick him into touch. Meanwhile the comically gigantic stopper (who could weigh as much as a small bungalow) lumbers about in futile pursuit of a flying winger, only to be knocked unconscious when a mud-soaked ball falls out of the sky and lands on his head.

THE RIO SUMMIT

England centre-half Rio Ferdinand fronts this current affairs programme. This week the Manchester United legend meets Burmese civil rights campaigner Aung San Suu Kyi and asks the burning questions, 'What's happening?' and 'Am I cool, or what?'

THE LOST WORLD OF BRACEWELL AND KENDALL

Amazing old film footage discovered hidden away at the back of a Merseyside chemist's shop a few years ago and now being seen on television for the first time. The films pull back the curtain on a now only vaguely remembered world in which footballers didn't have manicures, people stood up to watch the game and only children wore replica shirts. As narrator Harry Kewell observes, 'To the modern observer the 1980s seems like a distant planet in a universe far far away from the Emirates Stadium. Hahahahah, look at their hairstyles! It's like Alice bands hadn't been invented yet!'

GRAND DESIGNS

Kevin McCloud visits a Soho couple, Geoff and David, who bought a large art-deco property in north London several years ago and then pulled it down in preparation for the building of the home of their dreams. Three years later and it's still not finished, it's over budget, overdue, there's a massive dispute with one of the builders and Geoff is starting to wonder if he really should have tried to do all the plumbing himself. 'I've always had this incredible eye for detail,' reveals David, 'except when it comes to figures with a pound sign in front of them.'

I'M A FOOTBALLER GET ME OUT OF HERE!

A return of the popular reality show in which a number of top British strikers find themselves stranded at a relegated club and desperately try to 'do an Alan Smith' by escaping, while all the time pretending that they really want to stay. This year's inmates include Peter Crouch, Andy Johnson, Dean Ashton and Abi Titmuss.

GRAEME SOUNESS'S DRESSING ROOM NIGHTMARES

Rugged former Glasgow Rangers and Liverpool footballer Graeme Souness ventures into some of Britain's most appalling dressing rooms and sorts things out by shouting, swearing and jabbing his finger at people. This week the volatile Scot visits a north-east dressing room where failure is endemic despite the fact that millions of pounds have been lavished on it and those who work in it. 'To be honest, it's a *$@~# disgrace,' observes Graeme before drawing an unflattering comparison with the situation at Anfield in 1980.

CELEBRITY HATE ISLAND

Controversial reality show. Ten of the Premiership's most volatile footballers are placed on a tropical island paradise with a range of weaponry, in the hope of conjuring up Britain's first full penetrative onscreen manslaughter. Last week viewers voted to send obnoxious Roy and irritating Robbie into the 'slap shack' to see if they'd really do 'it' or just indulge in a spot of half-hearted 'handbags'. This week we find out the results. Warning – may contain strong language and shoving from the outset.

SERGEANT TREBILCOCK

Rerun of the classic sixties sitcom featuring everybody's favourite smooth-talking Cornish Cup hero. Tonight Colonel Catterick wants Trebilcock to carry on doing his milkround but our hero has other plans – an appearance at Wembley! Also starring Ernie Machin as Private Doberman.

EL LOCO-MOTION

Dance extravaganza filmed at Lima's exclusive El Loco Lounge nitespot and featuring many of the South American goalkeepers who down the years have earned the coveted 'Mad One' tag. In tonight's episode Ramon Quiroga introduces the syncopated stylings of Los Trios Chilavert, while Jorge Campos and Tijuana Trumpet invite viewers to 'Do The Hustle'.

WHOSE LINESMAN IS IT ANYWAY?

Witty panel game from Italy in which teams of top Serie A officials attempt to influence the outcome of an important Uefa Cup tie. Hosted by Brian Glanville.

SIDE BY SIDE BY TRONDHEIM

Award-winning musical outing from Norway featuring the stars of Rosenborg BK's 1988 championship-winning team. Bard Wiggen takes the honours with his rendition of 'Send in the Clowns' (dedicated to 'everyone at Fifa'), but Trond Sundby's solid glockenspiel work is not far behind.

THE STRANGE PASSION OF JAROSLAV KLAPKO

Cult animation from the Czech Republic, Smíček's controversial film tells the story of the eponymous hero's love affair with an inflatable banana and its consequences for his family. Amazing avant-garde soundtrack from the Josef Venglos Free Jazz Ensemble of Olomouc.

Chelsea

In 2000 Ken Bates stated his intention to make Chelsea 'the Manchester United of the South'. Football fans dismissed the notion on the grounds that there already was a Manchester United of the South – Manchester United.

Cincinnati Stratos

Many football fans on both sides of the Atlantic saw David Beckham's transfer to the LA Galaxy as just the Balco-style shot in the arm US soccer needed. One man who isn't holding his breath to see if soccer finally breaks America, though, is Sal 'the Big Canola' Cafeteria, and not just because he died six months ago either.

The former eighty-seven-year-old waste disposal magnate was once owner of leading Totally Awesome American Soccer League franchise the Cincinnati Stratos. In the late-1970s Cafeteria pumped millions of dollars into 'the Blues', recruiting such legends of the game as **Rod Rugg**, Mick McMugg and Trevor Thugg, the so-called 'Three Uggs' who had terrorised the East Midlands for several seasons with their brand of flare-based, fedora hat-wearing maverick mayhem. Added to the trio was Franky Van Swine, a Belgian midfield artiste with a left foot so cultured Joe Mercer once claimed he could 'quote Proust with it', and Ziggy Schtardurst, the crimson-haired German number-nine whose androgynous centre-forward play had electrified the Bundesliga and would lead to generations of Teutonic forwards experimenting with Kabuki theatre, silk mini-dresses and green lipstick (though not Rudi Voller, obviously).

Diana Rigg joined the squad midway through the first season, a signing that owed less to a decision to add greater dramatic weight and better diction to the Stratos line-up than to confusion over the pronunciation of the name Pelé. 'Sal phoned us up and said he wanted this superstar he'd heard of called "Peel",' recalls the Stratos's European agent Brian Wassock. 'We racked our brains and the only star called Peel we could think of was Emma Peel from *The Avengers*.'

'I was expecting a Brazilian soccer star,' Cafeteria would recall a decade later, sucking on a large Havana and wiping sweat from his forehead with a C note (far more absorbent than a B flat, you'll find), 'and instead I got this goddamn limey broad in a leather catsuit.'

As it was Dame Diana proved a better acquisition than Mike Pejic and started fifteen games at centre-back that season. But even this star-studded line-up failed to attract the American public and within twelve months the team had been disbanded. The players drifted back to Europe and Dame Diana left to play Hedda Gabler at the Old Vic. 'I beat her on away goals,' she now quips during her annual tour of working men's clubs with Tommy Docherty.

All that is left of that expensive experiment is a trail of memories. 'It could go the same way for Beckham,' said Rod Rugg when he recalled the demise of the Stratos. 'As they say, "*sic transit gloria mundi*". And funnily enough I did once have a bird called Gloria in a transit, though if memory serves it was a Tuesday and there was nothing sick about it. Well, not much anyway. Hurgh, hurgh.'

City of Rods

South American film directed by Brazilian Fernando Meirelles. A mesmerising sequel to his powerful *City of God*, the movie is set in a massive futuristic metropolis populated entirely by clones of forthright talkSPORT pundit Rodney Marsh. Designer João

Stepover describes *City of Rods* as 'a mad dystopia of leopard skin, tubular steel and white shagpile carpeting in which thousands of men with hair like loft insulation, who think wearing a white tie and a black shirt is kind of cool, battle for the airwaves using identical commonsense no-nonsense opinions laced with the odd quip that's guaranteed to get up the noses of the liberal so-called elite. It is scary, nasty, but with the technology we have you know that it could also become a reality.'

Coaches

At one time there was an apparently permanent, shifting tribe of unemployed managers in England, men with top-class experience and binding ties to neither club nor region who turned up at a ground like hired guns in a Hollywood Western, grimaced, snarled and were done away with before the watcher could say, 'Hey, wasn't he the bloke who was in that one where they lost the FA Cup Final? You remember, he had a big cigar and a funny sort of bumpkin accent?'

In the seventies and eighties notable itinerants included Ron Saunders, who looked like Jack Palance's hard brother, and Gordon Lee, who, with his flapping dark trenchcoat and gaunt, expressionless face, gave the impression that he slept upside down, suspended from the ceiling in a sleeping bag formed by his own membraneous wings.

If a club was in big trouble they could turn to Tommy Docherty or Malcolm Allison, a pair who spent their latter careers as football's answer to the Four Horsemen of the Apocalypse. Both had been successful, but by the time the Doc arrived at Wolves and Big Mal on Teesside, the two were so inextricably linked with financial ruin they were like pointmen for the official receiver.

These do-a-job-for-us managers have long gone and so too

have the coaches-for-sale who came after them. Terry Venables was once in the Frame for everything going, but no longer. Big Ron is retired in disgrace. Martin O'Neill settled. Glenn Hoddle is in a loss of lustre situation. Trevor Francis has passed into oblivion via Selhurst Park. Howard Kendall is a 'Where are they now?' column. Sources close to Kenny Dalglish remain conspicuously silent. Alan Ball is a squeaky memory and the considered opinion is that it will soon be Guus Hiddink's turn to manage Holland again. Roy Hodgson, who once lurked so successfully on the Continent, has now slipped so far out of the picture there isn't even speculation that he is in with a shout of getting into the Frame.

Sport is cyclical. Maybe Tony Adams, Stan Collymore or Steve Cotterill will come through; perhaps Howard Wilkinson will come back. Again.

Pini Colada

The Israeli super-agent leapt to the forefront of football's semi-consciousness in March 2003 when it was revealed that Manchester United had paid him £2500 for his part in the £2.75 deal that brought a hot bacon roll to Old Trafford the previous Tuesday. 'You cannot expect a bacon roll to negotiate its own contract,' said a forthright David Gill wiping grease from his chin. 'It needs a representative whose job is to try and stiff us out of as much money as possible and it's only fair that we should pay for that privilege.' As to securing the services of the twenty-minute-old pork-related butty, Gill professed himself delighted. 'Sir Alex had identified Bacon Rolly as the missing piece in United's breakfast jigsaw and we are very happy to have backed his judgement. It was a good deal for the club and one which, let's not forget, also included a complimentary sachet of brown sauce and a reusable paper napkin.'

Comfortables

A radical offshoot of the 1980s soccer casuals movement, the comfortables rejected stylish designer sportswear in favour of air-cushion-soled shoes, easi-fit slacks and fleece-lined anoraks with pockets large enough to hold road maps, a thermos flask and a copy of the *Non-League Directory*. On match days highly organised crews of travelling comfortables would often meet up with rival comfortable gangs at a prearranged place – usually a pub with real ale and a strict 'no jukebox, no TV, no computer games' policy. These notorious 'offs', with their frequent vicious tirades about the cost of **football pies**, the atrocious state of the toilets at the Fratton Park away end, and the flipping gyratory system on the M6 westbound, often went on right under the noses of the police, who appeared powerless to stop them.

Compliance Unit

One day in 2004 the Football Association issued a statement saying they were investigating transfer deals at Aston Villa, then a few hours later issued a second statement saying they were not investigating transfer deals at Aston Villa. To an outsider this may have seemed like bungling. In fact it was all part of the FA's strategy of lulling wrongdoers into a false sense of security by posing as total incompetents – a plan they have pursued with the utmost diligence for well over a century.

The FA Compliance Unit is the elite body used to catch miscreants. It is so secretive and stealthy that most football people do not even know it exists. Indeed, several members of the FA Compliance Unit expressed astonishment when they were told about it.

Adam Crozier set up the FA Compliance Unit, or FACU as it is robustly abbreviated, in 2002 to probe financial irregularities within football. In the days BC (Before Crozier) the Football Association adopted a more gentle policy, investigating fiscal crimes so slowly that by the time they had reached a verdict anybody found guilty had long since died. Since death is clearly punishment enough for any crime (with the possible exception of illegal use of the referee's toilet), no further action therefore needed to be taken and everybody was happy.

This is not to say the FA's investigative arm did not do a thorough job, far from it. Indeed, such was the fearsome reputation it built up under the great Sir Frederick Wall that when Sherlock Holmes retired Lancaster Gate became the globe's foremost consulting detective agency, called in whenever a case baffled the world's law enforcement agencies. Perhaps the most famous investigation began in 1963 when, at the behest of Lyndon Baines Johnson, a crack team of FA sleuths was sent to Texas to apply its singular methods to the Kennedy assassination.

Just forty years later and already the FA had come up with an opening pre-provisional conditional report that, according to insiders, dismissed the famous Zapruder film of the shooting as 'unsubstantiated speculation', the bullets found at the scene as 'gossip and innuendo' and the presence of the dead body of the thirty-fifth president in Dallas on the day as 'an unhappy coincidence'. The report concluded that there is no firm evidence of anything untoward having taken place and advised the American people to go and have a nice hot cup of tea.

Under Crozier's watchful eye the FA investigators gained an even greater reputation for toughness, albeit one that at times bordered on the ruthless. Some of Roy Keane's supporters, for example, believe that the paragraph in the Irishman's autobiography dealing with his notorious foul on Alf-Inge Haaland was inserted not by ghost-writer Eamon Dunphy, but by members of the FA's disciplinary committee who had a gut feeling

Keane was a wrong 'un but needed to firm up the evidence a bit to convince the jury.

Unsurprisingly the sleazy yet glamorous world of the FA investigators, populated as it is by rough-hewn larger than life characters such as Ted Wragg and Tord Grip, has attracted the attention of TV dramatists.

In January 2003 ITV began screening *Inspector Worse*, in which the late John Thaw gave a superb performance as the eponymous FA detective. In the series' opening moments Worse finds his assistant, Sergeant Ewsless, examining a potential crime scene.

> Worse: 'Well, well, what have we here?'
> Ewsless: 'The front door has been broken in with an axe, sir, and this cabinet over here, the one labelled 'Extremely Precious Chinese Porcelain', has been emptied. The housemaid saw the man in the act and describes him as being big, burly, wearing a black face mask, a striped jumper and carrying a large sack marked "swag".'
> Worse: 'Yes, yes, Ewsless, but is there evidence of anything illegal having gone on?'
> Ewsless: 'Not really, sir.'
> Worse: 'Thought as much. Now, let's go and have a nice hot cup of tea, shall we?'

The BBC responded to the new trend with a drama starring Amanda Burton as top FA pathologist Dr Edwina Croker. In the first episode of *Silent Witness* we see the charismatic, intuitive Croker in the autopsy lab quizzing her assistant, Dr McDunce, about a newly arrived corpse.

> Croker: 'Well, well, what have we here?'
> Assistant: 'A white male, found at six this morning, bound

and gagged. He had 1007 stab wounds in the back, any one of which would have been fatal and a note was attached to his body reading, "So perishes anyone who betrays the Red Hand".'

Croker: 'Any evidence of foul play?'

Assistant: 'Not that I can see.'

Croker: 'No, me neither. Now, let's go and have a nice hot cup of tea, shall we?'

Clearly much of this was a hugely exaggerated portrayal of the true nature of the FA Compliance Unit, but as with all fiction it held a kernel of the truth. It is far too early at this stage to determine the outcome of FACU's lengthy investigation into alleged transfer irregularities – the preliminary findings of which are currently on their way to Soho Square via a specially trained carrier sloth – but on past evidence the guilty men would be advised to put the kettle on some time around 2024.

Consolationist

A key position in any modern football team. The consolationist is tasked with shaking his head sadly and patting the arm of an opponent who has just been sent off or missed the crucial spot-kick in a penalty shoot-out, thus affording Lee Dixon the chance to murmur, 'And how great a sporting gesture is that, Gary?'

Conspiracy Theories

In 2003 Bert Konterman claimed to have an explanation for the number of positive dope tests in Serie A. The midfielder said that players such as Edgar Davids and Fernando Couto may have been guilty of nothing more than eating too much chicken. According to the former Feyenoord player Italian poultry was pumped full of hormones to make them grow faster and that was finding its way into the players via their health-conscious, white-meat-rich diets. Rumours that officials first became suspicious when Jaap Stam sat on a ball in the corner of the Lazio dressing room and clucked fiercely when anyone tried to take it off him remain unsubstantiated.

Konterman's fowl idea was given little credence in Italy, not because it lacked scientific foundation, but because it was nowhere near complex enough. While the British, for reasons too obvious to need explanation, tend to favour the cock-up theory of history, the Italians usually prefer to believe that unseen forces are manipulating events in a fiendishly Byzantine manner (within minutes of the World Cup draw in Busan in 2002, journalists in Turin were telling their English colleagues that Fifa had rigged the 'Group of Death' simply in order to get rid of England and 'her hooligans'). Simplicity has no place in the world of conspiracies. Here more is more. Any true Italian football fan would believe that the Dutch international came up with his chicken notion after having his freezer filled to the gunnels with goodies by representatives of the organic food lobby.

Italian fans are not alone in their belief in the sinister, of course. After watching Spain overcome Yugoslavia 4–3 in Euro 2000 Serbian fans were quick to explain away the Spaniards' thrilling last-minute win. 'Yugoslavia is a poor country,' they said. 'Spain is a rich country and so', and they held up their right hands and rubbed the thumb across the tips of their fingers. It was exactly the same gesture Romanians had offered two days earlier when quizzed on their national team's failure to beat Portugal. To argue against either was to feel naive to the point of prudishness. Cynicism has a masculine swagger to it that faith in the integrity of officialdom can never hope to emulate. It is also much more comforting.

While England spent months agonising over what elimination from Euro 2000 told us about our coaching methods, our schools system and the imperfections of our national psychology, these fellows simply shrugged defeat off with the word 'corruption' and got on with their lives, self-esteem undiminished.

Consummate Professional

Sometimes when sports people speak it is necessary to interpret carefully what they say. The phrase consummate professional, for example, is the short-hand form for, 'He was so peripheral I didn't even notice him until he thumped that bloke when the ref wasn't looking.'

The Controversy

Michael Owen was unequivocal when he spoke of it. 'As I say,' said the England striker furrowing his consonants thoughtfully, 'I can't talk specifically about the situation we were speaking about previously because I don't know what people have been saying about it, or otherwise. But in general when it comes to the sort of thing that's been discussed, then I've made my views known on past occasions and I stick with what I said at that time and I always will do, unless things change. And I've been around this game long enough to know that can happen often when you're least expecting it and sometimes when you aren't.'

His then manager Sven-Göran Eriksson was even more forthright. Pushing his glasses bluntly up his nose, the Swede told reporters, 'As I said, and I refer you back to that.'

Meanwhile, in Soho Square FA chairman Geoff Thompson was in no mood for compromise. 'As we have made plain over the years,' he stated, shuffling his papers with a deft and practised hand, 'we at the Football Association take alleged matters such as the reported "incident" extremely slowly. At the present time we remain firmly and 100 per cent behind whomsoever is in front of us.'

BBC pundit Mark Lawrenson was in a similarly no-nonsense mood. 'To be fair to the lad, he's taken a long look at himself in the mirror and he's held his hands up,' he told listeners on Radio Five Live. 'And at the end of the day, I've got to say, that when you look at what we've been looking at elsewhere in the world as we've been flicking through the channels trying to find the golf, then it really puts things in perspective, frankly.'

The president of football's governing body, Sepp Blatter, also felt moved to take a firm position on the mounting crisis. 'Clearly this is not something I or Fifa can get involved in, but it is certainly something I will be keeping an eye on,' the elegant Swiss squinted piercingly. 'I will observe the developing situation, yet I will take no part in it, you understand? It is like I am peering in from the darkness through high-powered night-vision glasses, the lenses slightly misted by the condensation of my hot breath, the frisson of excitement passing like a chill breeze across my tautening stomach as I struggle to make out exactly what is going on on the other side of that shower curtain . . . Er, ahem. Excuse me, I seem to be late for an important meeting.'

Fifties football legend **Keith Beast** meanwhile, was in despair. 'I cannot imagine what my lovely old mate Stanley Trout would make of this,' he told the small crowd who had gathered round him while someone called for an ambulance on their mobile and others whispered 'I wouldn't bother, mate. He's just fallen over with the drink.'

'And what would my boss Bert Cheesley have said?' Keith went on. 'Or Katie from the Oxo commercials? And what would Queen Boudicca have done about it as with bitter ashes of razed Londinium still smutted across her flushed Celtic cheeks she watched her rugged Iceni tribesmen crushed like hedgehogs beneath the unstoppable juggernaut of the Roman military machine? It makes you burp just to consider it. Sometimes I think I must be going mad.'

Britain's most celebrated sports columnist Frank Gutt of the *Daily Rail* predictably pulled no punches as he swung and slammed at the kidneys of the ravening beast that was threatening to rip out the very heart of English football and use it as the base for some new kind of expensive frothy coffee-related drink that doesn't even come in a china mug. 'On Saturday we called him reckless and hot-headed. Today he was unmasked as something much worse – cool and calculating. We had thought it a crime of passion, but it was actually a far more heinous and markedly less British act of brutality. A wild five-minute rampage of flailing fists or mighty axes when the blood is up and the ale is down is an act typical of our proud, fiery and honest island people, but this? This emits the garlicky stink of the assassination, carried out under the cloak of night, a stiletto planted between the shoulder blades of a slumbering foe by somebody with a vowel at the end of his surname and over-elaborate facial hair. Let's make no bones about it, what happened on Saturday was murder in the first degree. Bring back the rope. Carthage must be destroyed!'

When the gathering tidal wave of uproar was laid before the figure at the epicentre of the howling media blizzard, however, he remained defiant. 'As I say,' he retorted, shaving a single eye-brow into a stern yet quizzical slant, 'from where I'm standing I'm not going to sit here wearing my heart on my sleeve and then putting my hand on it and keeping my fingers crossed, because that's not what I'm all about as a person. And as to the other stuff, well, you know, it's time to draw a line under it in the sand and focus on the future, though not for too long or you'll go cross-eyed.'

And there, thankfully, the whole sorry business was allowed to rest.

Cousins

His cousin takes on a genial and benign role in the life of the foreign footballer. Or at least he does in Middlesbrough. Fabrizio Ravanelli's move to the north-east is said to have been directly influenced by his cousin, Silvio. As a student Silvio attended an English language course on Teesside and understandably fell in love with Boro after a visit to Ayresome Park. When the White Feather phoned to ask Silvio's advice about the wisdom of a move to the Riverside he was naturally enthusiastic. Later he joined Ravanelli as an interpreter and helpmate, and still lives in the town.

Ravanelli's co-troublemaker at the Riverside Stadium during the 1996–97 season was the Brazilian Emerson. The Rick James lookalike and occasional midfield general also had a cousin in tow, Fabio. Fabio had the same wet-look curls as Emerson, suggesting that the hairstyle was a family trait rather than just tonsorial whimsy. Mysteriously Fabio actually managed a first-team appearance for Middlesbrough as wing-back during a 3–0 win over Huddersfield, but his contract was terminated shortly afterwards and he has not been heard from since.

Most poignant of all is the tale of the third foreign cousin of the Bryan Robson era. When Jaime Moreno came to Ayresome Park from the Bolivian club FC Blooming in 1994, the young South American was, predictably perhaps, accompanied by his cousin, Javier. Jaime made twenty-seven appearances for Boro and now plies his trade with some success for DC United in the US. Javier, meanwhile, married a local girl and was last heard of running a pizza takeaway in Billingham.

Crime Campaign

In October 2006 Rio Ferdinand spoke out against the use of knives. 'The kids and the youth do not need them,' the Manchester United central defender told Sky. 'I mean, if you want to cut something up you can just use your fork, that way you've got a hand free for texting.'

Crisis in Refereeing

Chief Referee in the Land of Albion Keith Hackett adopted a radical solution to the refereeing crisis that gripped England during the 2005–6 season – putting both managers in charge of all decisions because 'they are the experts, apparently'. It was brought into force for the first time at Old Trafford. Despite the lack of match officials, the game ended in controversy as Chelsea equalised with a penalty in the ninth minute of injury time which José Mourinho awarded to his own side after Arjen Robben appeared to dive in the United area. 'Maybe when I see the replays of that decision tonight I am going to be a little disappointed with myself,' the Blues boss said afterwards with a sultry pout. 'But I have only a split second to make my mind up and I think it is a brave thing to do because not many referees have the courage to award one against United here.' Sir Alex Ferguson, meanwhile, was said to have been seen heatedly remonstrating with himself in the tunnel after the game. 'Fergie was incandescent about the amount of time he had added on,' revealed an eyewitness. 'He approached himself looking furious, told himself to back off and then there appeared to be some jostling and I heard an angry Scottish voice yelling, "You're a f***ing disgrace." Though whether that was Sir Alex yelling that at himself or vice versa I cannot be sure.'

Cup Final Build-up

We should have seen it coming, but it was a shock nevertheless. In February 2004 a secret poll carried out on behalf of this book revealed that when offered the choice between a long weekend in Tuscany and watching a fifth round FA Cup tie a staggering seven out of the nine people who could be bothered to respond to the email opted for a break in Italy ahead of Sunderland vs Birmingham live on BBC1.

According to tactical analysts, the Italian province had tactically outwitted the traditional gritty collision between two teams who hardly set the pulse racing by deploying olive groves in the hole behind breathtaking Renaissance architecture and the fact that even the most bog-standard trattoria is serving the sort of amazing food you'd drive two hundred miles to eat in this godforsaken country, darling.

Things were so very different in days gone by. Then the FA Cup was woven into the biorhythms of national life. Farmers sowed their crops on the day of the quarter-finals and harvested them at first round proper, snow never fell until the second round replays were complete and cuckoos refrained from calling until semi-final day.

Three decades ago today the nation rose as one, Brentford Nylons night attire sending showers of electrical sparks flashing across the greyness of the morning. In every living room across the land what we still referred to in those days as 'the television set' was switched on and all of England sat back and watched as 'the build-up' to the great day began.

First off FA Cup fifth round *Ask the Family*. Robert Robinson, hair teased over pallid pate in diligent homage to his idol Ralph Coates, posing conundrums to a couple of sets of parents and children specially selected from the home towns of the Cup favourites for their intelligence, thick glasses and taut air of emotional repression.

'Now,' the host would say as a mysterious black-and-white image flashed on to the screen, 'for the Alpaca family of Wolverhampton we have this photograph of an object traditionally associated with the FA Cup, viewed from an unusual angle. Can you tell me what it is?'

'We think it might be the faucet from one of the communal baths at Wembley,' Mrs Alpaca would venture after a hushed conversation.

'A good answer,' Robert would respond. 'But not the correct one, I fear. Though I can see why you think it might be. So, I pass it over. Any ideas, Mr Pimple?'

'Is it perhaps the Duke of Kent?'

'Let's have a look shall we. By Gad, sir, you're right! It is the Duke of Kent, patron of the Football Association, and viewed from, might I say (and I think I might), a position from which I imagine even the good Duchess herself has never seen him. Although in this permissive age we can't rule it out, or indeed in.'

A special FA Cup fifth round edition of *Tomorrow's World* followed. Raymond Baxter, swooping around the studio, talking in a voice that conjured the majestic drone of a Sunderland flying boat, would show us what football would be like in 2004. Holding in one hand a cardboard carton filled with some space age material the like of which we had never before seen and in the other a potato, he'd flash his what-will-the-crazy-boffins-back-at-HQ-come-up-with-next grin and tell us, 'And the crowds that flock into the hover-stadium on the wind-powered, aerial monorail won't be eating food as we know it. Not for these twenty-first-century fans the dehydrated Vesta Chow Mein or tin of ham and cheese toast toppers we enjoy before a match today, instead they'll be meeting all their nutritional needs with these things. They are called simply "fries" and incredible though it may seem these extraordinary, limp, greasy strips of pre-digested pap are made out of this, the common-all-garden spud.'

When FA Cup *Panorama* came on next the nation would

glance at the clock on the mantelpiece and groan as they saw that it was still only 4.45 in the morning and there was an age to go before Frank Bough would utter the magic words, 'And now let's go over to the Teleprinter.'

Curses

The late Wilf Mannion had an explanation for why the Middlesbrough side he played for had lost to Burnley in the FA Cup quarter-final of 1947. 'Ayresome Park was cursed by gypsies,' he said, pointing out that Derby County had been similarly afflicted until 1946 when, the jinx having been lifted, they went on to Wembley and victory. Asked whether the hoodoo might also have foiled Boro's chances of winning the First Division, Mannion was less certain, 'I think it was just the Cup it affected,' he said.

Nowadays, with science – in the form of physiotherapists, psychologists and dieticians – an increasing presence in the game, you might think that such superstition would be a thing of the past. Far from it. If anything, an even more mysterious spirit now rules the British game. And I'm not just talking about Malcolm Glazer. While modern tactical refinements mean that these days there are very few wizards on the wing, there seem to be an increasing number wandering about in the centre circle muttering imprecations.

Leyton Orient, for example, called in a druid to lift the curse of Brisbane Road. Something many Orient fans will feel should have been easy enough since chairman Barry Hearn only weighs about 170 pounds.

In Southampton, meanwhile, a white witch revealed that the then recently erected St Mary's Stadium was built on the site of a Saxon burial ground, a fact that was said to account for Saints' failure to win in their new home. In response the club allegedly brought in a pagan goddess (Where do they get these people from, by the way, the *Yellow Pages*? 'Goddesses, Pagan. *See under* Deities, Female, Pantheistic and Druidical Services') to placate the disturbed spirits.

Oxford United on the other hand adopted a more cosy, mainstream approach, calling in the Bishop of Oxford, the Right Reverend Richard Harries, to say a prayer of exorcism in the centre circle at their new ground, Kassam Stadium. Commenting on the reasons behind the exorcism, Oxford's club chaplain said, 'It is better to be safe than sorry.' One has only to imagine the sight of United's boss at the time, Mark Wright, spewing green vomit to know that he is correct.

After the ceremony a spokesman for the Bishop said, 'Hopefully Oxford United will feel they're on a level spiritual playing field as well as on a level grass one.' (And they wonder why people don't go to church any more.)

The Bishop's efforts seem to have been unsuccessful – Oxford went down to the Conference shortly afterwards. They should have known it would work out that way. In the early 1980s Birmingham City attempted to lift a longstanding curse on St Andrew's by bringing in a priest and painting crosses on the dressing room doors and the players' boots. This did little to drive off the evil spirits, though it is reported that when Pat Van Den Hauwe saw them his eyes began to revolve and a fearful howling noise rose from deep within him.

Later Barry Fry (something of an expert on curses judging by his efforts on that TV documentary a few years back) was told that to lift the Blues' malediction he should walk around the ground and urinate near each corner flag. The robust Fry duly performed the ceremony, though not without considerable effort. 'It's a pretty difficult exercise to squirt a little by the corner flag, walk sixty yards to the next corner and do it again four times in succession,' he explained later, adding, 'It didn't work. I got the sack.'

Even stranger were the efforts of Swansea City. Warned by Uri Geller, whose nephew had been playing for the Welsh club, that 'evil influences' were at work at the Vetch Field, forcing the club towards relegation (it's possible they spilled out from Swansea University's Egypt Centre where several staff are reputed to have resigned because of the paranormal vibrations given off by a collection of ancient death masks, though admittedly it is more likely to have something to do with John Hollins), the Swans decided to deal with them by bringing in a circus act, 'The Kenyan Boys'. Unfortunately on the day they were supposed to perform a dance to drive out the malignant forces, a more regular curse, the Welsh weather, struck. The Kenyan Boys refused to go out in the pouring rain. The dance went unperformed. The Swans went down.

– D –

Dadage

The era of a football fan's life in which he or she starts to sound like his/her father. Usually begins in the mid-forties and is characterised by a tendency to say, 'Cristiano Ronaldo? He's not fit to lace George Best's boots', 'There just aren't the characters in the game any more' and 'Call that a tackle! He couldn't tackle a fish supper.'

Dane-o-Block

Dane-o-Block was a piece of computer software that protected viewers from watching unsuitable material on their TV. When plugged into your digi-box it automatically changed channels whenever Peter Schmeichel appeared on the screen struggling not to say 'we' when he was talking about Manchester United. A Stubbsy-and-Lawro-Banter Filter was also available. Later the BBC made the machine obsolete by dispensing with the services of the former Manchester United keeper.

Dangling Qualifier

The language of footballers is skilfully covert. Like the piano style of Thelonius Monk or the forward play of Clive Allen, it is often not so much what they put in as what they miss that is truly important. Take, for example, the popular use of the dangling qualifier. This cunning verbal ploy leaves it up to the listener to imagine the statement to which the mitigating clause ought to be attached. 'To be fair', the footballer will say apropos of nothing, 'their fans were brilliant.' No sooner has he uttered this sentence than all across the nation people will be scratching their heads trying to work out what should have preceded it: 'The ground is a right dungheap, but to be fair . . .'? 'They played like a bunch of incontinent poodles, though to be fair . . .'? Thus a player makes a telling point for which no blame can be apportioned to him.

Demographic of Fans

Reports that the demographic of supporters attending football games is ageing were confirmed in a survey carried out before third round FA Cup matches in 2007. Asked to answer the question 'Do you think fans these days are older than they used to be?' 5 per cent of respondents replied 'No', 20 per cent replied 'Yes', while a massive 75 per cent said 'Colder? I should say we're colder. But you just can't buy a decent woollen overcoat any more for love or money. These days it's all just those Continental blooming anorak-type things. I wouldn't give you tuppence for them.'

Dentists

On the Continent players have strangely been lured towards dentistry as a profession for many years. Hugo Sanchez, the Mexican forward who won the European Golden Boot when he was with Real Madrid, was a dentist; Gheorghe Hagi, the Maradona of the Carpathians, owns a chain of dental surgeries in his native Romania; and Peter Kunter, Eintracht Frankfurt goalkeeper from 1965 to 1976, and Pak Do Ik, scorer of North Korea's winner over Italy in the 1966 World Cup, were also men who spent their time away from football poking around in people's mouths while muttering, 'C3, B42-5', to a receptionist in a nylon uniform.

Perhaps that is why the importance of teeth has caught on so quickly with foreign coaches. One of Jean Tigana's first acts on taking over at Craven Cottage was to have the Fulham players' teeth checked so that he could tell if their posture was correct. The Fulham manager's compatriot Gérard Houllier was clearly of a similar mind because Liverpool midfielder Steven Gerrard claimed that his groin problems had been alleviated by the arrival of wisdom teeth, while another Frenchman, Marcel Desailly, blamed Achilles tendon trouble on unspecified dental problems. It would be very easy to dismiss this as so much ridiculous mumbo-jumbo, which is just as well because it is.

Diamond Stud

Vital component of footballer's attire and the way he describes himself to girls.

Diving

During the 1920s the British boxer Phil Scott rose into the upper rankings of a then formidable heavyweight division by use of a simple but effective tactic: the minute an opponent took aggressive action against him the Londoner would fall to the canvas clutching his groin and squeaking, 'Foul!' He carried out this manoeuvre so frequently that he was nicknamed

Faintin' Phil, the Horizontal Heavyweight, or more floridly the Swooning Swan of Soho.

The names that Robbie Savage has been called during his career are a good deal less poetic, but there are certain similarities between the Welsh midfielder and the English fighter. It was said of Scott that, unlike other old pugs, he wouldn't be able to run a public house after retirement because every time the bell rang on the cash register he would fling himself to the deck. It would be likewise hard to imagine the Savage opening a butcher's shop after he hangs up his boots, for he would surely be incapable of seeing a leg of lamb without falling over it.

Neither Scott nor Savage excites much admiration. One pugnacious boxing referee who had officiated over Faintin' Phil commented, 'He is the yellowest bum I ever saw. For ten cents I'd take him into a cellar and give him a licking myself.' The Welshman, meanwhile, provoked the normally amiable Jim Smith to let rip. The Bald Eagle claimed that Savage thrived on notoriety (a suggestion which will delight those readers who like me have longed for the day when the sporting scene produced a worthy successor to long-haired bad boy grappler Adrian 'The Blond Bombshell' Street, though until Robbie dons thick eye shadow and a feather boa he won't be all the way there, obviously). 'We've all seen players who were clever at getting penalties,' Smith thundered one Saturday, 'but he's not even clever.'

The implication of Smith's remark was that had the player's antics a bit of finesse about them, he would have been a good deal less vexed. You can see his point. The cat burglar and the conman make popular heroes in books and films, but nobody likes a mugger.

In fairness to Savage, it should be said that diving is not an easy art to master. In fact of all football's skills it ranks as the third hardest, just behind the bicycle kick and blowing your nose with your hand without getting snot all down the front of your shirt. For those wishing to really make a go of it and save themselves from humiliation the trick is to pick from one of the tried and trusted styles and then work at it and work at it until they have got it right.

THE ABSENT-MINDED SPRINTER

By far the simplest of all diving techniques and one used by many top talents including Luis Figo and Robert Pires. The diver rushes forward normally until opponents close in, at which point he suddenly suffers a temporary loss of memory and leaves his feet behind. His head and torso continue on their forward journey while his boots remain rooted to the turf inevitably causing the player to topple earthwards. A nice embellishment to this approach is for the diver to kick one of his own ankles as he falls and then cast about urgently as if looking for the culprit, in the manner of Eric Morecambe pretending that guest star Glenda Jackson has pinched his bottom.

THE UNBEARABLE LIGHTNESS OF BEING MICHAEL OWEN

Some players are clearly too saintly to actually dive. They are simply the victims of bodies so lacking in ballast that the merest brush of a sleeve can send them crashing to the ground. England striker Michael Owen, with his pleasant face, sensible haircut and general air of an aspiring junior executive who's just checked into a luxury hotel and taken full advantage of the in-room trouser press facility, is clearly not the sort of man to try and pull the wool over anybody's eyes, and yet . . . He has fallen over an awful lot, most notably in World Cup games against Argentina. This is not cheating, though. It is just that

Michael is so lacking in substance that the very breath of a South American defender is enough to unbalance the poor little fellow. Clearly not many players are so blessed, but using Zen actualisation techniques and muttering the mantra, 'I am as thistledown wafting on the breeze', even the burliest of strikers can achieve similar results.

THE OSCAR NOMINEE

Most diving is purely utilitarian, but some players like to bring a pinch of melodrama to the act, engaging in wild histrionics that call to mind the movie actors of the Silent Age. The great German striker Jurgen Klinsmann, for example, would soar into the air, his body jerking hideously as if being subjected to a massive electric shock, and on hitting the ground execute a series of rolls culminating in a final spasm and a cry of existential anguish such as you might imagine emanating from the character in Edvard Munch's *The Scream*. By such methods he succeeded in getting Argentina's Pedro Monzon sent off in the 1990 World Cup Final. Klinsi was a diver of extraordinary dramatic talent. Even he, however, must bow before the greatest single exposition of the craft, which was performed in 1989 by the Chile goalkeeper Roberto Rojas during his nation's match with Brazil. Faced with certain defeat and elimination from the World Cup, Rojas hit on a brilliant scheme – forcing the match to be abandoned. When a firework thrown from the crowd landed in his penalty area Rojas hurled himself down amid the smoke, took a razor blade out of his glove and slashed open his scalp. Carried off on a stretcher while his team-mates created a riot, his plan seemed to have worked when the game was stopped. Sadly his antics had been caught on camera and after Fifa reviewed the evidence it was Chile not Brazil that were kicked out of the tournament, while Rojas was banned from the game for life.

Like a cruise missile, some forwards can pilot themselves through the air and into the opposition penalty area with pin-point accuracy no matter where they start their dive (though unlike cruise missiles they rarely veer mysteriously off course and crash into a nearby hospital). One of the great exponents of this style was Francis Lee of Manchester City who, during the 1970s, won and then converted so many penalties that many believed his surname was actually Lee Pen. Whenever, or wherever, a defender's leg was left outstretched Lee could contrive to trip over it and fly into the box, his chunky body and swift progress through the air calling to mind an alarmed grouse. Some have recently claimed that Ruud Van Nistelrooy, late of Manchester United, was even better than Lee, but those who witnessed the great man in his pomp will hear none of it, though that may simply be a case of the past lending disenchantment.

Dogs and Footballers

The bond between dog and footballer is a historic one. When Jack Charlton lived in the village of Great Ayton while managing Middlesbrough the lawn in front of his house was littered with large and well-gnawed bones. Presumably these belonged to his Labradors, though a feeling persisted among some that they were actually the limbs of forwards he'd taken as souvenirs during his playing days at Leeds. Big Jack was not alone. Peter Shilton had a Dalmatian and Andy Gray an Old English sheepdog. Even Sir Alf Ramsey liked dogs. He had a miniature dachshund named Rusty. 'He's a lovely little fellow. He hasn't a bad thought in him,' he told the Dagenham *Post* and somehow you feel that the words 'Unlike Rodney Marsh' were there, hanging and unspoken.

At one time if footballers were not being photographed making a trip down the local coal mine (a tradition sadly abandoned of late largely because of the closure of the pits, though surely after a poor away result at Blackburn Arsène Wenger must be tempted to make Jens Lehmann and Co. go on a trip around a call centre?), they were being snapped with their dogs. By tradition these were usually something big and hairy – the canine equivalent of Micky Droy or Trevor Hockey – and named Rocky or Butch.

In the seventies and eighties you could hardly pick up a paper without seeing Kevin Keegan with his arm around a big, fluffy-haired, affectionate mutt with its tongue lolling comically out of one side of its mouth. And if he wasn't with Terry McDermott, then chances were he'd be with his dog.

Sadly the once great bond between footballers and dogs has now been all but broken. Only that old school warrior Roy Keane still carries on the tradition, walking dear old Trigs ceaselessly whenever a crisis looms (by now the poor thing's legs must have been worn to nubbins). But, figuratively at least, Keano walks alone. Nowadays if you see any of his fellow players having a cheek licked by something with a wet nose and a waggy tail the chances are it will be beneath the headline, 'Actress/Model's Secret Night of Cocaine and Passion with Soccer Star.'

Once it was pastoral utility breeds, now it is members of Girls Aloud. No doubt they are just as loyal and affectionate, and from the look of Cheryl Tweedy I'd say she'd be capable of clearing a garden shed of rats as quick as any Patterdale terrier, but they do not occupy the same place in the hearts of the British public. And nor, as a consequence, do footballers.

The widespread perception of the probable and improbable England boss, Steve McClaren, is of a man erring towards the chilly side of blandness – a left-over rice pudding on the managerial dessert trolley, if you will. But if Mac were to get himself seen around town with a couple of bearded collies, or a pair of

Ramsey-esque wire-haired dachshunds getting their leashes tangled around his legs, that would surely change.

Besides in the cut-throat environment of modern professional football dogs have an important role to play. As top psychologists such as Willi Railo would probably say, the dog is the footballer's waggy-tailed emotional safety net.

Dressing Room

Towards the end of his days at Leicester City Peter Taylor told the world, 'Some people have been saying that I have lost the dressing room. I have not lost the dressing room.' Rumours that a large, tiled chamber with a door marked 'Home' had been handed in at a Loughborough police station were clearly unfounded.

It's easy to see why Taylor was worried, though. A poor start to the season would be demoralising enough without the players having to spend the time before kick-off scurrying along behind their manager as he raced around the corridors beneath Filbert Street muttering frantically, 'It's here somewhere, I know it', and his assistant counselled, 'Just try and think where you were when you saw it last, gaffer.' This is not prematch preparation, it is a scene from *This is Spinal Tap*.

If Taylor had lost the dressing room the effects would indeed have been disastrous. Not least because Muzzy Izzet and his colleagues would have had to get changed on the bus like a school team, with a subsequent collapse of spirit caused by anxiety that passing girls might see their pants. As it was in their next game they were able to concentrate for the full ninety minutes on football. Undistracted by the thought that at the final whistle they would have to wash the mud off their legs from the outside tap the groundsman uses for his hosepipe, they got a last-minute equaliser.

Strange though it may seem, the substance of Taylor's comment was not that unusual. In fact it reflects an obsession among members of his profession. Football managers place great emphasis on locating things. During the close season they look for the missing piece in the jigsaw in the form of a striker who knows where the goal is, and their teams often fall apart after losing their shape. The latter is a mysterious thing that has never been fully explained but is believed by many to be a symbolic device akin to the Holy Grail which once misplaced causes the kingdom to fall into lawlessness, crops to fail, storms to rage and the team to concede several second-half goals to Newcastle United. Losing their shape is the worst thing that can happen to a team, but mislaying anything can have terrible consequences for the coach.

Bryan Robson, for example, resigned as manager at Middlesbrough because he said he had lost the crowd at the Riverside Stadium, a search down the back of the sofa and in the pockets of the suit he last wore at his brother-in-law's wedding having proved fruitless. When Kenny Dalglish was in charge at Liverpool, meanwhile, he apparently fretted that if players spent Friday nights with their wives and girlfriends they might get so carried away they lost their legs. Apparently on Saturday mornings the Scot was often to be found in his office, phone clamped to an ear, saying patiently, 'And are you sure they're not in your other trousers, Aldo?' It was an attention to detail that brought trophies.

Spending so much time looking for stuff while simultaneously struggling hard to ensure the kids don't take what they already have out into the garden and lose it in the sandpit has lead to a tendency among football managers to put rather too high a value on ownership. Possession is said to be nine-tenths of the law – among footie folk that would be considered to be erring rather too dramatically on the side of the dispossessed.

Bob Dylan

Bob Dylan's brief attachment to Hartlepool United sparked some of the greatest rock songs ever written about the game of football. The Alan Sunderland-haired singer arrived in England during the 1963–64 season to hang out with the luminaries of the British folk scene such as the Knitters, Bernadette Earnest, Wilf Suffering, the Welsh-Dresser Family and Big Iain Smock. These folk folk were not interested in football, preferring to spend their Saturday afternoons whittling, weaving and recalling great mining disasters. Bored, Dylan had gone off wandering on his own in the hope of finding an eighteenth-century miscarriage of justice on which to pen a few bitter stanzas when, attracted by talk of 'some mystery voodoo cat' named Ernie Pythian, he found himself entering the Victoria Ground.

Dylan was no novice when it came to soccer. Though he had briefly been an apprentice with local US League side the Duluth Foot Servants, he was not offered professional terms (an incident later recalled in his song 'I Shall Be Released'). However, it was on the terraces at Hartlepool, watching Ambrose Fogarty, Bob Brass and Stan Storton that Dylan's mind was opened to what his music could become – frenzied, wild, angry and filled with arcane, yelped phrases, 'Track him, keep your shape, put it in the mixer, get tight on them, don't follow leaders, watch the parking meters.'

The result was an outpouring of creativity the like of which the world has never before seen as Dylan penned a sheaf of songs that would shape a generation including 'Fifteen Believers All Dressed in Blue' (a reference not, as some writers have suggested, to the Scotland rugby union team but to the crowd at the Victoria Ground for a Tuesday evening Durham Senior Cup tie against Easington Colliery), 'Typically Holker Street' and 'Your Brand-New Leopard Skin Pill-Box Hat', a satirical broadside aimed at Malcolm Allison.

Perhaps most splendid of all was a song that looks forward into the future at Hartlepool with uncanny accuracy, 'Visions of Joe Allon'. The resonant opening lines sum up the experience of watching football with extraordinary lucidity: 'Ain't it just like the ref to wave play on when you've nobody free?/ Your forwards stand there forlorn, gesturing oh so vacantly/ And a bloke proffers up some midget gems saying, "Go on, take two or three"/ He says, "We were rubbish last week an' all/ And we never even got a sniff of the ball/ When we lost at Roots Hall".'

Sadly the songs were never recorded in their original form. The reason for the lyrical changes was simple: Joan Baez. Dylan's raven-haired muse and inamorata was a passionate advocate of rugby league and forced him to excise all mention of what she termed 'twenty-two big jessies running round kissing one another'. Her attempts to get him to insert references to Hull Kingston Rovers and Billy Boston were less successful, though some Dylanologists insist that the later song 'Idiot Wind' was inspired by recollections of the commentary style of David Coleman.

– E –

Elegiac Reaction

Most people will have heard of an allergic reaction; in football, however, the elegiac reaction is becoming increasingly common. Instead of greeting victory with the familiar vindictive fist-waving and taunting of 'the doubters' by 'ramming it down their throats', top players suffering an elegiac reaction tend to respond to a win or a defeat by talking mournfully about the need to 'put things in perspective' and drawing attention to the grave situation in Chechnya.

Emotions

The emotional response of footballers to any situation used to be much more muted than it is today. In the 1950s, for example, goal celebrations were not the passionate frenzy that is such a jolly aspect of the contemporary scene. Back then the scorer simply received a pat on the shoulder from the man who supplied the final pass and he reciprocated with a robust punch on the chin and a cry of 'Take your hands off me or I'll see you're thrown in jail, you pervert.'

In the past a 'good communicator on the pitch' was a man who kept his own counsel. Should a player have blurted out even a quick 'Man on!' to a team-mate, you can rest assured he would have been taken quietly aside afterwards and told in no uncertain terms that in future he was to bottle such things up until he got home, at which point he was free to take them out on his family in the form of unwarranted outbursts of sarcasm.

Contrary to popular myth, this sangfroid was not due to inner resolve on the part of the English sportsman and his admirers, but stemmed from the lasting effects of the severe rationing of frivolity during and immediately after the Second World War. Incredible though it may seem to us in our own emotion-rich times, between 1939 and 1953 government restrictions meant that British children were forced to make do with half a dozen chuckles, a couple of chortles and a cheery 'Wotcha, mister!' per week, while married couples got by on a yearly allowance of eight ounces of monkey business and as much give-over-Cyril as they could produce in a lean-to greenhouse.

The rest of England's supply of good humour and affection was commandeered as part of the war effort, the plan being that when sufficient was stockpiled it would be dropped on the Germans, who would then easily be overpowered in the ensuing explosion of merriment, guffawing and hanky-panky. Unfortunately by the time the required mega-tonnage had been accumulated US scientists had invented Bob Hope and Dorothy Lamour and so there was no need of it.

In the mid-1950s, thanks to the development of the Goons and Diana Dors, Britain at last felt able to dispense with its war-time reserve. The entire supply was taken out in a convoy of little ships and dumped in the North Sea. Inevitably it entered the food chain. And twelve years later, thanks to our nation's appetite for fish and chips, it kick-started the swinging sixties.

Entertainment

It has been suggested that under José Mourinho Chelsea surrendered the tag of 'the Entertainers', a title they picked up during the days when their starting line-up was packed to the gussets with mercurial talents such as Micky Droy, Ray 'Butch' Wilkins and Mike Brolly.

However, to say that José Mourinho's side was not entertaining betrays a lack of understanding of modern entertainment. In the seventies, when Chelsea earned their soubriquet, it is true that a single episode of *Seaside Special* (featuring Guys 'n' Dolls and Bernie Clifton) drew an amazing sixty-seven million viewers. The fact that this was thirteen million more people than actually lived in Britain was explained by some families loving the show so much they bought two TVs and watched it on both at the same time. Things have moved on since then, though, and what we call entertainment has changed. While Eddie McCreadie, John Hollins and suchlike were undoubtedly the footballing equivalent of Val Doonican singing a jaunty Irish ditty about Father O'Flannery's Ferret while the Young Generation jigged about in the background in hip-hugging slacks and polyester polo necks, that time has gone.

Sad though it may be to admit it, we no longer live in a world of Ali Bongo, Lieutenant Pigeon and that bloke who used to sing 'Mule Train' while smacking himself over the head with a tea-tray.

Yes, we all remember with affection the famous glamour days at the Bridge when pop stars such as Leapy Lee and Hugo Montenegro and his Orchestra were begging for jobs as ball-boys, Peggy Mount made the half-time tea, and Peter Osgood, Alan Hudson, Charlie Cook and the rest were frequently joined in the post-match bath by glamorous A-list megastars such as Derek Guyler, Pinky & Perky and Truman Capote (at that point still basking in the glory of creating a new literary form – non-fiction journalism). But we have to let it go and move on.

Nowadays what constitutes entertainment is altogether different from those innocent times. Look at the TV schedules and you will see that what the public wants is reality shows, preferably featuring celebrities (or realebrities as the smart set call them). Watching a former Royal equerry bury his face in a bowl full of maggots, or a woman who once had an affair with a bloke who was once married to someone who was once in *Driving School* trying to explain what Sweden is to the pudding-faced bloke from Bros – that is entertainment today. The sitcom, too, has changed. Out have gone finely crafted gags about Mrs Slocombe's pussy, or Chinese people's accents and in has come naturalistic comedy of cruelty and social embarrassment.

Stamford Bridge is a reality, it is filled with celebrities, and who can deny that watching José Mourinho's side is much the same as watching Antony Worrall Thompson trying to shin-up a tree in his underpants?

As to the excruciating Dave Brent-style moments, well, the modern King's Road Entertainers have that well covered, too. 'Did you see Peter Kenyon last night? God, when he did the "Everyone wants to be loved" stuff'! I could only watch it through my fingers.' Variations on those words have been heard hundreds of times during the past three seasons.

Etcetera Affected Disorder

In February 2004 BBC pundit Mark Lawrenson became the first sports personality to give an interview in which over half his answers were the word etcetera. Asked to sum up his feelings at cracking the fabled 50 per cent and so on and so forth barrier, Lawrenson responded: 'I've etc. But etc. You have to etc, etc, etc.' Lawrenson's chief rival, Newcastle striker Alan Shearer, who many had tipped to be the man to take things on to the next etc, remains philosophical. 'At the end etc. Records etc,' he told the assembled media etc.

European Cinema

Leaving aside the efforts of **Ingmar Bergman** and official **World Cup Films** the great auteurs of European cinema have generally ignored the game of soccer. Only a very few stand-out movies exist. These include François Truffaut's homage to male friendship *Jules et Jim Rosenthal* ('They shared a life, a house, a woman and a lip-mic', the poster strap-line proclaimed) and Paolo Pasolini's lurid *44 Days of Sod 'Em*, an account of Brian Clough's time as manager of Leeds United. In 2007 it was announced that controversial Danish director Lars von Trier was planning to feature a top Premiership club in his latest collaboration with elfin Icelandic chanteuse Björk. The script of the film, *The Morons*, has yet to be completed, but von Trier says the movie will be true to the Dogme manifesto and offer cinema-goers 'a truly grim and disturbing tale filled with characters who range from the deeply unpleasant to the outright repellent'.

'Clearly it is an absolute honour for our football club to be associated with this prestigious project,' Freddy Shepherd then of Newcastle United said when von Trier named St James's Park as his venue of choice for filming. The irrepressible Toon Chair-gadgie added, 'And I have to say that I am really looking forward to working with that Berk.' Asked if he meant 'Björk', Shepherd replied, 'Oh, is she in it as well? I was talking about Douglas Hall.'

– F –

Fair Play League

With only a couple of Saturdays left in the 2003–04 season, things were balanced on a razor's edge. A slip-up by a defender, a flag raised by a linesman, or the short-circuiting of the immersion heater for the referee's bath are all it takes for fate to snatch a lucrative European place from a club's sweaty grasp. No wonder people were calling it the most exciting Fair Play competition in decades.

The automatic UEFA Cup spot for niceness goes to the most well-behaved team from the country that tops the UEFA Fair Play table. At that stage England led with an average of 8.2 out of 10, with Sweden lurking just behind on 8.16, closely followed by Poland, Finland, France, Russia and Ireland. Unfortunately this did not mean much as the last table the European authorities had seen fit to issue was back in February.

Why UEFA had waited so long to update things was a matter of conjecture. Either they were determined to crank up the tension, or the means of calculating the damn thing was so fiendishly complicated it baffled even the imaginative accountants at HQ. Clearly bookings and sendings-off came into it, but UEFA observers at matches also measured less tangible matters such as how the crowd behaved towards opposing teams and the way the host club treated match officials. Basically it is a combination of statistics and the spirit of the game – Rudyard Kipling meets the Duckworth-Lewis method.

In the Premiership Fair Play table clubs whose berths in the

Champions League and UEFA Cup are already secured occupied the top five places and so realising a European dream had come down to a battle royal for sixth between Manchester City and Middlesbrough.

Both Kevin Keegan and Steve McClaren claimed not to be influenced by considerations of fair play. And the Boro boss's insistence on playing the Riverside's resident hothead Franck Queudrue (six yellows and two reds so far that season), instead of somebody less likely to get involved in trouble (Mad Frankie Fraser, for instance), seemed to bear this out. However, when the two teams met at Maine Road in April the contest was so limp the considered opinion of most who witnessed it was that had they been boxers both would have had their purses withheld.

The general verdict was that, safely ensconced in mid-table, neither club had anything to play for. Others, though, wondered if in actual fact the exact opposite was the case. The teams had too much to play for to risk anything. As it was, a momentary lapse in concentration from Ugo Ehiogu gifted Keegan's men a 0–1 win on bookings. Altogether a good result for the home side, but with three hours-plus of football still to come it could still go either way. Or even to Scandinavia.

No wonder supporters of both teams were sweating. Other clubs simply had to win games, but for Boro and City there was an ocean of imponderables to take into account. A pitch invasion in London, some noisy and ill-informed chanting about the excellent Paul Durkin's sexual habits, or Robbie Savage paying a repeat visit to the wrong toilet, could tip things in Sweden's favour and end with the English winner being thrown into the hat with the most morally upright teams from any other countries that have averaged 8 out of 10 or over. The first two names drawn out also gain entrance to the UEFA Cup, as Ipswich Town had the previous year. Many considered this a torture too far. Bad enough that a supporter's mental equilibrium hangs on the performance of the eleven malingering fops who constitute their own team, without stirring in the efforts of the club catering staff, mixing in the activities of a load of tattooed fat boys in Burberry baseball caps 250 miles away, then chucking a lottery on top of it as well.

With so much to consider there was little wonder that on Monday mornings fans of both sides anxiously scanned the Internet looking to see how many yellow cards there were in the Polish top flight, or in the hope of discovering a mass brawl involving Trelleborgs and BK Hacken (unlikely, obviously, the Swedes having cunningly stopped playing altogether until the decision was made), or of finding that the tea lady at Krylya Sovetov stood accused of serving stale fig rolls to the linesmen.

And who was to say that the Belgian FA's swingeing assault on bankrupt top flight club Mechelen – relegated to the third division, starting the following season on minus-nine points and forced to change their name to Geel Red KV – might not have some effect on the UEFA table and lead to mighty Sint-Truindense or unfancied Mons edging out Keegan or McClaren's men?

It was a tense and difficult time, one that was not made any more bearable by the antics of some Premiership managers. Sam Allardyce asked for empathy when he savaged referees whose alleged blunders cost Bolton Wanderers vital points. But did the Trotters' boss care that his outbursts could be jeopardising the chances of an exciting away trip to Poltava or Brno for fans of another Premiership outfit?

In the end Manchester City took it.

Fairy Tale Characters

It is fair to say that characters from fairy tales and nursery rhymes have not always had a positive impact on the game of professional football. Prince Charming's transfer to Real Madrid had a much bigger effect on merchandising than it did on the field of play; the Gingerbread Man, once tipped as 'the new Franz Carr' by the media, failed to build on his natural assets of pace and stamina; and Old Mother Hubbard resigned after just seven days in charge at Elland Road telling friends that the Leeds job 'wasn't as advertised in the brochure'.

And then there was the chaos created at Wembley Stadium when Ken Bates elected to put the Three Little Pigs in charge of the building project. Things began badly when the third Little Pig fell out with his partners over their insistence on constructing the new 90,000-seat venue from organic, renewable materials (i.e. straw and sticks) rather than the bricks he had advocated. From then on the situation went downhill faster than the Grand Old Duke of York.

'It was a disaster,' recalled former FA chief executive Adam Crozier afterwards. 'The local authority vetoed the original plans because they said any stadium built of straw and sticks was likely to blow down. But whenever we tried to contact the two Little Pigs to discuss changes the secretary told us that they were unavailable, one apparently having gone to market while the other went "Wee, wee, wee" all the way home.

'We tried to get the third Little Pig back on board,' recalled Crozier, 'because he had always seemed to take a more pragmatic attitude to health and safety issues than the other pair, but by that stage he had been stolen by Tom the Piper's Son and eaten.'

Fans

Football fans come in many guises. You can identify most by their characteristic cries. Here are a few you may find yourself sitting next to.

THE SOCIAL REALIST

'A lot of pressure at this point in the season? You call this pressure, £20,000 to kick a ball about twice a week? This isn't pressure, lad. Pressure's when you're standing two hundred feet above the ground on a six-inch steel beam with no safety harness and a man chucking white hot rivets up to you, one per minute. You're that concentrated on them rivets you never hear the gale coming and the next thing you know it's pulling at your clothing. It's tugging at you. It's trying to pull you over the edge. It wants to smash your body to pulp on the cold, hard earth . . . No, that's pressure, lad. Mind we had some laughs an' all.'

THE WELL-ROUNDED MAN

'Well, you know the quality of light in Valencia is extraordinary, it's almost as if the very air is alive – GET STUCK IN BROWN, YOU FANNY MERCHANT – I think it's something to do with flat landscapes and water because, and this will sound funny – WHERE'S YOUR FLAG, LINESMAN, WEDGED UP YOUR ARSE? – the only other place I've encountered anything like it was on the salt marshes near Holkham. It was early evening, a thunderstorm was brewing and it gave this amazing golden tinge to everything that was positively ethereal – JESUS CHRIST, WILKO, YOU BLIND BANDY-LEGGED POOF – and really quite enchanting.'

MR HANDS FREE

'Can you hear us? Where are you? West Stand? I'm in the North Stand. Top left, about three rows down. Can you see us? I'm wearing that Hackett sweatshirt. Can you see us? I'm waving. Can you see us now? I'm stood on my seat waving both arms. Can you see us now? I'm jumping up and down on the seat and waving both arms. Can you see us now? I'm in the North Stand, top left, wearing a Hackett sweatshirt, I'm waving both arms and two stewards are escorting me down the steps. Can you . . . Bollocks, the signal's gone . . .'

CORRECTIONS AND CLARIFICATIONS

'Actually, mate, I think you'll find it's four defeats in six matches not five. Actually, the goal difference is currently minus-seven, which is actually one better than United's. Actually he wasn't playing at right back in that game because Ouija was injured and Séance was suspended, so actually he was utilised on the left of central midfield. Actually he was signed for £1.78 million not £1.77 million. Actually he's Moldovan not Russian. Actually my parents were married when I was conceived. Actually I think you'll find they use butterfly grips to seal a cut like this not stitches.'

THE EXPLAINER

'No, Jake, he looked as if he were offside, but he wasn't because he was inactive. It means not active. Yes, I know he was running, but I don't mean active in that sense. Well, I mean active in the sense of being active in a football sense, obviously. Look, let's say my glove is the player with the ball and my mobile is the ball, then . . . Give me your Mars Bar a minute. I'm not going to eat it. No, I promise. Well, clearly. All right, then: YES, I promise. Satisfied? Look, just give it me, will you. We didn't come here for chocolate. We came here for football. Well, if that's your attitude, young man . . . So, look, the glove slots the mobile through to the Mars and this programme is the defender and . . . Was that a goal? Who scored it? Oh, for Heaven's sake, here's your bloody Mars Bar.'

THE PENITENT

'It's never been the same since they abolished the maximum wage . . . I don't know what they're cheering that for he's barely struck it from thirty-five yards . . . They wouldn't be singing his name if they'd seen George Gizzard play . . . Bertram Chunk, now he was a footballer . . . He's not fit to lace Goddard Stump's rupture appliance, yon fella . . . Oh, give him a jelly, referee . . . When you think of how Cliff Triffid carried on battling away in midfield even though he was in an iron lung they make you laugh this lot . . . They're all pathetic . . . All right, I've suffered enough. I'm off. See you in a fortnight . . .'

SEEING THE BIGGER PICTURE

'Well, it's very tight, isn't it? I mean, we're fourteenth, but if we lose by two clear goals today, Wanderers and City don't get beat, United pick up the points at home, and one of the bottom three scrape a win, then suddenly we're in the drop zone. Whereas if we can avoid defeat, Town get gubbed away and any of the front-runners stumble, then suddenly we're just a couple of results away from the play-offs. Mind you, there's no guarantee that Athletic won't pull something out of the hat away in the Midlands and then it only takes City to pick up maximum points, Wanderers to score twice and not lose and . . . did we just score? That's good because if it stays like this and the result at East Road goes our way . . .'

THE CHOIRMASTER

'BLUE ARMY. BLUE ARmy. Come on, join in! What's the matter with ya? Let's get behind the team. QUE SERA SERA . . . Christ! Where's your passion? You might as well be sat at home watching Neighbours. THE REFEREE'S A WANKER. I'm glad I'm not in this section every week. I've had more fun at a funeral. HIT HIM ON THE HEAD. HIT HIM ON THE Oh what's the bloody point? You're all middle class, you lot.'

THE WALKMAN RELAY STATION

'SMITHY LOOKS ON FIRE, DOESN'T HE? WHAT? WHAT? I CAN'T HEAR YOU. ALAN GREEN'S YELLING. YEAH. HANG ON. PENALTY AT ST JAMES'S. SHEARER TO TAKE IT. HAHAHAHAHAHA, WANKER . . . ROVERS 2–0 UP. PARDON? I'VE GOT THESE ON, YOU'LL HAVE TO SHOUT. THERE'S A GOAL AT GOODISON. SMITHY GOT IT. WHAT? WELL, HOW COME YOU KNOW ALREADY? OH, RIGHT, SO WE ARE . . . SENDING OFF AT PORTMAN ROAD . . .'

THE INSPECTOR

'Sit down, I can't see . . . Sit down . . . I said, Sit down . . . You're not sitting, you're crouching . . . Sit down . . . Because I didn't pay £30 to stand . . . Every week the same thing . . . Sit down . . . Oh, right, and what about the fella behind me? What if he doesn't want to stand? He's a war veteran, you know . . . Sit down . . . You paid for that seat. Now put your arse on it . . .

Sit down ... Right, I'm off ... What do you mean, "Sit down"? ... I know there's five minutes left, pal ... Because if I nip away now I'll not get stuck in traffic ... Sit down your bloody self ... Well, I'm sorry if you missed a goal but if you'd just let me out instead of arguing ...'

THE SIMPLE PLANNER

'Where's our width, eh? Where's our width? Look! Look! Stood there in the middle like a bunch of grapes. WHAT ARE YOU DOING, HAVING A GOSSIP? GET IT WIDE! No one on the wing again! They're not going to waltz through the centre of this defence, are they? USE THE FLANKS, UNITED! Look at this pitch. Forty-three games on it and there's hardly a stud mark down either touchline. SPREAD IT! Look! Look! Acres of space, acres and we're all clustered round the centre spot. ARE YOU AGORAPHOBIC OR WHAT? WHERE'S OUR WIDTH?'

Fans Out Campaign

There were scenes of unrest at Villa Park in October 2005 when Aston Villa chairman Doug Ellis launched his 'Fans Out' campaign. The chairman's day of action began by his refusing a complimentary match-day programme and continued with him releasing a balloon on to the pitch before kick-off. After a sit-down protest in the directors' box at half-time, Ellis then invaded the players' lounge after the final whistle and stayed there smiling insipidly until he was dispersed by police. 'Every Villa chairman I have spoken to is sick and tired of these fans,' Mr Ellis told reporters afterwards. 'I intend to carry on with a well-orchestrated series of protests until they have finally turned their back on this club and been replaced with some wealthy new fans, possibly from Venezuela or the Far East, who will put some much-needed cash into the club shop and snack bars. Until that happens this club is going nowhere and neither am I.'

Fear Factor

The fear factor is an ever-present in football. Its effect on players can be catastrophic, leading many coaches to quote the famous words of John F. Kennedy: 'There is no factor to fear but the fear factor itself.'

Fiasco Exhaustion

Fiasco exhaustion, or FE as medical professionals know it, is sport's equivalent of compassion fatigue. Those struck down by FE find themselves overcome with lethargy at the very mention of 'an exciting and innovative concept by one of Britain's leading experts in the field of stadium design'. They become so listless they are unable even to work themselves up into a mouth-frothing fury at the mention of Ken Bates and luxury hotel and conference facilities.

In 2005–06 FE reached epidemic proportions across England. A survey carried out by the Department of Health during the summer of 2005 revealed that when asked, 'What precipitated the National Stadium crisis?', one in four British schoolchildren said they weren't sure but they thought the Romans might have had something to do with it. Asked the same question, three in four British adults say, 'Pardon? What was that again? No, sorry. It's weird but every time you start the question my mind just goes "Please hold the line", and starts playing the theme music from *Ski Sunday*.'

An article in the medical journal *The Lancet* recorded: 'The FE sufferer wants to yell, "If I hear the words New National Stadium ever again I will put my underpants on my head and run down the high street jabbering like Peter Alliss", but he cannot summon the energy. He becomes instead supine. "Build it where you want, from what you want and at whatever cost you decide, but just stop bothering me with this incessant bloody prattle" becomes the sufferer's attitude. It is as if when it comes to Wembley the human mind's natural immune system has become so overloaded it has simply ceased to synthesise cynicism and outrage any more.'

Fire Extinguisher

A large red object that shoots foam at fellow hotel guests. A vital part of player relaxation therapy (or 'horseplay' as it was once known) when taking a mid-season break in Dubai.

Alberto Flange

One of the greatest players of his generation, the balding moustachioed Chilean's remarkable style of play is best encapsulated in the following description from the *Tip-Top Football Book For Boys* (1965): 'Alberto Flange (Racing Concombre (France) and Chile) is a cunning central wing-nut whose perpendicular thrusts and whirling strategic lunges can dizzy even the most resolute half-back phalanx. Known in his native land as "El Banjo", this languid and metaphysical Andean boulevardier is at his most perspicacious when plucking the chords in no-man's-land from whence a sudden anonymous eructation can rapidly turn an opposition counter-riposte into a dangerous precedent. Twice winner of the prestigious Chorizo

Gordo, the thirty-two-year-old from the land of the rustling vicuña is considered by many experts to be the most redoubtable exponent of oblique probing the game of soccer has ever known.'

A Football Man

In January 2005 A Football Man was unveiled as the Big Club's new manager. A Football Man succeeded A Man the Fans Could Never Really Relate To, who had left the club ten days before by mutual sacking.

Speaking for the first time from his freshly designated parking place, A Football Man (whose appointment had been an open secret with local bookmakers ever since his name appeared in the frame after he threw his hat into the ring, following a six-month sabbatical to pursue unemployment and other opportunities outside the game) said he was delighted with his new role. 'Everyone knows that the Big Club is a genuine football club,' he said. 'The whole place lives, breathes and sweats football. It's 110 per cent wall-to-wall solid football through and through, from the carpet tiles to the tea lady's hair and the heavens beyond, and you can't beat that in mine or anyone else's book.

'Make no mistake, the job here is massive,' Football Man said. 'But that is what attracted me to the salary. The players' heads are down, their tails are between their legs and the crowd is on their backs. I don't make promises, but one thing I will promise is that I will bring back effort, pride, character and card schools to this club. We are in the trenches. It is a time for the players to roll their sleeves up, dig deep and say, "Just deal the cards, fat man" in a Clint Eastwood voice. That way even if they fail they can at least look themselves square in the mirror and say they gave it the best shot with the hand they were dealt because if they don't they will kick themselves for the rest of their lives and they'll deserve to.

'It's a pressure cooker situation. But I love a pressure cooker. I love a battle. I love a Chinese-style steamer pan. I love being up the creek in a hole with my back to the wall and a corner to turn and a mountain to climb. People who know me will tell you that I relish a challenge.'

A Man Who Knows Him said, 'He relishes a challenge.' Asked what he thought the man he knows would bring to the challenge he relishes, A Man Who Knows Him said, 'Football Man is a great motivator. He knows when to put his arm round your shoulder and when to kick your backside and when to put his arm round your backside and kick your shoulder and sometimes both at once, if he deems it necessary so to do.'

'I don't suffer fools gladly and that applies to myself as much as anybody,' Football Man continued. 'But I come in with no preconceived ideas – except about bringing back hanging to protect Britain's kiddies, obviously. All the players will start with a clean sheet, but if they blot their copybook I will mark their card and they will be on their bikes showing me a clean pair of heels before their feet touch the ground.'

This was believed to be a veiled reference to Want Away Striker, who earlier in the week had issued a come-and-get-me plea in an attempt to end his English nightmare. However, last night Want Away Striker moved to distance himself from himself, saying, 'You shouldn't believe everything I say in the newspapers. Most of it is just paper talk and the rest is an old story I rehashed from mistranslated quotes that I made up a long time ago. What is happening, Signor Capello? Did you lose my mobile number? No, I never said that.'

Supporters of Big Club had never warmed to A Man the Fans Could Never Really Relate To, but they were ecstatic about the appointment of Football Man. Said one excited season ticket-holder who had once met a reporter at a party and given him his telephone number in case he ever wanted any plumbing done, 'Although he has never actually won anything, Football Man is a twenty-four-carat winner. He will put a spring back in the face of this football club and smiles in a few bellies. Ever since he walked through the door there has been a buzz about the place, which is probably because he brought his beehives with him.'

A widely respected former player who now works for local radio in between pubs concurred. 'Except when it is all about results, the game is all about confidence. Football Man will get the dressing room behind him and he will get the dressing room bubbling again. And everyone in football knows that if you have a bubbling dressing room behind you and pulling in the same direction when it comes to turning things around, then that is half the battle. But half a battle does not win a war and Football Man will know that better than anyone, even me probably.'

In all the elation surrounding A Football Man's appointment, one voice sounded a note of caution, however. An Embittered Ex-Pro commented, 'I wish him well, but nothing is as good as it was in my day and there are far too many foreigners.'

Football Party

Short-lived political group founded by Jimmy Hill and presided over by José Mourinho after he had turned down the offer of the post of Pope because it was 'something in the way of an assistant position'. The Football Party's aims can be gleaned from a look at their 2004 manifesto.

'Under the Football Party public transport will be totally scrapped and the money used instead to provide every citizen with a sponsored Lexus (though only real wallies will drive them, obviously, because all the top lads have Humvees). The speed limit will be raised to 150 mph and there will be random compulsory breath tests with anyone caught under the legal limit fined two weeks' wages for "not being a good laugh". Road tax on Italian marques and sports utility vehicles will be abolished.

'On a law and order front we will see an introduction of instant punishments. Instead of entrusting minor felons to the costly and haphazard legal process, police officers will be empowered to order the offender to run ten times round the park with his shirt off, do a hundred press-ups, or wear a baseball cap bearing the legend "Plonker" for a week.

'A panel of retired referees, comprising the likes of Jeff Winter, Graham Poll and David Elleray, will replace the Law Lords. This will fundamentally change the nature of the decision-making process, while preserving the irrational and arbitrary element of British justice that has made it the envy of the world. Legal terms will be redefined with manslaughter becoming "an overenthusiastic challenge", attempted murder "handbags" and mass murder "something of nothing, really, Gabby".

'With the Football Party in power the nation will feel more secure. We will insist that the Minister of Defence is always over six foot tall, and everybody feels a lot happier with a big lad in there. Defence spending would be increased tenfold because without that platform the people further forward won't have the confidence to go out and express themselves.

'On the education front we will radically overhaul the national curriculum, making it vocationally focused to ensure that British school leavers are more capable of meeting employment needs. Lessons will run from ten until one with compulsory afternoon snooker sessions. "Making up a CD to play in the dressing room to get the boys wound up before kick-off" will become a major facet of the music syllabus and new GCSE subjects will include card games, organising a sweepstake and shopping for labels.

'Higher education will be abolished altogether because nobody feels comfortable when there's a "prof" around. Instead university degrees will be awarded based on continual assessment of life skills with a Ph.D. from the University of Hard Knocks going to anybody who left school at sixteen with no qualifications but is now driving a Ferrari, has a six-bedroom house next to a golf course or owns three-eighths of a racehorse.

'With five years until the next election we have plenty of time to get our ideas across to the public. And rest assured we will be doing so from now on using wild hand gestures coupled with yells of "channels, channels", forehead-slapping, scowling and the occasional hurled water bottle.'

Foreign Non-Investors

In November 2006, following in the footsteps of Russians, Venezuelans, Dubaians, Serbs and Thais, an Uzbek gas baron became the latest foreign plutocrat not to buy a Premiership club when he failed to pursue an interest in Leicester City beyond the back pages of the tabloids. 'This is fantastic,' said the dapper forty-five-year-old billionaire of his entirely hypothetical interest in the Foxes. 'As a boy I dreamed of being spuriously linked with a struggling English team long enough for their long-suffering fans to begin fantasising about a forward line of Henry, Ronaldinho and Klose and then suddenly disappearing never to be heard of again.'

Forgotten Men Card Game

On 7 April 1966 Alf Ramsey announced a preliminary squad of forty players for the World Cup finals. Later he added Bobby

Tambling to the list. This family game focused on the nineteen men who didn't make it to the final twenty-two. Using skill and judgement, players tried to match the face cards with the name and club badge cards. Were there really three Blackpool players on Alf's list? What did D. Temple look like? Is that Paul Reaney? Provided hours of brain-teasing fun until bankruptcy removed it from the shelves.

George Formby

Goofy Lancastrian comedian and singer Formby appeared in one of British cinema's best-loved football films. *A Right World Cup Lather* was shot at the 1938 Mondial. In its most famous scene the buck-toothed minstrel shares a comic duet with victorious Italian manager Vittorio Pozzo, 'I Wonder Who's Kissing My Trophy Now'. The song's well-loved chorus, 'It's one foot long, strong and neat/ When you polish it, it comes up a treat/ Your girl will smile and say "How sweet!"/When you put your little Jules Rimet trophy in her hand', was once whistled by milkmen from Land's End to John O'Groats.

Forward Exoneration Unit

Sometimes the England football team has lacked world-class players, sometimes it has lacked luck and sometimes it has lacked a top-quality coach. One thing the England football team has never been short of, however, is excuses.

Those unversed in the mysterious ways of what Pelé memorably dubbed 'futbol' may judge this to be simply a happy coincidence. Nothing could be further from the truth. It is all down to the ingenuity, hard work and careful planning of the men and women of the Football Association's Forward Exoneration Unit

'Excuses don't make themselves,' Jez Beevor, the FA's Chief Technical Director of Long Term Mitigation Operations, said in the build-up to Germany 2006. 'Tiredness due to playing more club matches than any other nation, a lack of opportunity for homegrown talent due to the influx of foreigners, insane managerial appointments – these things don't just happen by accident. You really have to work at them. And believe me, we do.'

Beevor's Soho Square office is plastered with flash cards bearing the slogans he uses to instruct and inspire his staff: 'The Buck Stops Somewhere', 'The Team That Excuses Together Loses Together' and 'Don't Fail To Prepare, Prepare To Fail'. When he talks to his staff, Beevor explained, 'I always get them to visualise the England team and its supporters as a group of claustrophobics desperately seeking a way out of a small, dark place called defeat. It's up to us to light the exit sign for them.'

As long-term followers of the England national team will know, the Forward Exoneration Unit is not a new thing. It was set up in the 1920s by FA secretary Frederick Wall, an Edwardian visionary who realised that English football's reputation would not long survive prolonged exposure to foreigners who had already begun amassing an armoury of cunning tricks such as passing to one another, kicking with both feet and tactics.

'Without forward planning in the area of exculpation, palliation and extenuation,' Wall noted, 'our bloated sense of self worth and ingrained complacency will be gravely damaged. Imagine for one instant what would happen should the Manchester cotton worker or Yorkshire miner wake up to the fact that the heroes they watch every week are actually a bunch of blundering half-wits marshalled and championed by a hierarchy of incompetent poltroons. The effect on national morale would be catastrophic.'

Wall entrusted the task of preventing such an outcome to a military intelligence officer, Colonel Hilaire St Cloud, who had previously done a splendid job convincing everyone in Blighty that the Germans weren't actually as good at fighting as we were, they'd just had the wind behind them for most of the Great War.

St Cloud came up with the perfect excuse for England not winning the World Cup – not entering it. Unfortunately after the Second World War the public foolishly started clamouring to pit our players against the Continentals and so the FA had to think up something else to assuage their inevitable disappointment.

In the 1950s that generally wasn't too difficult. Most English people had never travelled abroad, so when the cream of England's professional footballers came a cropper in World Cups it was a simple matter to persuade the public that it was due to the spicy local grub, terrible heat and the hostile crowds of swarthy men wearing greasy vests and reeking of garlic, even when the tournament was held in Switzerland or Sweden.

Cheap airfares and television coverage put a stop to that get-out clause, however. 'It's a cliché,' Beevor admitted in 2006, 'but there really are no easy excuses in international football these days. You're constantly looking for that little something extra, that little bit of quality: **The Robbo**, **The Hud**, Peter Kenyon sat in the stand waving a huge contract at your key central midfielder, a jumping penalty spot. And sometimes you just have to fall back on your classic set-plays – key player out injured, Sol Campbell having a goal disallowed, or Becks getting sent off – and hope that's enough to get you through.'

Unfortunately the English public refuse to buy into the sort of convoluted global conspiracy theories the Italian public gobbles up, leaving the Forward Exoneration Unit often feeling a little exposed at the back. 'The Italians are the masters of the paranoid grievance defence, but that's not something that's part of our culture,' Beevor explained.

After the debacle in Germany, Beevor heaped praise on England coach Sven-Göran Eriksson. 'Let's face it,' he said, 'Sven did a fantastic job in drawing the potential sting out of the catastrophe in Germany. Everyone quickly became convinced we would have lifted the trophy if only an Englishman had been in charge. That's a fantastic situation to have found ourselves in. But we can't get complacent about it. In football it only takes a second for things to go horribly right.

'At the end of the day, though, I think our record speaks for itself. We have never yet gone to the World Cup without a fantastic line-up of plausible reasons for failure. And if we ever did, I'd have to say there'd be absolutely no excuse for it.'

Future England Manager Syndrome

Many regard Future England Manager Syndrome as the biggest menace to English football since the invention of foreigners. At the end of the 2006–07 season Stuart Pearce became its latest victim.

It was inevitable, of course, because Pearce had been tagged as a 'future England manager', three words that have the same enervating effect on English coaches as the sign of the black spot did on the crew of Captain Flint's pirate ship.

Potential victims of Future England Manager Syndrome (FEMS) are easily spotted. They are generally former international players, they have neat hair, trim waistlines and a habit of using phrases such as 'steep learning curve', 'put it down to experience and move forward' and 'we have to remain positive and focused'.

FEMS should not be confused with its near relative One Of A Bright New Generation Of English Coaches Who Could

Really Make An Impact On The Premiership If Only One Of The Bigger Clubs Had The Courage To Give Him A Shot At It Virus (or Cotterill's Disease as it is colloquially known). This has struck a number of managers over the years, including Micky Adams, Mike Newell and Adie Boothroyd, but while sufferers such as Kevin Blackwell are often bad for quite a while after being diagnosed they generally make a full recovery and are soon making rueful self-deprecatory remarks to Five Live's Mark Clemmitt again from their office at Spotlands or wherever.

The effects of FEMS on the other hand are much more horrifying and the chances of a full recovery are virtually nil. Perhaps the effects of this debilitating mental complaint are best illustrated by considering the fate that befell Peter Taylor in 2001. One minute the former Crystal Palace winger was busy preparing the England squad for a friendly in Italy as caretaker boss, with his Leicester City side sitting top of the Premiership and everything apparently grand. Then people began to point at him and whisper, 'The chance has come too soon for him this time around, but in six or seven years . . .' Sure enough within what seemed like days Taylor was being chased from the East Midlands by an angry mob carrying placards emblazoned with images of Ade Akinbiyi.

No sooner had Taylor fallen victim to FEMS than another Future England Manager, Trevor Francis, found himself booted out of St Andrew's. When Francis first went into coaching his cocktail of England honours and 'Continental experience' (a rare and valued commodity albeit one with hints of the seamy – the sort of quality that might be advertised on a postcard stuck in a phone box) was thought to make him an ideal man to lead the national team 'one day'. Indeed, the then Birmingham City boss was reportedly the only other candidate the FA International Committee seriously considered before awarding the job to Kevin Keegan (how desperate a sentence does that look, by the way?). Later when Crystal Palace boss he was sacked on his birthday.

Then there was the case of Bryan Robson. Once being groomed as a successor to Terry Venables, Robbo took the long walk at the Riverside Stadium in the summer of 2001 with cries of derision ringing in his ears. And it has been more or less downhill ever since.

David Platt's CV closely mimicked that of Trevor Francis, which perhaps explains why FEMS struck before he had even hung up his boots at Highbury. Tasked with leading Nottingham Forest back to the big time, he was quickly struck down by the acute uselessness that is one of the disease's most obvious symptoms.

Some experts argue that it is not the tag of Future England Manager that is the problem, but the men it is applied to. The days when the FA could reject out of hand candidates for the national job such as Brian Clough are long gone. As a consequence any coach who puts a decent run together and isn't the subject of an ongoing police investigation comes under immediate scrutiny. The FA itself talks of fast-tracking top players through the coaching system, presumably so that their managerial careers can be ruined by the FEMS tag even before they have begun – a fact of which the wily Alan Shearer is surely all too aware.

The only manager who has so far withstood an acute case of FEMS is Steve McClaren and he only did it by actually becoming England coach. This was an appointment that called to mind the immortal words of Jesus Gil when he observed of the wisdom behind his latest managerial appointment: 'It may be that he is not the right man, but when all the other trains have left the station you can only take the one that is left.' Yet scientists nevertheless believe that if they can find what made Steve McClaren immune to the worst ravages of FEMS (possibly a thick skin, a massive ego and a sincere smile that nobody quite believes is genuine, or maybe just the antibodies of another common complaint, Sir Alex's Successor Complex), then they may be able to find a cure. For the sake of all those other Stuart Pearces out there we can only pray they succeed.

- G -

The Game as it is Meant to Be Played

'That's the sort of game the fans up here love,' Alan Shearer once remarked after Newcastle had beaten Man City 4–3 at St James's Park. The implication of the former England captain's words was clear: somewhere in another part of England there are supporters who really can't abide seeing their team win 4–3.

Initially this may seem unlikely. After all, every fan in the entire country claims to have been raised on a diet of exciting football. Listen to supporters and you'll find that all clubs in the British Isles have a tradition of stylish, cultured one-touch play, or a rich history of encouraging artistic ball-players, or of celebrating tricky wingers. 'They love their centre forwards up here,' the pundits gleefully observe, and never once do we hear anybody voice the opinion that, 'The number-three shirt is a big one to fill at this club'. There are a plethora of Schools of Science but not a single side that boasts of being an Academy of Brutalism.

Since Five Live came on air not a single fan has called up the *6–0–6* phone-in to say, 'Four–three, Spoony! Four bloody three. I'm gutted, mate. When will this manager be made to understand that this is not the City way? The fans at this club have been brought up on bitty, fractious, disjointed fare, where the ball is treated not as a friend or lover but as if it were a cold-calling tele-seller who has rung just as the milk pan comes to the boil. We don't want flair and thrills. We want football AS IT

IS MEANT TO BE PLAYED – nine across the back, a lard-arsed centre forward with sharp elbows, and big speculative punts that hang in the air like a marital argument. We want to watch something that's the visual equivalent of tinnitus. We don't want the game to leap up and smack us between the eyes. We want it to drizzle down our cheeks like a stranger's spittle.'

Despite the lack of any corroborative evidence, such fans must exist. After all, there are people who turn their noses up at chocolate and don't laugh at Tommy Cooper. We may imagine them sitting in the stands at the Emirates, inwardly groaning at Arsène Wenger's team and muttering, 'It just needs somebody to take their foot off the ball. The big problem's the ref. He's letting the game flow and as a result neither side's getting a chance to build up a real head of incoherence.'

Or we may picture them sitting at home, pupils peeping through the bunker-slits of their eyelids, jaws grimly configured as a sprung gin-trap, watching a video entitled *The Magnificent Number Fives – Celebrating a Century of Centre-Halves*, or flicking through a coffee-table book on knee injuries, occasionally emitting a bitumen-rich gurgle of bitter pleasure when they come across a ripped ligament they hadn't previously heard of. 'If God had meant us to play football on the grass, he wouldn't have made all that sky,' they may mutter in the sort of voices you could surface a road with. 'The game's not about glory, it's about winning, it's about playing with a bit of bile.'

It is pleasant to think, too, that they are not just confined to these islands, that they are an international brotherhood. Pleasing to imagine, for instance, that in Italy or Argentina when a forward takes a mighty swipe at a volley, misses it totally and collapses to the floor like a badly erected tent, there is someone who points and says, 'And, you know, if Carlton Palmer had done that we'd be showing clips of it for weeks to come.'

Or that in Rio and Amsterdam there are exasperated men on the terraces bawling, 'For Christ's *sake*, Brazil, where's your negativity?' or 'Stop fannying about, Ajax, and give it a welly', all the while dreaming of the Reebok Stadium.

Serge Gainsbourg

In the autumn of 2006 fans of esoteric pop and international soccer were treated to a digitally-interfered-with reissue of Serge Gainsbourg's classic 1969 album *Requiem Pour Un Banjo*, the sleazy old roué's psychedelic tribute to Racing Concombre's Chilean midfield librettist **Alberto Flange**. Against a swirling backing track featuring vocals by Brigit Bardotte, Georges Pompidou, and Guido and Genaro from *Jeux Sans Frontières*, and some 'pure Roquefort, man!' Hammond organ from a youthful Maxim Bossis, the gravelly-voiced Gainsbourg told the tale of Les Rayons Verts' symbolist number-ten shirt from the moment he first burst on to the French football scene like an exploding toad to the day he was forced to flee the country after allegations that he had had sex with a mimer (Flange, of course, always denied the charges, saying that he was unable even to touch the mimer in question because she refused to come out from inside an invisible box, but a jury made up entirely of men with white faces and gloves convicted him in absentia). The album included the never before released track 'Je T'Aime (Mon Concombre Magique)', featuring **Victor Umbrage**'s legendary petroleum jelly solo.

Gamesmanship

In football the line between gamesmanship and cheating is a fine one. So fine, in fact, that people who can pinpoint the exact moment when an action crosses it are rarer than photos of Paul Scholes with his mouth closed.

According to the then West Bromwich Albion manager Gary Megson, Sheffield United leapt across the line with both feet and studs showing one Saturday afternoon. In Megson's view the Blades deliberately set about getting their game with the Baggies abandoned by reducing their team strength to six through a combination of sendings-off and injuries. 'That was cheating,' he said pointing a figurative finger at his opposite number Neil Warnock.

While it was hard not to sympathise with Megson, it is altogether more difficult to agree with him. For while the spirit of the game on the field is protected by the law against ungentlemanly conduct (a pleasant catch-all term which were it fully enforced would surely terminate the careers of many international players and indeed anyone else without the good sense to run on to the field wearing a Norfolk jacket, capacious corduroy trousers and a pair of stout brogues), off the field it is a free-for-all. Clubs can narrow the pitch to frustrate the opposition's wingers, bring in the advertising hoardings to thwart long-throw experts or let the grass grow long to hinder slick passing, and nothing can be done. When he was manager of Gremio, 'Big Phil' Scolari instructed ballboys to disrupt the game by throwing extra footballs on to the field when the visitors were in possession. Far from being sent away in disgrace, Big Phil got the national team job.

This was not the first time Neil Warnock has incurred the wrath of an opposition manager (nor would it be the last). Ex-Burnley boss Stan Ternent once accused the former chiropodist of sending someone to stand behind the dressing room door to listen in on his half-time team talk. If there is a narrow margin between gamesmanship and cheating, there sometimes seems to be an even narrower one between gamesmanship and puerile silliness.

During one World Cup qualifying campaign, for instance, the coach of the Fijian football team, Billy Singh, accused his

Australian opponents of attempting to unsettle Fiji by planting something smelly in the away dressing room. Anyone who has ever spent time in a male dressing room will wonder how Singh could be quite so sure it was the Australians who had created the odour, or indeed how he had detected it at all above the general hum of sweat, socks and the night before's curries. At the time the view of many psychologists was that had they been truly cunning the Australians would not have secreted something that gave off an evil pong in the lockers, but a sweet bouquet of flowery scents that would have undermined the Fijians' warrior spirit.

Undoubtedly the modern master of this kind of petty-irritation gamesmanship was John Beck. During his first spell at Cambridge United Beck ensured that the away dressing rooms at the Abbey Stadium were overheated and that the showers were freezing cold. The sugar that accompanied the half-time tea was laced with salt and the balls handed out for the warm-up had been soaked overnight in water. Even more remarkable was the effect his directives to the groundstaff had on the pitch. The grass in the corners was so tall Dennis Wise would have needed a periscope to find his way out of it, while the centre of the field was a wide band of damp sand. 'If you think it's bad now, lads,' one wag remarked when Middlesbrough played there in 1991, 'wait till the tide comes in.'

Under Beck Cambridge were promoted three times and reached two FA Cup quarter-finals. When they were winning staff and fans at the Abbey Stadium derided the complaints of the opposition as the whingeing of sore losers. Once the team went into its own spiral of decline, however, players queued up to denounce Beck and his methods. Gamesmanship, like history, is defined by the victors.

Genetic Science

When he was still a Liverpool player Kevin Keegan told reporters, 'A team of eleven Berti Vogtses would be invincible.' Nowadays thanks to scientific advances it seems that Keegan's nightmare vision of an unbeatable squad of chunky German battlers with Mr Whippy hairstyles has moved a step closer to becoming reality.

People will say that it could not happen. Others believe it already has. After all, they argue, there is surely something deeply suspicious about the fact that the national team of the Netherlands, a country long at the forefront when it comes to genetically modified vegetables, fielded two sets of twins (the Van Der Kerkhofs and De Boers) during the last three decades of the twentieth century while the other major footballing nations (and England), excepting Germany who had the Forsters, fielded a grand total of none.

Not that cloning would necessarily be a negative thing. Sportsmen and women would be seen not as one-off creations but what contemporary artists style 'ongoing multiples'. In this brave new world Rio Ferdinand could honour his advertising and lifestyle commitments *and* knuckle down and concentrate on learning to breathe through his nose. Steven Gerrard would be able to play wide on the right and in central midfield for England. Arsenal would be able to sell Thierry Henry and hold on to him simultaneously, and Clive Tyldesley would have a nervous breakdown and be forced to resign.

In the long term, however, it would surely be bad for business. At first, as Kevin Keegan so rightly said, a team of eleven Berti Vogtses would indeed be invincible, not just for their tenacity but for the problems it would create for the opposition in designating markers at corners ('Woody, you take Vogts. Ash, you get on Vogts and I'll watch any late runs Vogts makes from the edge of the box'). Opposition managers would soon work out ways of dealing with them, though. Probably by fielding their own team of eleven Berti Vogtses. Clearly one set of Berti Vogtses would cancel out the other, resulting in a stalemate.

The effects of this discovery would not be pretty. Soon the Champions League and Premiership would be full of teams of Berti Vogtses battling grimly with one another. It is the sort of deadlock that is only ever likely to be resolved when one team gets the benefit of a ludicrous refereeing decision. Admittedly this could easily be arranged simply by producing dozens of Graham Polls, but the fun would soon pall, as would the excitement of seeing Cristiano Ronaldo engaged in an endless attempt to lure Cristiano Ronaldo into a rash challenge, or Ben Thatcher thumping himself.

Faced with rebellion by the sporting public, the authorities would have to outlaw cloning. As Kevin Keegan sensed back in the early 1970s, we are facing a strange and uncertain sporting future. A world in which the past threatens to overwhelm the present and the star of the 2010 World Cup is sent home in disgrace because he tests positive for being Ferenc Puskas.

Getting the Ball

Whenever a player is sent off for crunching into an opponent with all the finesse of a drunken clog dancer with a dead leg, his manager and the TV pundits will defend him by complaining that he 'got a bit of the ball'.

This phrase has been repeated so often that it is hard to avoid the conclusion that if some football folk had their way the He Got The Ball Principle would replace presumption of innocence as the cornerstone of the English legal system. A defence attorney would then address the jury: 'While it is true that my client murdered Mr Smith in cold blood, cut his body into pieces using a chainsaw and then buried it at various locations across the Home Counties, I would remind you that *he did get the ball.*' The judge bringing an end to the consequent wild hullabaloo in court only by rapping his gavel and croaking, 'Case dismissed. Release the accused.'

Goal Drought

After a 0–0 stalemate with Charlton in 2006 Rafael Benítez begged the authorities to take drastic steps to ease the Anfield goal drought. 'The goal table on Merseyside is dangerously low,' said the Liverpool boss. 'There are only a finite number of goals to go around and if we do not recognise that in the future we may reach a situation when the scoring reservoirs dry up completely and we are forced to import goals from Russia down a big pipe.' Liverpool chairman Rick Parry backed up Benítez and called on the government to install goal meters at every amateur club, school, park and house in the region. 'Goals are a precious natural resource,' he claimed. 'And the public must be made aware that they cannot go on wasting them. It breaks my heart when I walk down a street and see kids spraying them about all over the garden like there's no tomorrow, when poor Robbie Fowler is choking for one.' A government spokesman said that they were taking the situation very seriously. 'But our policy is to try and look for green solutions to the current crisis,' she told the BBC. 'I would ask Liverpool to consider sharing the goals they do use between more than one player, recycling Ian Rush and John Toshack and possibly even trying to extract every last drop of goals from Peter Crouch by squeezing him in some kind of vast mangle.' Luckily things were resolved when one went in off his **Backside**.

Gobtometrist

Name given a player who waits till TV cameras have him in close-up before **spitting** copiously.

Gods

One weekend in 2005 Leicester City released thirteen first-team players. The following Monday Foxes' boss Micky Adams gave details of the clear-out to the press. 'Unfortunately,' he said, 'Father Christmas is no longer at this football club.'

That Keith Gillespie, Frank Sinclair and Craig Hignett were axed from City's squad surprised nobody, but the news that Santa Claus had also been given his marching orders was quite a shock. Not least because many members of the public had forgotten he was still at Leicester. After signing for the club during the reign of Peter Taylor, the whiskery Laplander had quickly become the Winston Bogarde of the Walker Stadium. So much so, in fact, that many people had started to think that he didn't actually exist.

'Father really struggled to adapt to the heat,' one Foxes fan who had seen Christmas playing in the reserves told *6–0–6*. 'He could still turn it on when he was in the mood. But one great performance a year is not enough at this level.'

Others connected with Leicester were less kind about the festive legend. One member of the Foxes squad, who asked not to be named in case he didn't get any presents this year, told the local newspaper, 'When Santa arrived he made Mario Jardel look like a praying mantis. He needed to shed about eight stone, but if you pointed it out to him he just went, "Ho! Ho! Ho!", like it was all a big joke.'

Peter Taylor, who brought Christmas to the East Midlands, had hoped that if nothing else signing the man from the Arctic

Circle would have helped foster team spirit. 'We thought he'd give the dressing room a lift with his positive attitude and hearty laughter,' Taylor recalled later. 'But it just didn't work out. He kept calling the other lads his "little helpers" which really pissed them off and I nearly put my eye out on the antlers.'

Predictably the news that Father Christmas's sponsored sleigh would no longer be a fixture in the car park at the Walker Stadium led to further complaints that too many Continental legends view the Premiership as nothing more than a chance to top up their pensions.

'There's no doubt that when they were abroad a lot of these guys were fêted like gods,' Gordon Taylor of the Professional Footballers' Association said. 'But too many of them have come to England for one last pay day. Look at Hercules. He had a huge reputation but he hardly pulled up any trees at West Ham, did he?'

Then there was Hermes' unsuccessful spell at Stamford Bridge. The man the press in Greece nicknamed 'The Winged Messenger', because of his speed and the accuracy of his delivery, had lost much of his pace and, according to John Terry, 'did nothing in training but stand around trying to flog the rest of the lads expensive handbags and head-squares.'

The prevailing feeling among many English managers is that too many of those who have built up a mythical reputation abroad are arriving in England when their best days are behind them. 'We brought Baal over from Carthage for a trial,' Portsmouth boss Harry Redknapp commented last year. 'He still had the touch and vision but it was obvious to me that he no longer had the fire in his belly.

'To sign him would have involved this club making a huge sacrifice. Literally. His agent was asking for thirty sacks of gold a week plus a yearly bonus of two hundred noble born children. To me he was just trying it on.'

The claim that many of the 'Galacticos' are greedy is another one that is heard a lot around the Premiership. Birmingham City, for example, were stunned when, during contract negotiations, Jehovah's representatives insisted on a contract clause that completely banned the other members of the Blues team from making any money from 'graven image rights'. 'He didn't want supporters at St Andrew's to adore anyone else but him,' Steve Bruce recalled of the aborted deal. 'It was totally unbelievable.'

However, not everybody is so quick to condemn. Former Liverpool boss Gérard Houllier has since pointed out that while Father Christmas and others may have failed that was no reason to turn our back on what the rest of the world has to offer. 'The old days when British fans would worship a big tree stump have long gone,' the Lyon boss said. 'The game now is about pace and movement. You just don't get that from huge rocks or caves, no matter how many dead rabbits you give them.'

Gordon Taylor dismissed Houllier's comments, though, as simple prejudice. 'It's the old inanimate objects stereotype again, isn't it? I'm sick of hearing that about our English idols. If you want pace and movement, what about the Green Man? OK, the other players often don't spot him on account of the way he blends in with the grass, but he's second to none when it comes to getting about the field. And what about lightning? It's, well, like lightning, really. You put those two in the centre of midfield, the big lads Gog and Magog at the back, and up front you'd be hard-pressed to find anyone better than the Wicker Man – the lad's on fire at the moment.'

In 2005, meanwhile, Chelsea chief executive Peter Kenyon was photographed in a West End hotel with a mysterious figure. 'He had long flowing robes, a beard and spoke in a strange ethereal voice,' said an eyewitness. 'At first I thought it was Demis Roussos, but then I realised that it was, you know,

Him.' The news that Chelsea were about to, quite literally, have God on their side was greeted with joy at Stamford Bridge. 'Almighto will be a great buy,' said Frank Lampard. 'He has brilliant movement and seems to be everywhere on the pitch at once. He will definitely take us on to the next level. Well, he will just so long as we agree to adhere to a few simple life rules he has established.'

The deal eventually fell through, however, after God stormed out during a trial match. 'I admit I have not been at my best recently,' he later confessed. 'But my game is very much about confidence. I need to feel people really believe in me.'

Gravity

British football folk once set great store by a forward's ability to defy the laws of gravity. A top-class targetman of the fifties such as Tommy Lawton could, apparently, launch himself into the sky like a rocket and then stay there, returning to earth only when food and Brylcreem supplies ran low. Later players such as Ian St John perfected the knack of lurking above the ground until a cross eventually found its way to them or they were knocked unconscious by a passing sputnik. When Denis Law was described as 'hovering around the penalty spot', it was meant quite literally.

One of the game's greatest soarers was Wyn Davies, once memorably described in Newcastle's *Evening Chronicle* as 'the Magpies' leaping Welsh dragon'. On a video dedicated to St James's Park centre forwards, *The Magnificent Number Nines*, one of Davies's former team-mates, Scottish centre-back Bobby Moncur, tells how in training he would jump for the ball with the Welshman. Defender and attacker rose together but as the Scot began to descend he would look up and there would be

Davies loitering casually at the apex of his leap. 'He was just hanging there in the air,' a still-amazed Moncur announces to viewers.

You might be tempted to imagine that such an astonishing thing could only possibly result from the use of banned substances. But that would be an outrageous libel against Bobby Moncur.

– H –

Norman Hartnell

British fashion designer widely credited with helping Wales and Juventus legend John Charles develop the awesome heading power that became his trademark. Charles himself privately acknowledged that much of his own aerial prowess was developed when Leeds United sent him to work with dress designer Norman Hartnell. 'It was the air kissing that did it,' the giant centre forward would later confess. 'Every time anyone came into the room, it was thrust your head past their left cheek, pucker and back. Thrust your head past their right cheek, pucker and back. After the first week I was buying my shirts three collar sizes bigger.'

The strenuous work paid off and Charles was soon on his way to Juventus. But the Gentle Giant never forgot the lessons he had learnt in haute couture. Watching film of Charles in his pomp in Turin, you can occasionally hear above the noise of the crowd the sound of the Welshman squealing, 'Mwwwwah, dahling', as the ball cannons from his forehead.

Heritage Transfers

For Roman Abramovich the main concern about Chelsea is the club's lack of heritage and history. That was why in the summer of 2005 he and chief executive Peter Kenyon were alleged to have 'tapped up' a key member of the Manchester United dream team – Old Trafford.

According to a statement issued by United, the stadium rejected the Russian's approach out of hand saying, 'I am part of the very woof and weave of this famous old club. My fate is inextricably linked with that of Manchester United by an immutable bond of loyalty and large amounts of steel and concrete.'

But those close to Old Trafford told a different story. According to people who know it well, the stadium was sorely tempted by Abramovich's multi-million-pound offer. 'Traffie sometimes feels it is in danger of getting stale in Manchester and would have relished the fresh challenge in fashionable west London,' a friend of the ground said. The same source believes the Home of Legends rejected the deal only because of fears that as soon as he owned the 76,000-seat Theatre of Dreams the Siberian intended to send it to Portsmouth on a year's loan.

As the move for Old Trafford demonstrated, Abramovich was acutely aware that it takes more than just several dozen new players to make a football team into a worldwide phenomenon. United's powerful global brand is based on the club's rich history. Chelsea do not have United's illustrious past and that is something the Russian is still working to rectify. The billionaire, though, is too impatient to wait for the past to build up over the course of time in the traditional, pedestrian manner. As one of his main advisors told *The Economist*, 'Roman wants a history and he wants it now.'

To this end it has been reported that within a few days of taking over at Stamford Bridge the Russian had approached Arsenal about buying a section of their past from 1934 to 1994 for a sum of money sufficient to cover the cost of building the new Emirates stadium. According to the advisor, 'Roman was planning to recoup a considerable sum by selling off minor parts of Arsenal's history to less successful clubs. He had already received a firm offer for the 1987 League Cup Final from Middlesbrough, with Newcastle United – eager to add to their European pedigree – locked in negotiations for the penalty shoot-out defeat to Valencia in 1980.'

Arsenal's refusal to part with any of their double-winning seasons, or Liam Brady, eventually scuppered the deal, but it is thought that Chelsea have recently been approached by Celtic who have offered to lease them the 1960s.

The benefits of becoming the first British side to win the European Cup are obvious for Chelsea, but the deal also fits the Scots' long-term strategy. The Celtic board believe that if the Londoners take a decade of the club's history it will smooth the way for the Old Firm to join the Premiership. 'After all, if you already have a side in the English top flight such as Chelsea who dominated Scottish football throughout that fantastic ten-year period under the brilliant stewardship of Jock Stein, you can hardly complain if a couple of other teams from north of the border join too, can you?' said a source close to Dermot Desmond.

In Glasgow fans have reacted angrily to news that their past might be about to be sold to the Russian oil magnate. 'I had been looking forward to telling my grandchildren about watching the likes of Jimmy Johnstone,' said one disconsolate fifty-year-old supporter, 'and now it seems it may all have happened four hundred miles away and I couldn't afford the train fare, or the time off work. They say I can tell them about seeing Terry Venables and Bobby Tambling instead, but it's not the same. The moneymen have made me a stranger in my own life.'

A spokesman for Chelsea expressed sympathy for Celtic's supporters, but said should any such deal come off in the future it would be a good one for both clubs and that many Blues fans were already enjoying sitting in the pub reminiscing about Billy McNeill's quiff: 'They say you cannot put a price on memories, but we just have.'

Heroes Left Unsung

When the football season draws to a close much is tradition-ally made of the game's 'unsung heroes'. In truth in these days of blanket media coverage there are few people involved in the football, however peripherally, that haven't been celebrated in verse and music. Such is the clamour it would be no surprise to find that Philip Glass has composed an opera about the editor of Cowdenbeath's match-day magazine, or that Britain's Eurovision entry is a ditty en-titled, 'Boom Boom La La My Baby Works in the Mill House Paddock Tea Bar'.

One group of genuinely unsung heroes does remain, how-ever, their contribution to our joy and despair completely ignored by the record books. Stalwart fellows all, they are yet but fleeting shadows on the pages of history, a vague outline that is gone as swiftly as a David Beckham hairstyle. They are the forgotten men. They are 'subs not used'.

By dint of their non-activity, subs not used are a great com-fort to middle-aged men who can daydream about sitting on a bench in a nice warm tracksuit without having to confront real-ity. Yet while it may appear that any idiot could take up a subs not used berth in a Premiership side, that is by no means the case. The role of sub not used is an important one filled with unique psychological and physical pressures. These stem from the two main functions of the sub not used, the first of which is to bounce stiff-leggedly along the touchline like Spotty Dog from *The Woodentops*, in order to distract opposition fans from mocking Mark Viduka's waistline or offering ribald suggestions as to what the runic messages carved into Djibril Cissé's head might mean. The second is to chew gum and stare at the pitch with psychotic intensity as if hoping by the power of the mind alone to make an opponent's leg fall off. Unless that is you are Robbie Fowler and Steve McManaman, in which case you just look unbothered, nudge each other and giggle a lot like you were in double French, or something.

Generally the psychology of the sub must be handled carefully. All those years on the bench can have left him with football's equivalent of cabin fever – dug-out flush. Like a long-term prisoner, the 'institutionalised' sub finds the freedom of the open pitch hard to handle. Let out without strict supervision he is likely to become overwhelmed by the choices on offer and end up getting sent off for a frantic assault on an opponent or even a vicious challenge on a ballboy. Subs not used are men who really must be kept inside for their own good.

This is why in the 1960s sub not used became a recognised position. The first, and some would say the greatest, sub not used was Mick Bates of Leeds United. Bates was clearly made of stern stuff, as anyone would have to be if they were to spend most of their working life sitting on a wooden plank sandwiched between Les Cocker and Don Revie. Mick was a midfielder but he was incredibly versatile. In fact during his twelve years at Elland Road I think there wasn't a Leeds player anywhere on the pitch whom he didn't at some point fail to replace.

Nowadays the laws have changed to allow coaches a greater number of subs they can safely ignore and so the sub not used can afford to specialise more. Often an ageing player – usually a goalkeeper – is brought in as a sub not used not for what he can offer by not going on the field but for what he 'brings to the dressing room'. Tradition dictates that this is usually a pair of clockwork false teeth, a laughing bag and an obscene imitation of Groucho Marx that involves pulling down his shorts and sticking a false nose and glasses above his genitals.

Thus do the subs not used play a vital part in a team's success. As Barry Davies used to say, 'Cometh the hour, cometh not the man.'

Damien Hirst

Contemporary British artist. Hirst once confessed that, 'Whenever I take a chainsaw to a dead cow I always ask myself, "Is this how Norman Hunter would do it?"'

Holding Clubs to Ransom

Top footballers holding their clubs to ransom is nothing new, but last year things took a fresh and sinister twist. It was reported that a leading Premiership striker had cut off his left foot and posted it to his chairman with an attached note saying that a package containing a body part would arrive every day, 'until I am allowed to leave and join the team my agent has dreamed of me playing for since he was a boy, or I am reduced to a worthless and bloody stump'.

A couple of years ago the striker's left foot alone would have been worth several million (Spanish club Betis, it will be recalled, bought Brazilian star Edmilson in instalments, starting with his knees), but in these days of collapsing transfer values it would probably command no more than a few quid from the local dog food factory. As the chairman commented bitterly, 'I could call his bluff, but what good would that do? I either give in and get something for him, or wait twelve months till his contract expires and watch him hop away on a free transfer.'

Though by no means as dramatic, the situation at other clubs is equally fraught. One top Midlands side hit problems on the first day of preseason in 2006–07 when their latest signing climbed up a tree at the training ground and vowed not to come down until he was paid a loyalty bonus and given a testimonial in advance. 'You cannot put a price on loyalty,' he told reporters through a megaphone, 'but I want it up front.'

At a club recently relegated to the Championship,

meanwhile, it is reported that three England squad players tunnelled under the pitch and declared their intention of staying down there until they were allowed to move back to the Premiership. 'You do not become a top player to win nothing,' said a spokesman for the trio. 'People will say, "Well, you are the players, so if you have won nothing it is your own fault". That is rubbish. Football is a team game, which means that failure is never the responsibility of one, two or even three brilliantly talented stars, but of everybody else. As long as you can look yourself in the mirror and say, "Hello, handsome, I bet that shirt cost a packet", then that should be good enough for anybody.'

At one time the board of directors of the relegated club would have been able to act quickly to bring the situation to a close using poison gas or dynamite, but since the day when Jimmy Hill finally broke the employers' iron grip on the game, by threatening to get every professional player in Britain to hide under the bed for the duration of the 1962–63 season, their hands have been tied.

Holdontologist

Name given to the player, usually a winger or forward, who wins a throw-in near the opposition penalty area, grabs the ball and then makes to take a quick throw once, twice, three times, before letting it roll down his back and then running off and leaving it for his full-back instead.

Home Phone-In Karaoke Machine

A Japanese device that was a major craze in the 1990s. The Home Phone-In Karaoke allowed everybody to reproduce the trenchant opinions and brilliant banter of their favourite football phone-in in the comfort of their own living room. Users simply picked up the receiver, selected the topic of their choice and read out the words that appeared on the LCD screen while the machine accompanied their nonsensical twittering with jingles, traffic news, or an optional range of backing vocals, including 'My views on referees are well known', 'It's common knowledge that Alex and I have our differences' and 'It's a total nonsense. Simple as that, folks'. The gizmo offered literally half a dozen phone-in favourites to choose from, such as, 'The ref this afternoon was a total joke', 'Gérard Houllier has lost the plot' and 'What effect does that have on the kids that are watching, Mark?' In Christmas 2001 a Golden Oldie with David Mellor attachment proved a huge hit, allowing punters once again to experience the thrill of football's favourite former Conservative MP talking in a matey voice and saying patronising stuff such as: 'That's a very wise and intelligent view and, if I might say so, most articulately expressed by one so young.'

How to Go to Football

For the novice attending his or her first football match, one important fact must be borne in mind – no matter what the TV companies, advertising copywriters and sportswear manufacturers may think, people do not go to footie matches to be entertained. They go to rant, to torment, to sneer, to experience childlike glee and black despair, but most of all they go because a football ground is the only place on the planet where a forty-year-old accountant with three children, a tracker mortgage, a Renault Megane on nought per cent finance and a rapidly expanding waistline can make obscene gestures at Robbie Savage without anyone thinking it in the least bit inappropriate.

There are two types of people who go to football matches. The first group wear thick coats apparently made from old boiler lagging and arrive at least half an hour before kick-off. They then mill aimlessly around glancing about the concourse in the hope of seeing the players' miraculously overdressed wives and children arriving. The second group wear only the flimsiest shirt no matter what the weather and keep warm by a combination of beer and layers of aftershave. This group never get to the ground until thirty seconds before kick-off. If you decide to join the latter body, remember that in your rush to get to your seat you must shove, barge and stamp on everyone who has arrived sensibly early because they are the sort of middle-class tossers who are ruining football.

When you get into the ground you will see lots of men and women in big, fat luminous coats that make their arms stick out from their sides like the wings of a wet cormorant. These people are the stewards. But don't let the word steward fool you. They are not here to provide any kind of service.

FIRST HALF

Football fandom is a participatory sport, so get involved. Pick a player from your team and shower abuse on him at every opportunity regardless of how well or badly he's playing. Don't forget that everything that goes wrong is totally this man's fault. When the ball is booted forty yards and runs out of play exclaim, 'Where's his bloody anticipation?' Nothing should deter you. Just because the player you have chosen to target beats five opponents and finishes by blasting in a shot from thirty yards that is no excuse to ease up. Simply wait until the celebrations have subsided and then grimly observe, 'The wages he's on he should be doing that every week.'

Always remember that the referee is devoutly biased against your team. Fate may be blind, but refs are merely blinkered. It is essential to abandon any attempt at taking a balanced view of things. Fairness and perspective have no place in football. When abusing the match officials try always to include at least one reference to his or her rectum, for example: 'Where's your yellow card, ref, up your arse?' or 'Get your flag down from your backside, lino, and start signalling.'

The vast majority of people only go to football so they can get really really cross about something. Give them a helping hand by adopting an irritating habit. You might bring a klaxon, phone up your mates on a mobile every five minutes and hilariously pretend to be John Motson commentating on the match, or simply get up and go to the lavatory just when a corner is about to be taken.

Or better still adopt a few key phrases and shout them randomly throughout the game. Try to make them technical sounding yet senseless: 'Our forwards just aren't working the big slots', 'We need to get more conscious in the third phase', 'We've gone baggy in the drop-off zone', that sort of thing.

HALF-TIME

Always bear in mind that at football matches you must do everything in advance to 'avoid the rush' – even if it's just the rush of people doing things in advance. So if you plan to eat at half-time leave your seat at least ten minutes before the whistle. You may miss goals and action, but you will get your offal, nose and throat in a bun quicker and force people on your row to stand up and let you through, and that's what counts.

Never offer any appreciation for the half-time entertainment. Whether it is a primary school penalty prize, a junior dance troupe from a local care home, or an internationally renowned opera singer, simply stare at them with blank indifference and then as they leave the pitch remark in a loud voice, 'Well, what the hell was that in aid of?'

If you go to the lavatory always take a drink or some food in with you. Remember, as long as you've got one hand free you can still eat a hot dog. And don't whatever you do wash your hands afterwards. You don't want people thinking you're some kind of hygiene-obsessed sicko.

SECOND HALF

For a little variety you might like to select a member of the opposition to subject to a series of ribald witticisms. Bald players or those who have just gone through a well-publicised marital break-up are particularly amusing. Everyone appreciates the man who starts the 'If you've shagged his wife stand up' chant, especially when he's sitting in the family enclosure.

The most important question you must address in the second half is when to leave. You have two choices: you can leave five minutes early to 'get away before the traffic', or you can stay to the bitter end and then hang around the players' tunnel to make rude hand signals to the opposition's coach driver. Whichever choice you take, you must stick to it no matter what is happening on the field. Only the most irresolute or feckless fan bases the decision on when to leave the ground on how the match is progressing.

As the game goes on you may like to add to the mounting tension. Every time the opposition cross the halfway line say, 'This looks dangerous' or 'They've got men over, here.'

No matter what the score greet the final whistle by yelling 'Eighteen quid to watch that crap, I must be mental.'

LEAVING THE GROUND

Whether you go early or stay to the end one or two important points of etiquette must be observed.

Always bounce down the steps rapidly, as if you have just remembered you've left the oven on.

At some point remark loudly yet gnomically to a stranger next to you, 'I'll not give him long after that result', and then look away as if you weren't really talking to him at all.

Always step out on to busy roads without looking. You are part of a football crowd and traffic has to stop for you. It's the law.

The Hud

England supporters have long relied on the psychological equilibrium provided by **The Robbo** – a key player who selflessly injures himself before a tournament so that we can all blame the team's failure to get beyond the quarter-finals on his damaged metatarsal. In the absence of a natural Robbo, the selection choices of the manager become absolutely vital.

For this reason the job of the England manager has always been the most complex in international football. On the one hand he must attempt to win the tournament by selecting the best team available, on the other he must also shield the fragile psyche of the English support from the brutal blows of failure.

To achieve this the manager has a couple of courses open to him: he can make a bold decision to leave out at least one key individual from his eleven, so that when things go wrong

England fans can shrug and mutter, 'Well, I said we'd get nowhere without Bowles/Hoddle/Le Tissier (strike out where non-applicable) to bring a bit of creativity', or he can persistently select someone of less obvious gifts so they can shake their heads and say, 'I'm sorry, but Wilkins/Mariner/Batty? I mean, what do you expect?' Thus do the English mentally preserve our status as a 'major football power' while appearing in far fewer finals than the Czechs and generally accruing a record comparable to that of a small Nordic kingdom where lakes outnumber people.

The history of the England team is littered with brilliant blocking manoeuvres designed to take the sting out of defeat. Losing to the USA in 1950 might have severely damaged national confidence had not the selection panel cunningly dropped Stanley Matthews for the match. Even in the hour of our single triumph, Alf Ramsey had provided a well-positioned cushion to land on by ditching the country's greatest goalscorer Jimmy Greaves. And in 1970 he proved it was no fluke by favouring Jeff Astle ahead of Peter Osgood.

Shortly afterwards the Football Association took over responsibility for national morale once more, appointing Ron Greenwood as manager and thus leaving the whole country content in the thought that no matter how pitifully we performed, 'It would all have been very different if only they'd had the guts to go with Cloughie.' Surely there is no victory so rich in savour as the one that might have been?

Later the managers were back in action. Graham Taylor picked Carlton Palmer. Glenn Hoddle, a master of his craft, dropped Gazza from his squad and refused to play David Beckham in France 1998 until a tough second-round tie against Argentina had been safely secured. Kevin Keegan omitted Michael Owen and, with England 1–0 up against France in Euro 2004, Sven coolly bided his time before throwing on Emile Heskey.

'On the continent they would have built a team round Alan Hudson', people used to say in the 1970s as England failed to make it through qualifying yet again. Many will feel that the only thing that should have been built round Alan Hudson was a big brick wall topped with razor wire, but nevertheless the psychological value of Hudson (or The Hud as the role was named in his honour) cannot be underestimated. He, Tony Currie, Rodney Marsh, Frank Worthington and the rest of those talented players routinely left out of the starting line-up at least gave England fans something to fall back on, an excuse. The way things are going, though, future England managers will not have the luxury of omitting anyone, no matter how wonderful and creative they may be, because there will only be eleven English players to pick.

Already there is hardly anyone fans want to see in the squad who isn't. There are no alternatives. There is nowhere to hide. To be honest, if it wasn't for the reemergence of Phil Neville the damage international football could inflict on English self-esteem would be incalculable.

Image

In football the phrase 'There just aren't the characters in the game any more' hovers as persistently as the scent of yesterday's Brussels sprouts. It was a view substantially reinforced in 2004 by the news that Arsenal were attempting to address their financial frailties by bringing in pop impresario Simon Fuller to advise on team matters. Fuller, of course, is the man who gave the world the Spice Girls, S Club and *Pop Idol*. And Highbury's pulsating business brain Peter Hill-Wood believed he could work a similar feat of marketing and merchandising magic on the Gunners.

'Arsenal are not a manufactured band/team,' Fuller insisted at the time. 'All the ingredients were already in place when I discovered them. All I've done is try to delineate their separate personas a little more clearly. So we've got the sensible, quiet one the mums adore, Sol Campbell; the boring one who can actually play, Dennis Bergkamp; the funky, funny one who's really kinda sexy in a kooky kinda way, Thierry Henry; and the one all the girls think is really cute, but their boyfriends just don't get it because he just looks a bit like a troll to them, Freddie Ljungberg. That's what I've worked with. I haven't asked to bring anyone in, although obviously a red-head and something for the dads would be ideal.'

Fuller, however, denied that the rebellious one who looks like he knows a bit more about you-know-what than he really ought to (Ashley Cole) will leave Arsenal in the summer and be replaced by an out-of-contract Geri Halliwell.

Meanwhile, Arsène Wenger proclaimed himself delighted with the appointment. 'It is no secret that we lag behind Manchester United when it comes to revenue,' the Frenchman said, 'and when you examine the situation you see that is because three years ago at Old Trafford they took the decision to bring in Prestige Management to help Sir Alex. Now, when you have the people who built up the careers of pop sensations Busted, McFly and V working for you, it is obvious you are going to do very well. And that is what has happened. They have brought in the one with the pretty face and the chest that is muscularly masculine and yet rendered strangely unthreatening to pre-pubescent girls by its hairlessness (Cristiano Ronaldo) and the one with the lumpy head the young lads like because he looks like he'd be a good laugh if you went go-karting with him (Wayne Rooney), and financially they have kicked on from there.'

Asked if he thought football was in danger of becoming a load of lightweight synthetic pap, Wenger replied, 'Well, you know, I prefer seventies stuff like Leeds United and Terry Mancini, but the kids enjoy this and who are we to judge they are wrong?'

Immutable Laws of Soccer

The first immutable law of football is that players always score against their former clubs. The second immutable law of football is that immutable law number-one only works against your team, never for it.

The third immutable law of football is that anyone who played in a team with a boy who went on to become a professional will always insist that there were much better players in the side. The speaker will invariably say something along the lines of, 'He wasn't bad, but he wasn't the best either, not by a long chalk. There were three or four kids who were more talented.' The speaker then adopts a slightly self-satisfied expression and goes on, 'The thing was, though, when all the rest of us started getting interested in girls and drinking and that, he just got on with his training. Dedicated, he was.' Dedicated is one of those words that while appearing complimentary always carry the inference of a flaw, a lack of something – imagination or testosterone usually.

The gratifying implication of this tale is that the professional player is actually just one remove from those adolescents who misspend their youths translating Ovid into early English or doing equations. They are a muscle-nerd whose bulging thighs and ability to chest down a medicine ball without yelping are the athletic equivalent of a pair of baggy corduroys and a certainty about what logarithms are for. Since usually the player in question is Mick Duxbury, Kevin Richardson or Martin Keown, it is just about possible to believe it, too.

But there are people around who insist that despite scoring nine and a half million goals in representative football (I may be one or two out here so don't quote me), Michael Owen is not a 'natural goalscorer', a phrase that suggests goalscoring is some primal human urge and the days before the advent of football were marked by the sight of men instinctually volleying hedgehogs through the uprights of Stonehenge they knew not for why. And so there must also be those who are prepared to apply the third immutable law to players of greater stature even than Scott Minto. That as you read this there is some bloke propping up a bar in Rio de Janeiro, adopting a slightly smug tone and saying, 'When I was fourteen I was in a Sunday morning side with Kaka. And you know what? He got subbed at half-time week in and week out. Oh yeah, loads of lads with more flair in that side. Normano, Herberto, Plato, Schopenhauer, they were all better than him. But Kaka, see, he worked at it, didn't he?'

Impediments to Success

Leicester City's flirtation with changing their name back to Leicester Fosse was a move broadly to be welcomed, especially for those who pine for a return to the days when Middlesbrough Ironopolis and Darlington Rise Carr Rangers made typesetting the pools coupon on FA Cup first round day a nightmare for printers.

The reasons for the proposed name change were sound enough. Acting Leicester chairman Jon Holmes pointed out that of the fifteen Citys in the Football League only one, Manchester City, has ever won the championship. Teams called City, Holmes concluded, rarely win the title. This is indeed true, but since it is even truer to say that teams called Leicester *never* win the League, perhaps Bob Fosse would have been a better solution.

Whatever the rights and wrongs of Holmes's analysis, it was at least good to see somebody within the upper echelons of the game finally beginning to take such matters seriously. Far too often the lessons of the past go unlearned by those who run the English game. Why else would Newcastle United (No problem with that suffix, clearly) persist with their striped shirts when anyone can tell them that these are a bigger impediment to them lifting the Premiership title than even Kieron Dyer's shooting? Surely a man of Freddy Shepherd's experience is aware that no team playing in striped shirts has won the title since the Second World War? In Spain and Portugal things are different, admittedly, while in Italy it is generally the plain-shirted teams who struggle, but this is England where a different set of rules apply. After all, the success of hooped shirts north of the border has been of limited benefit to QPR.

Incident

Any offence or accident, no matter how serious, committed by, or involving footballers. Example: 'After the players left the club there was an incident. Thirty-seven people were later treated in hospital for cuts, lacerations and the effects of inhaling smoke.'

Injuries

In the build-up to an international football tournament phrases such as 'medial collaterals' and 'anterior cruciates' bounce around pubs and sitting rooms like household words. For in keeping with Britain's new and more European atmosphere, injuries nowadays have a distinctly Latin flavour to them. We have ciabatta and pesto, so why not lateral meniscus damage, too? In the past British players rejected all body parts that didn't have a robust Anglo-Saxon name – hamstrings, hocks, fetlocks, withers and the like. As a result there were far fewer injuries than there are today. Unfortunately any advantage accrued by our national elevens was mitigated by the fact that the lack of fancy Continental limb joints meant that our players could only run in straight lines, forcing managers to persist with the rigid WM formation decades after it had become obsolete everywhere else.

International Managers

One Sunday a caller to *6–0–6* offered the view that Joe Cole had 'the same centrifugal force as Maradona'. It turned out he meant centre of gravity, but for a moment he unleashed on the nation the notion that the Argentine number ten kept control of the ball simply by spinning round so fast it stuck to him.

At one time our ignorance of overseas stars would have given credence to the idea of a twirling midfield genius from the banks of the River Plate. Not any more. Long gone are the days when the only between-World-Cups glimpse British fans got of the great players of South America and Continental Europe was in Soccer Stars sticker albums. Even here identification was often made difficult by the choice of mind-bending background colours and the habit of sticking heads on to bodies that were plainly not their own (a tradition apparently still practised by whoever made Carsten Jancker).

In the modern era footballers are as much international brands as Burger King and Body Shop. You do not need to wait for the Mundial to come around for your chance to see them. They appear on our TV screens daily.

All of which puts added pressure on the managers. It is them we must look to to provide the unexpected. Because while foreign players have become as familiar to us as the menu in KFC, the coaches still retain a whiff of mystery about them. Although in the case of José Camacho and his one-man protest against anti-perspirants, it might be slightly overpowered by more recognisable odours, obviously.

The World Cup is one of the few chances we get to see old favourites such as Cesare Maldini, whose rapidly wrinkling face suggests that somewhere in an attic there is a painting of him that is swiftly returning to raw canvas, and Bora Milutinović still sporting an extraordinary, thatched hairdo, which surely represents the most elaborate cover-up since Watergate.

The newcomers to the scene, though, produce the real excitement, men such as Bruno Metsu. While most of his players are well known from their exploits in the French league, Bruno is a refreshing novelty not least from having made the singular mistake of confusing Michael Bolton with a fashion-leader.

There is often a rare glimpse, too, of crazy-maned Winfried

Schäfer. The German is, according to Barry Davies, a fully qualified train driver on the Bundesbahn, though he looks more like the sort of bloke who would turn up on *Rock Family Trees* talking about his days playing rhythm guitar in the Steve Gibbons Band.

The best Uruguayan players are star turns in the Champions League, not so Uruguayan coaches, such as Victor Pua. Affectionately nicknamed 'Fatso' by home supporters, Pua is so wide he doesn't so much stand in the dug-out as wear it.

Most of us have grown weary of watching Roberto Carlos blasting free-kicks into the stands of the Bernabéu. Thankfully his countryman Luiz Felipe Scolari is less familiar. Big Phil has more hand gestures than John McCririck and slaps his own pate with such force when a chance goes begging you really feel that health groups should campaign to have compulsory head-guards introduced for the technical area.

Argentina were once led by barmy disciplinarian Daniel Passarella. Passarella refused to pick any player with long hair or a beard. His successor Marcelo Bielsa had other things on his mind. He took two thousand football videos with him to the Korea/Japan. Three games a day was plainly just not enough for the man.

Of course the players, with their shimmies, feints and step-overs are marvellous, but they are also as ubiquitous as the golden M. In these days of globalisation it is left to the men who shout at them to remind us of the glorious and unexpected diversity of our small, blue and perpetually spinning planet. Walrus moustaches, wobbling bellies and worrying shirt-and-tie combinations all held together by football and centrifugal force.

International Retirement

Footballers generally announce this exclusively in a tabloid newspaper the morning after being dropped from the squad, and then spend the next five years hinting to journalists that they might reconsider their position if the manager declares his immense respect, admiration and adoration for them live on prime-time television.

Irritating Vowel Syndrome

During a January 2003 edition of *Final Score* Mark Lawrenson collapsed during an exchange of banter with Ray Stubbs and was rushed to hospital, where he was diagnosed as suffering from an acute case of Irritating Vowel Syndrome. 'I just dernt kner what came erver me,' he told speech therapists.

– J –

David James

England goalkeeper. Rumours that during his spell modelling Armani underpants James used a performance-enhancing stair rod have never been proven.

Mildred Jessup

When it comes to football **landladies** you'd be hard-pressed to find any finer than Mildred Jessup, a woman who has tutored some of the game's finest talent – among them such household names as **Rod Rugg**, Bryan Lump, Ron Lamp, Trevor Limp, **Roy Keane** and Eric Cantona – in matters of bathroom etiquette and cruet usage. Mrs Jessup was twice winner of *France Football*'s prestigious European Football Landlady of the Year award ('And I'd have won a third time if it hadn't been for that Mrs Gonzalez of Real Madrid waving her *Olla Podrida* in front of the judges two years ago,' she snaps with an edge of bitterness) and she is adamant about the secret of her success: 'Tinned peas,' she says, plumping her antimacassars, 'When Mr Rowbottom brought the lads to me and said, "Put some beef on them, Mrs J", I reached straight for the marrowfats. There's a lot of goodness in a pea. A bowl of marrowfats and a bottle of Mullarkey's brown ale before bed and they'd soon start to thicken out. "I don't know what you're trying to do with them boys, Mildred," Mr Jessup sometimes used to say, "fatten them or inflate them".

'He was normally a perfect gentleman, Mr Jessup, but he'd travelled in ladies shoes after the war and sometimes slid into vulgarity. Though never of course in front of my boys. And they always remain my boys, no matter how big a star they become. Sometimes when I see a newspaper headline saying "Bryan Lump voted S-E-Xiest man", I say to myself, They wouldn't say that if they'd smelled his sock drawer.

'I remember one time Mr Jessup caught a whiff of it. "Blimey," he said, "what's he got in there, a pair of badgers?" He had quite a colourful turn of phrase, Mr Jessup. I often thought that if it hadn't been for his waterworks he'd have gone on the boards.

'All this S-E-X business and Bryan, when I read it, honey, I have to laugh. Because in my day somebody like Miss Great Yarmouth Maplins would have thought twice before dining out with a lad who made gravy lakes in his mashed potato. Because while Bryan looks like butter wouldn't melt in his mouth, I'd have to say his table manners left a lot to be desired. "Put a ball in front of that lad and he's a genius," Mr Jessup used to say, "but put a bowl of Weetabix in front of him and it's goodbye tablecloth".

'Rod Rugg, now he was a different matter altogether. They say he was a right dirty beggar on the field, but I find that hard to believe. He was fastidious when it came to napery, wouldn't so much as touch a chocolate biscuit unless you served it him on a fresh doily.'

Mrs Jessup's most famous boarder was the *enfant terrible* of French football, Eric Cantona. The first meeting of these two great figures of the English game is the stuff of legends. As Mrs Jessups recalls it, 'I said to him, I said, "I don't care if you are having a 'Mickey Rourke Day', young fella me lad, you put a mug of hot Horlicks down on an occasional table without a coaster under it ever again in this house and you'll be down the road so fast your feet won't touch the ground." I think I got my point across because I noticed he'd had the Mr Sheen out when I came back from the butcher's.'

Cantona soon blossomed in the disciplined new environment and the rest, as they say, is a lot of made-up stuff with the odd fact tossed in at random.

Roy Keane

The following entry is about Roy Keane. Throughout it, in the style of the tabloids, we will be using asterisks to cunningly conceal the expletives. We do this not because we believe in censorship, but simply because it saves having to search the keyboard for the correct letters. A process which, to be honest, I find a time-consuming pain in the a***.

Over the years we have heard a lot about the Real Roy Keane, a person, any number of important writers have assured us, the public does not get to see. As a member of the public I, naturally, do not know the Real Roy Keane. Nor, I must confess, have I ever met the Unreal Roy Keane. I have at times in the past, however, communicated with the Surreal Roy Keane, a large-breasted wardrobe named Yolande, who wore a false beard and recited the tennis commentaries of John Barrett after first removing all the consonants, but I am better now.

As one Old Trafford insider who cannot be named for legal reasons and because I have just made him up and can't be f***** to come up with anything even semi-plausible told me, 'The Roy Keane none of us knows is very different from the man who bestrides the football field like some growling Martian war tractor. Though I don't know him – none of us does – I have spoken to several other people who don't know him either and through that have formed the idea that in private Keane is a small creature, painfully shy and yet filled with impish fun – a bit like a red squirrel.'

Another source told me, 'Obviously I have not seen the Roy Keane nobody has seen – nobody has – but I once loitered around outside the door of his house long enough to gain an impression of a wraith-like and almost formless being, throbbing with profound wisdom and terribly fond of decorative thimbles.'

Undoubtedly then the Real Roy Keane is, to paraphrase Winston Churchill, a riddle wrapped in a mystery and shoved up the b******* of an enigma.

Kids

It is often said that footballers are role models for our children. Possibly so, though many would like to see that situation reversed. According to these wise old heads, the game would be greatly improved if instead of children copying the players, the players copied children. The feeling among this cadre of experts is that football needs to return to the exuberance and innocence of its spiritual home – the field round the back of the housing estate. Some may argue that an increase in childishness would result in a breakdown in discipline. Not a bit of it. It seems unlikely, for example, that we would have half as much arguing over decisions if the ultimate power of arbitration was taken out of the hands of referees and given instead to the Big Tough Boy Whose Brother Is In The YOI.

To take football back to its roots will require radical action, but if Sepp Blatter and his Fifa henchmen could get the following proposals in place in time for the qualifying rounds of the next World Cup, we would all feel the benefits.

First of all the pitch, much work needs to be done here. Goalposts, of course, must be replaced with jumpers, while the exact position of the 'bar' will be determined by a long argument between the goalkeeper ('It went about a foot over me hands and I was jumping *this* high') and the player claiming the goal ('No, you weren't. You were leaning backwards and your elbows were bent'), and eventually resolved by a wrestling match (one fall or submission to determine the winner. No kicking, gouging or pulling down your opponent's shorts to reveal his buttocks to passing girls).

One touchline should be clearly demarcated by a wall, fence or line of parked cars and the other should lie at a point so far away none of the players can be bothered to run after the ball once it has gone beyond it.

To spice things up still further at random moments during the game the dimensions of the pitch should suddenly be altered when: a game featuring younger players starts up in one corner; a gang of youths on bicycles turn up to practise skids and experiment with cigarettes and spitting; an elderly couple in a spotless Ford Mondeo set up a picnic table and chairs near the halfway line and declare that, 'If that ball comes anywhere near our cups you lot are for the high jump.'

The game will last from 'after lunch' until 'tea-time', a duration calculated by having a traditional British grandmother boil a cabbage until it is cooked to her satisfaction – roughly four and a half hours. Half-time will occur when the two biggest lads are thirsty and will last as long as it takes for the puniest player to go to the shop and bring back crisps, pop and a selection of flying saucers, liquorice laces and some of that sherbet that turns your tongue blue.

The game will end when the cabbage has reached the consistency of pond slime and the granny appears at the edge of the playing surface yelling, 'Your tea's on the table. Come in this minute. I don't care if you are 3–2 down. Your granddad didn't die in two world wars so you could let good food go to waste. And stop that chuntering or I'll have the FA suspend you for a fortnight.'

In keeping with widespread playing-field practice, experts

would also like to see Fifa introduce new rankings that mimic the popular 'you get two of the little kids and we'll have our Gary' system. Under these rankings an established star like Ronaldo will be the equivalent of 1.5 members of an international U-21s squad or a dozen U-12s. This will lead to greater tactical flexibility for coaches as they weigh up the possibilities of selecting the best available players and using a 4–4–2 system or opting instead to give youth a chance in a 12–12–28 formation. It will also allow good players to show off a bit more by dribbling round whole teams of little 'uns sometimes while doing a silly walk or using only their weaker foot.

It would create some compelling matches, too. Who would not be fascinated to see how the current star-packed Arsenal squad's attacking invention coped with the packed defence of an entire Teesside primary school representing Gareth Southgate's Middlesbrough (assuming Boro could afford their wages, obviously).

Team selection duties would not stop there. The coach would also be expected to designate one team member who will play the entire match wearing wellies and another who is not allowed to get dirty because 'we're going to my aunty's house after and my mam says if I've got any grass stains on these trousers she'll brain me.'

Most managers are resistant to the idea of learning from kids, but most teams would surely benefit from the introduction of some of the classic positions from the world of kids' football. These would include:

RUSH GOALIE

Of all kids' football innovations this is clearly the one with the most obvious applications in the adult game. Picking a goalkeeper of proven footballing ability (or better still a footballer of proven goalkeeping ability) and instructing him to rove about the field as he sees fit would add flexibility to any team and allow managers to switch formations effortlessly from 4–4–2 to 4–5–2, 4–4–3, or even a Continental-style 4–6–1. With practically every player in the professional game now totally committed to wearing gloves, there is plainly no reason why Fifa shouldn't introduce the popular 'Change of goalies' rule for the 2010 World Cup.

THE HOGGER

A key component of any kids' football team, the hogger's role is simplicity itself: he gets the ball and dribbles past opponent after opponent, then turns round and dribbles past them again. While dribbling he is totally oblivious to kicks, trips, dead legs, punches on the arm and attempts to break his mesmerising spell over the football by offering him bags of sherbet flying saucers or claiming that the woman in a car that has just driven past didn't have a bra on, or anything, honest. He is also totally deaf to his team-mates, who are lined up in front of goal unmarked and yelling, 'Pass it here! Pass it here! Away and pass it, man, you ball-greedy get!' Capable of retaining possession for twenty minutes at a stretch, unless distracted by the sound of an ice cream van or his mother grabbing him by the ear and dragging him home for his tea, in the professional game the hogger would be particularly useful in away ties in Europe, or as a sub to be brought on when you are already 1–0 up.

GOAL HANGER

A totally different animal to the goal scrounger (who loiters about the penalty box in the hope of deflecting in somebody else's shot), the goal hanger literally hangs around in the opposition goalmouth, distracting the keeper by reciting sketches from *Little Britain*, getting him to do his impression of Mr Bean and begging to have a go with his gloves in exchange for a swig of Lucozade and two Yugioh cards. When the ball comes his way, however, the hanger is lightning quick, slotting it coolly home and then doing an elaborate Bart Simpson-style goal celebration that expends far more energy than he does during the game. Draconian offside laws make this a difficult role to replicate in the professional game, though rapid advances in mobile phone technology may make it possible within the next twelve months.

TITCHY KID

Titchy kid uses his small stature to create mayhem by peskily jogging alongside bigger opponents, poking them in the ribs and saying things like, 'What's the weather like up there?' and 'Watch out, or I'll bite your kneecaps.' At set-plays titchy kid is traditionally carried into the penalty area on his tallest team mate's shoulders where he unsettles the opposing goalkeeper, usually by grabbing his cap and throwing it into a puddle. It's surely high time England used Michael Owen and John Terry in such a manner at corners.

RADGIE BAIRN

Radgie bairn is basically titchy kid after he has drunk a litre of Irn Bru and eaten a family size bag of Haribo Tangtastics. Fired up with E-numbers, he hurtles hyperactively about the pitch yelling, 'I'm radgie man, me woohoo!', tackling everyone including his own team-mates and booting the ball as hard as he can in whatever direction he happens to be facing. In the Premiership the radgie bairn would ideally be brought on towards the end of a game when you were in front and would be used to disrupt the tempo and rhythm of the match until the opposition threatened to leave the field unless 'he stops acting mental and plays properly'.

LITTLE BROTHER

Not to be confused with titchy kid, little brother is only there because 'our mam said I had to bring him with us.' Little brother traditionally rejects normal football boots or training shoes in favour of a pair of Wellingtons that are three sizes too big for him. This means that when he kicks the ball his welly flies off after it bemusing goalkeepers and causing defenders to dive for cover – a free-kick technique that has yet to be fully explored in grown-up football even by dead-ball masters such as Thierry Henry.

Rudyard Kipling

Rudyard Kipling's poem 'If' is particularly popular with football managers and pundits. They have trotted out this verse for generations as if it held some sacred truth. In fact it makes no sense whatsoever. 'If you can meet with triumph and disaster/And treat those two impostors just the same,' it counsels. What does that mean? Why are triumph and disaster impostors? Does the poet believe that the only true and genuine result is a draw with a replay a week on Wednesday? And if so how will the Cup competitions ever be resolved?

Kookachoo (Horace Virgil de Homer Sapho Junior)

The seminal Brazilian ball-playing wizard of the 1950s, Kookachoo's career was cut tragically short due to his insatiable love of the horses. The FC Bogus of São Paulo left-winger infamously missed the 1958 World Cup final because he was in bed with the winner of the King George the Fifth Diamond Stakes and Devon Loch. Later drowned while working as a herdsman on a salmon farm.

Svenbo Krump

One of the first and best-loved of the legion of foreign players to arrive in England during the 1980s was Faroese striker Svenbo Krump who enjoyed a brief, successful spell at Kenilworth Road in 1983–84. When he signed for Luton the tall, blond forward from the Land of the Midnight Cheese was already well known to many in this country thanks to his appearance as the cartoon character Mike the Second Boyfriend in the popular 1960s public information film *Learn To Swim* (Krump's one line, 'Hallo!', was dubbed by a young ingenue at the Mrs Irma Bassett's Stage & Secretarial School, Basildon, a certain Glenn Hoddle). 'We knew we were buying a player who could swim like a fish,' Hatters team-mate Paul Walsh commented later. 'What we didn't know is that he thought like one, too. And I mean that in a really positive sense. Svenbo was very much the salmon and the goal was the spawning ground to which nature compelled him to return.'

The rampaging Krump made a major impression at Kenilworth Road where his boss David Pleat notes he played 'like Iain Dowie on asteroids'. 'He's a man whose abilities you should never overestimate,' the once and future Spurs manager has said. 'He was very affirmative, had a great orbit and his ability to anticipate precipitation has always been exceptional. Sometimes maybe you'd question his thickness around the no-loading zones, but then when you're mentally askew you can often times get away with it. And he was propitious in that area, most certainly.'

Another colleague, Ricky Hill, is equally complimentary. 'Svenbo had this way of carrying himself on and off the field,' he confirmed, 'which obviously saved him having to walk like the rest of us.'

One man who watched Krump regularly during that spell, former midfield juggernaut turned TV thief **Rod Rugg**, says that the Nordic striker always had an 'aura about him'. Was it an aura of calm decisiveness or an aura of natural authority? 'No,' he replies with a rumbling laugh, 'it was more the 'Ammer 'Ouse of Aura. The bloke looked like Frankenstein! Hurgh! Hurgh!'

If Krump was a myth in Luton, he was to become a legend in his next port of call, the Ex-Former Yugoslav Republic (Twice Removed) of Potya, where first as player and later as coach of VK Mustikka he fired the imaginations of a public starved of fantasy of all but the most brutal kind. 'He was like a great stork of hope,' VK Mustikka president Haka Flugg recalls of the man nicknamed the Hamershaven Harpoon, 'who made a nest on our chimney and set the whole place alight.'

Popular local singing duo the Frisky Chicks, whose infectious international hit 'Frisky Fella (Squeeze My Patella)' will be played before every Champions League match until further notice, even released their own tribute to the coach. 'Frisky Svenbo' was the EFYR(TR) Potya's fastest-selling record ever and there is hardly a child in the country who cannot sing its catchy chorus: 'Frisky Svenbo/ Hey Frisky Svenbo/Frisky Svenbo/Hey Frisky Svenbo/ Frisky Svenbo, yeah.'

– L –

Labels

Wearing clothes by fashionable designers such as Versace, Armani and Moschino plays a vital part in an English footballer gaining the respect of his team-mates. And it helps him remember his kids' names, too.

Landladies

In 2006 FA Technical Director Howard Wilkinson decided to put English football back on track by reinvigorating a proud tradition and forming a Football Association-backed elite brigade of football landladies.

These indomitable figures were once a beloved feature of our footballing landscape. They nurtured the top stars, feeding them up on stodgy grub and bourbon biscuits and protecting them from the prying eye of the media and the attentions of any girl they considered 'a bit on the brassy side'. In a sixties BBC documentary about George Best, for instance, who could forget the sight of the Belfast Boy, under the watchful eye of landlady Mrs Mary Fullaway, carefully fashioning an attractive Mother's Day card out of a paper doily, some glitter and a tub of rubber-solution glue? If only his fingers had been so fumblingly incompetent when it came to zip fasteners, the whole history of the game would have been so very different.

Wilkinson had long been a champion of these sturdy women who he sees as an important pivot in a player's learning curve. 'You can't expect a player to understand zonal marking, if he's still eating his peas off a knife,' the technical director has observed, citing the link between table manners and tactics that has been acknowledged by top soccer bosses from Vittorio Pozzo to Sir Alex Ferguson.

It is a little known fact that Eric Cantona refused to join Sheffield Wednesday not, as was reported at the time, because Owls manager Trevor Francis wanted him to play in a trial, but because he discovered that Wednesday intended to billet him at a luxury hotel rather than with one of the legendary *dames-de-terre-de-football Anglais*. Sensing the Frenchman's discontent, Wilkinson offered him an alternative, a back bedroom at number seventeen Maiwand Terrace, two meals a day, use of the cruet and unlimited hot water (on alternate evenings), under the watchful eye of **Mildred Jessup**, a woman whose firm line on winceyette pyjamas would later see her smack **Roy Keane** on the nose with a rolled-up newspaper.

In his forthcoming autobiography, *Ici, L'Enigma*, Cantona relates his delight when the Leeds boss made his proposal: 'It decided things for me. You see, in France the English football landlady is an almost mythic figure. She is an existential hero who is honourable, independent and totally unwilling to compromise, especially when it comes to letting anyone take more brown sauce than she considers decent.

'And of course Mrs Jessup's name was well known to me. As twice winner of the prestigious *France Football* European Football Landlady of the Year award, she was a true idol, worthy of a place in the pantheon beside Mrs Sophia Panini of Turin, whose pinny Paolo Rossi wore beneath his shirt during the 1982 World Cup, and Holland's Miss Bettina Bunge, whose concept of "Total Bed & Breakfast" had revolutionised the world of lodging with half-board in the seventies.'

Under the FA's scheme a taskforce of strict yet caring middle-aged women trained by Mrs Jessup would become an integral part of Steve McClaren's England set-up. They would make sure that the players drink regular cups of weak tea, buy them sensible underpants and regularly check under their beds for the presence of 'mucky books'. Wilkinson believes the results would be a marked improvement in the national team's mental attitude and an end to the current problems of on-the-field indiscipline that have seen three Englishmen sent off in twelve months. 'Mark my words,' he said, 'there will be no players taking an early bath with Mrs Jessup about. Unless, of course, it's Tuesday between seven and eight, which is when she normally puts the immersion on.'

Lawyers

By 1999 the game of football had become the playground of the legal profession. Players sought compensation for injuries sustained in collisions with opponents; libel writs flew in all directions; contractual obligations were the subject of suit and counter-suit; and a young midfield star at a leading Premiership club launched a multi-million-pound class action against the tailor whose assurance that 'all the lads will be wearing chiffon harem pants and a yashmak in a few months time, honest!' had brought on a severe bout of post-traumatic stick disorder, which had left him powerless to leave the golf course.

In a climate so litigious that burly centre-backs and combative ball-winners tended to seek the advice of counsel before launching two-footed tackles at the upper thighs of opponents (a lengthy process which, while it disrupted the flow of the game, at least offered a possible explanation for the lateness of one or two of Paul Scholes's efforts), it was really no surprise when Aston Villa announced that their latest big-money signing would be the elegant defender, George Carman QC, bought from Lincoln's Inn in a cash plus Stan Collymore deal.

'We have been watching Georgie for some time,' a plainly elated Villa boss, John Gregory, explained. 'He is a versatile lawyer who reads the game, and lots of big, thick dusty books, really well. I think he can do a great job for us sitting in front of the defence and breaking up opposition attacks with his crunching but perfectly legal objections.'

The Villa captain of the time Gareth Southgate also welcomed the arrival of the silkily skilled silk: 'Miranda (that's George Carman, by the way) is a great addition to the squad. When everything gets a bit frenzied on the field and the affidavits are flying, you need someone who can slow things down with a quick injunction, or by calling a series of extremely dull expert witnesses to testify on your behalf over a disputed throw-in.'

The England centre-half also explained why chambers had been prepared to accept Collymore as part of a package, which would see the errant striker exchanging Old Trafford for the Old Bailey. 'While Stan has no formal legal training, he has spent an awful lot of time on the bench,' Southgate said, adding, 'Hahaha. I had to get that one in.'

Villa's new boy, Carman, quickly proved his worth to his latest employers during a Wednesday night friendly in Norway, coming off the bench in the seventieth minute, with his team trailing 1–0, and promptly secured a three-week adjournment to prepare the case against a goal kick.

The legal eagle's telling intervention came as no surprise to one watching expert, Ron Atkinson. It was during his days in charge of Manchester United that Big Ron established the modern blueprint for the use of footballing barristers when he secured the services of one of Britain's most famous Learned Friends, on behalf of the Red Devils. 'It was clear from the first training session,' Atkinson recalled in his autobiography *Ron for the Money*, 'that Horace Rumpole simply didn't have the stamina to last a full match. But if things were going against us, maybe we were the odd goal down at home, I knew I could bring him on for the last ten minutes and see if he couldn't conjure something with a magical little precedent, or wrong-foot the match officials with one of his little burden-of-proof lollipops. For a couple of seasons there, Rumpole of the Bailey was very much our get out of jail card.'

The arrival of George Carman at Villa Park started a predictable rush from other Premiership outfits eager to get themselves attorneyed-up. Arsène Wenger, Gérard Houllier and Gianluca Vialli became locked in a three-way bidding war for the services of Belgian ace Jean-Louis Dupont, whose scintillating display in the Bosman case caught the eye of practically every manager in Europe; Leeds United secured the services of Kavanagh QC; and the late master of the rolls, Lord Denning, was said to be the target of Middlesbrough boss Bryan Robson, who believed the deceased peer would bring top-level experience, expertise and a much-needed dash of pace to the Boro midfield.

While some praised the forward thinking of the clubs in protecting themselves against potentially destructive litigation, not everyone was pleased with the trend. Reacting to the news that Frank E. Bailey had just signed a £40,000 a week deal with Newcastle United, PFA chairman Gordon Taylor commented, 'Believe me, the only people who'll be happy with this situation are the lawyers.'

Leadership of the Conservative Party

When then Middlesbrough boss Steve McClaren resigned from his part-time post on the England coaching staff in 2004 rumours quickly spread on Teesside. Cynical talk had the rubicund Yorkshireman clearing the decks in preparation for a top job he believed would soon fall vacant. The pessimism proved ill-founded, however. Ten days later McClaren was still in charge at the Riverside and, contrary to all speculation, Iain Duncan Smith remained leader of the Conservative party.

So was McClaren really serious about swapping Boro red for Tory blue, or was the timing of his decision and that of the presumed plot to oust the Quiet Man simply a coincidence? The answer to both questions was – probably not. While sources close to the Middlesbrough manager said that the chance to lead Her Majesty's Opposition had come a couple of years too soon for him, his manoeuvres may not have been entirely without political motives.

Insiders at Conservative HQ in Smith Square had been reluctant to use the term 'stalking horse candidate' since the time eleven years before when John Major came close to being toppled by Desert Orchid, but the feeling remained that McClaren's move may have been a finely timed decoy run designed to open things up for the man IDS's opponents really wanted – Terry Venables.

The *Daily Mail* (whose readers have long nursed the suspicion that anyone whose first name begins with three vowels must be of foreign extraction) had always touted Venables as 'the only realistic English candidate' for the job of Tory leader. And while the former England coach had never publicly expressed any interest in the position, the feeling in the game was that he would not pass up the chance of reviving a sleeping giant with the potential to become a leading power in Europe alongside the likes of the Christian Democrats, Silvio Berlusconi's Forza Italia and Real Madrid.

The idea of bringing in Venables had been floated around Smith Square for some time. Tory grandees were won over to the notion of using sporting talent to reinvigorate the party's fortunes by the efforts of Sebastian Coe. Lord Coe, it will be recalled, worked wonders with William Hague, briefly giving the Conservative leader the illusion of three dimensions by engaging him in regular bouts of judo.

Alas, the splendid Olympian's offers to roll about on the carpet with Duncan Smith, in the style of Alan Bates and Oliver Reed in Ken Russell's *Women in Love* (albeit fully clothed, obviously), were rejected. IDS apparently preferred the more cerebral exercise provided by regular sessions of Buckaroo with Oliver Letwin ('It is a game which requires delicacy of touch, sound balance and nerves of steel,' an IDS supporter later explained, 'and it's not as noisy as Hungry Hippos').

With Lord Coe having stepped down to spend more time with himself, a number of other sporting candidates were considered. Kevin Keegan was among the early favourites. At Newcastle and Manchester City the former England boss has shown he had a knack for reviving apparently comatose behemoths, but the fact that, in his own words, 'My father was a miner. He worked down a mine', was thought to count against him. There was also a fear that he might too easily fall prey to Chancellor of the Exchequer Gordon Brown's infamous mind games. The Scot's uncanny ability to get under the skin of opponents having been dramatically demonstrated during the previous election when Charles Kennedy, live on Sky TV, delivered his now notorious 'I would love it, just love it if the base rate of inflation in this country rose above that of the EU average (allowing for seasonal adjustments)' diatribe.

Charismatic German coach Klaus Toppmöller was also believed to have been strongly favoured by Europhiles within the party, though the idea of appointing the wild-haired German was never seriously considered, most feeling the chain-smoking, heavy-drinking 'Toppi' was too much like Kenneth Clarke to gain wide enough acceptance among the rank and file.

And so Venables emerged as the candidate of choice, his chirpy Essex manner, flashy dress sense and history of wheeler-dealing apparently putting many senior Conservatives in mind of Teresa Gorman in her pomp.

Venables' supporters felt his ability to get the best out of wayward yet gifted mavericks like Paul Gascoigne was critical in a party that in recent years had failed to fully integrate the considerable talents of Jeffrey Archer and David Mellor. They also believed he had the tactical sense to maximise the talent available and, in one fan's words, 'make the team more than the sum of a lot of spare parts'.

Venables, they felt, would take on Labour at the next election with a Christmas tree formation, the muscular and uncompromising Michael Portillo employed as a lone forward, supported from midfield by the bustling runs of Anne Widdecombe.

Unfortunately Venables turned the job down and it went instead to David Cameron.

Hannibal Lecter

In the winter of 2005 the charismatic cannibal Hannibal Lecter launched a shock bid to take over Liverpool. The strangely attractive serial killer quickly outlined his plans to prevent Steven Gerrard from leaving Anfield, reassuring fans that he would extend the England midfielder's contract, reassure him that the club's ambitions match his own and pan-fry his thighs in Normandy butter and serve them on a bed of wild rocket. 'I'd like to see him walk away on a Bosman after that,' the super-intelligent murderer joked darkly. Some fans expressed concerns that Lecter simply intended to bleed Liverpool dry. He denied the allegation. 'I love the game. As they say in the adverts: "Drink football, sleep football, eat footballers". Mmm! Do I scent roasting?' Sadly some other strange Americans bought the club instead.

The Libertarian

Sven-Göran Eriksson was not generally regarded as a great tactical innovator, but in 2005 he confounded his critics by playing Shaun Wright-Phillips in a new role in the England side to face Austria. The Chelsea winger was to be the libertarian – playing so far over on the right he was actually on the left a lot of the time. 'Shaun will be taking a position he feels comfortable with,' England assistant Steve McClaren explained, 'while simultaneously filling a problem area for the team'. A spokesman for the Libertarian Alliance was unimpressed, however. 'Despite the evidence of our own eyes we firmly believe that all footballers are mature individuals who should be free to make up their minds over where they go on the pitch and what they do when they get there without the interference of the Nanny coach,' he said, adding, 'though that shouldn't stop him from axing Fat Frank Lampard clearly.' The libertarian should not be confused with the Blaireo, a left-winger who drifts over to the right at the first chance he gets, like Joe Cole.

Victor Loaf

In 1955 Vic Loaf, steel-rimmed midfield chassis of England coach Walter Winterbottom's WMD formation, revolutionised British football when he became the first professional player ever to take control of himself by buying out his contract.

Loaf was working under the financial constraints imposed by the maximum wage. As a result he was forced to buy himself bit by bit from his club. 'It all started when I got a double-up on the greyhounds one night and used it to purchase my left thigh,' the stout middle-half recalled in his autobiography, *A Slice of Loaf*. 'At first my chairman at Town, Alderman Alf Offal, was happy to take the money, but once I started getting close to having a controlling stake in myself he became altogether more awkward, especially when it came to the sale of that part of my anatomy which he knew to be vital to a man about to embark on the rigours of married life, namely my pipe-tamping thumb.

'Though never what you might term a "Red", at one point I even went so far as to threaten the withdrawal of my left thigh, right knee, both elbows, ribcage and the top half of my head from competitive matches. Offal got on his high horse at that. He claimed that if I did so I wouldn't have a leg to stand on in the eyes of the law. There was some argy-bargy between the lawyers, though, and in the end he relented. I eventually purchased the final part of yours truly, my pituitary gland, on 21 June 1955. After consulting my good lady, Bertha, I then sold myself to a local joiner for the princely sum of seven pounds, six shillings and tuppence. I have never looked back since. Though that is largely because Alf Offal chiselled me out of two vertebrae.'

Low Centre of Gravity

A low centre of gravity has long been the Holy Grail of the English football gaffer.

According to ancient runes, a low centre of gravity allows players to turn faster and also makes them difficult to knock off the ball. In Paul Gascoigne's case this natural advantage was achieved by being a bit on the chunky side. But there is clearly more to it than that. Otherwise Premiership teams would be packed full of average-sized lads with equatorially propor-tioned waistlines, which is clearly not the case. Well, not since Barnsley dropped out of the top flight, anyway.

For while chunkiness is one way of ensuring the sort of weight-to-height ratio that, according to mythology, produces a Wayne Rooney, it is the distribution of the poundage that is all important. To put it in layman's terms: the bottom half of the player's body must be considerably heavier than the top half (this is known to soccer technocrats as 'The Weeble Syndrome' in honour of the popular round-bottomed 1970s toys which, as older readers will recall, were celebrated with the words 'You can make them wobble but they won't fall down'). There are three basic methods of achieving a low centre of gravity: mighty thighs and a huge bottom (a technique invented by Kenny Sansom and perfected by Roberto Carlos); short, thick legs and a long, skinny body (Brian Kidd in his pomp); or mas-sive feet (if only Ian Thorpe had been Brazilian). Players lacking these characteristics can attempt to compensate by fill-ing their boots with lead or wet fish, but it is generally at the expense of basic speed.

LSD

As you may have guessed from the utterances of Ted Croker and Graham Kelly, mind-expanding drugs have never been in vogue at the Football Association. Not since that unfortunate incident involving Sir Alf Ramsey and the revolving paisley-patterned llama, anyway. And that was, as has been well documented since, a total mistake. The England manager agreed to 'drop acid' only because he thought it meant he would be able to bring an extra centre-half into the squad instead. As it was, but for a brief, tight-lipped freak-out that saw Bobby Moore and Co. running on at Wembley to the accompaniment of Caravan playing 'In the Land of Grey and Pink', little harm was done save for Peter Storey being suspended for six matches after following his coach's instructions 'to, like, love Günter Netzer out of the game, man', a little too enthusiastically.

– M –

Magic of the Cup

Third round day is every true football fan's favourite Saturday/Sunday and Monday of the season. The reasons why are best summed up in the following award-winning piece by journalist and broadcaster Frank Gutt:

Old Trafford is a world away from the gritty, down-at-heel realism of Sixfields where Northampton Town meet Manchester United in the FA Cup tomorrow. Yet United manager Sir Alex Ferguson wouldn't exchange his cherished theatre of dreams for all the hand-painted dug-outs, breeze-block tea bars and touchline advertising hoardings extolling the services of local undertakers in the world.

'OK,' the avuncular Scot says when the vivid contrast is drawn to his attention, 'I admit that Old Trafford has little in the way of quirky architecture and there are no hand-knitted woollen teddy bears in the club colours for sale in the megastore, but for those of us who love Manchester United this sparkling state-of-the-art super-stadium is home.' And as the man known to everyone at United from the loftiest retail sale-point service trainee down to the humblest marketing director simply as 'the Boss' casts a loving eye over the palatial surroundings his cheeks glow with undisguised whisky.

'It's unbelievable, isn't it?' says United's bubbly, dressing-room joker Gary Neville as he looks forward to the resonant tussle with the Cobblers. 'None of the lads can get their heads round it. I have to keep pinching Rio Ferdinand to make sure he's awake.'

Like all of the United squad, the veteran right-back is a part-time footballer fitting a couple of hours' training a day around a busy schedule of film premieres, shopping and searching for a saucepan in his luxury city centre penthouse.

'Some days it's tough,' says the commendably honest Mancunian whose working day can begin as early as 10 a.m., 'dragging yourself out of bed the morning after the opening night of the Rod Stewart musical and going off to the training ground. Especially when you know the minute you're finished you've got to leg it over to Harvey Nichols to check out the latest range of designer clobber, then get back home again in time to download the Joss Stone CD on to your iPod.

'To be frank, there are times when you wonder why you're putting yourself through it,' Neville admits, 'but then something like Sunday comes along and reminds you.'

Though the manager is one of United's only full-time employees, his day is no less full than that of his players. 'I'm a real jack-of-all trades round here,' the Boss chortles. 'Coaching, shouting, throwing cups, becoming embroiled in bitter legal wrangles with majority shareholders, you name it I do it!'

But things have certainly come a long way since Ferguson swapped a secure position in Scotland two decades ago for the uncertainty of Old Trafford. 'Oh aye,' he recalls, emitting the friendly chuckle that is never far away from his lips. 'When I first arrived it was a total shambles. I had to clean out the dressing room myself. Took me weeks to get the remains of Paul McGrath off the floor.'

It was the thought of games with the likes of Northampton Town that kept the Boss going through those troubled times. True to his combative nature, however, he is not prepared simply to sit back and enjoy the occasion. 'Absolutely not,' he says, 'this isn't just about soaking up the atmosphere and swapping jerseys, we've got to go out and try and win.

'Obviously the Northampton side are not household names

and they never will be, no matter how many times they appear on *Football Focus* being patronised by Garth Crooks, but we mustn't let ourselves be intimidated by their awesome lack of reputation.'

It's a robust view that Neville endorses. 'We know we can't hope to match Northampton when it comes to heartwarming life stories and unsubtle yet endearing blond highlights,' he says, 'but we are much fitter and more skilful than them, so on the day who knows?'

United's optimism is bolstered by the knowledge that the history of the FA Cup is littered with heroic pixie-crushing feats such as mighty Arsenal's celebrated triumph over tiny Farnborough in 2003, or gigantic Liverpool's unexpected win over plucky Yeovil in 2004.

'It's the uncertainty: the fact that with a little lack of luck the form book can come straight in through the window and even the feistiest underdog can get spanked on the nose with a rolled-up newspaper. That's what makes the FA Cup a competition rivalled only by the battle for that all-important fourth Champions League spot in the affections of football fans the world over,' Neville says.

And for a club such as United, advancing to the fifth round can have far-reaching fiscal implications. 'You can talk about links to the local community, social hubs and the fostering of civic pride,' says Sir Alex, 'but working at Old Trafford makes you realise what football is really all about – money. When I walk out of here after a good financial result and see the smiles on the innocent faces of our shareholders I know why I got involved in the game in the first place.'

Neville, meanwhile, takes an even more romantic view of what a totally expected victory tomorrow might mean. 'No disrespect to Northampton, who have done really well to establish themselves as a struggling lower division outfit and built up a well-deserved reputation for teetering on the brink of oblivion, but I'd love to draw a real minnow like Telford next,' he says with a gleam in his eye.

Such is the magic of the FA Cup, who is to say that his wish won't come true?

Magic Sponge

For over a century the magic sponge was an essential item in every trainer's kitbag. Then came the leaner, fitter age of the physio and the painkilling spray. Soon magic sponges were surplus to requirements. Without concern for their future, football, the master they had so faithfully served, wrung them out and tossed them aside.

There are a thousand magic sponges out there. This is the story of just one of them: Ronnie Soft (Manchester United and England). Once celebrated by the Stretford End with his own chant ('Ee-ay-ee-ay-ee-ay-oh/Down your waistband Ron will go'), now a washed-up husk earning a precarious living wiping the flies off motorists' windscreens at a busy road junction in Hulme.

'The United scouts spotted me while I was still at school. It was the autumn of 1967,' Ronnie recalled twenty years later. 'I was a bit wet behind the ears but even then there wasn't a marker I couldn't handle – or a stick of chalk or crayon come to that. They took me on as an apprentice. I spent a few days at Old Trafford just absorbing things; my new environment, the atmosphere, some excess embrocation off David Sadler's knee.

'Despite the fact I was doing quite well, it still came as a shock when one day Sir Matt Busby called me into his office and told me that on Saturday my place was in the bag.'

On that afternoon in front of 60,000 people the nerves that were eventually to prove his undoing surfaced for the first time. 'I felt clammy all over,' Ronnie would later confess. 'Then

Brian Kidd took a blow in the nuts and the next thing I knew Mr Compson the trainer was signalling that it was time for me to do a job for the team.'

Soft's impact was immediate. 'I made quite a splash,' he would tell his first biographer Michael Parkinson in 1970, 'most of it over Kiddo's jock-strap! And that was it, fame. My life was changed for ever. It happened so fast the details never really had time to sink in.'

By the time the European Cup Final came around Ronnie was an international celebrity, but his edges were beginning to fray. 'I know it was stupid and unprofessional, but the night before the Benfica game I allowed George Best to take me out on the town with him. Bloody hell, I soaked up some stuff that night. Lager, whisky, champagne, beeswax furniture polish . . . if it was on the table I polished it off. When I woke up next morning I was on the floor in the gents' toilets of a fashionable West End night spot.

'I got back to the team hotel in time for breakfast, but Sir Matt only needed to take one sniff at me to know that I'd literally been out on the piss. Luckily he was a kind man and chose not to comment. But I sensed that the writing was on the wall and nothing I could do would erase it.

'After that my career never really recovered. Sure I had some great moments with a bruise on Denis Law's knee and there was that steamy night in the laundry basket with Pan's People's knee socks, but my life was sliding. It came to the crunch in 1971 when Wilf McGuinness took me to one side and introduced me to a new lad. "From now on this fella's going to give you a hand," he said waving a can at me. I asked what it was. "It's an anaesthetic spray," he said.

'Why is it that funny shape? I asked. "Because it's an aerosol," he said. Well, you're telling me it was. Soon I couldn't get a look in for that little squirt.'

Within six months Ronnie Soft had left Old Trafford on a

free transfer to a local window cleaner. 'Yes, I do feel bitter,' he confided in a newspaper 'Where Are They Now' feature in 2002. 'Football squeezed what it could out of me and then threw me out like an old rag.'

Make a Name for Himself

In the opinion of many managers (but mainly Sam Allardyce) too many referees these days are trying to make a name for themselves. They do this by sending players off for minor infringements such as dumb insolence and making V-signs at them while pretending to scratch their noses. Since many referees are called Mark Clattenburg or Uriah Rennie, the desire to make a name for themselves is not surprising. What nomenclature the officials are hoping to fashion by this ruthless exploitation of power is never discussed, but in all likelihood it will be something hunky and masculine such as Spartan Beltsander or Stud Router. If things continue as they are there is a serious threat that in future the Premiership referees list will read like the cast of a Jackie Collins mini-series.

Managerial Types

Managers have always come and gone, their respective styles enjoying a vogue and then falling gradually out of favour. One minute it's fedora hats and champagne, the next cool analysis and pasta. Looking at the Premiership now it is plain, for example, that there is no longer any room in the modern game for the Caledonian Warhorse, a once ubiquitous managerial figure easily recognised by his grim, rubicund face, blue lips and the accompanying voice – like gravel in a cement mixer. Formative years in the Lanarkshire coalfields gave the Caledonian

Warhorse a sense of perspective ('People talk to me about pressure. This is not pressure. When you're working in a fourteen-inch seam and dust begins to trickle from the roof – that's pressure, laddie'). He was never an inspired appointment but he selflessly took pressure off the directors, who knew that sacking him was guaranteed to make them popular on the terraces.

Latterly a new hybrid, the Intense Celt, has replaced the Caledonian Warhorse. He comes with staring eyes, gritted teeth and a notepad and pen. In interviews he affects the manner of a religious zealot about to administer a well-deserved strapping to a boy caught crumbling communion wafers into a cardinal's hat. Like his predecessor he builds from the back.

Gone too is the Gent. The last exemplar of this style to be found in the English top flight was Roy Hodgson. The Gent always looked smart in neatly-pressed blazer and grey flannels and sported a hairstyle that hinted at an era when Britain was big and powerful and people got excited when they saw a banana. The Gent's approved technique was to move into a club, upset a couple of key senior players and then resign before his reputation was too badly tarnished. A decade or so later he would then express regret that he left when he did saying, 'I fully believe that had I weathered that minor storm, we would have turned the corner and Athletic would now be a major force in Europe.'

A continental breed, the Boulevardier, has superseded the Gent. He is highly regarded in Europe (though by whom nobody ever says) and impresses everybody by having 'a philosophy'. The Boulevardier takes a holistic approach to fitness – 'If you look at a technical player such as Seedorf, you will see that his balance all flows from his ears.' However, his insistence on training often alienates English footballers who prefer more traditional ways of keeping fit such as snooker, wine bars and lap-dancing, and he is forced instead to bring in lots of players from abroad whose names nobody can remember.

Maradonas

Football's least exclusive brotherhood is the Maradonas of Society. Turkey's Emre Belözoğlu is the Maradona of the Bosporus, while Albania's Edvin Murati is the Maradona of the Balkans. The talented Emre once plied his mercurial craft for Internazionale. He moved there from Galatasaray where he linked up with Romania's Gheorghe Hagi, who was the Maradona of the Carpathians.

Murati was once said to be attracting the attention of the bigger Italian clubs. If things had worked out supporters at the San Siro could at one time have found themselves watching a match in which the Maradona of the Bosporus and the Maradona of the Balkans lined up for Inter against a Torino side boasting the New Maradona, Carlos Marinelli, or one from Napoli featuring the Maradona of Maradona, Diego Maradona's son Diego Junior. Sadly the Maradona of the Desert, Saudi Arabia's Saeed Owairan, has retired and it seems the days of the Maradona of the Caucasus, Georgia's Georgi Kinkladze, have passed. Though, thankfully, the Kinkladze of the Baltic, Marian Pahars, is still scampering merrily about.

This is not the first time such a situation has arisen. Peter Marinello was the Scottish George Best, Ryan Giggs was the Welsh George Best and the New Maradona's former Middlesbrough team-mate, Alan Moore, brought things full circle when he briefly became the Irish Ryan Giggs.

It perhaps says something for the British imagination that none of these titles makes adventurous use of topographic features. Had Marinello been the Best of the Pentlands or Moore the Giggs of the Great Sugar Loaf things might have been different.

The puzzle is how players come by these tags. When it comes to the Maradonas Of and the like, the phrase frequently used by the media is 'They call him . . .'. They call Gerald Vanenburg the White Pelé, they call the Saudi keeper Tommy Lawrence of Arabia, and so forth. Who 'they' are remains a mystery. We are told, for instance, that 'they called Nat Lofthouse the Lion of Vienna'. It's hard to imagine life chez Lofthouse resounding to the sound of Nat's wife asking, 'Do you fancy a cup of tea, the Lion of Vienna?' Nor does it seem likely that his arrival in the public houses of Bolton would have been greeted with a joyful cry of 'Hey up, it's your round, the Lion of Vienna.' Although life was more formal in the 1950s, so perhaps that was the case.

Some people may feel this 'they' is a journalistic equivalent of the royal 'we', or the managerial 'I' (as in, 'I'll check if we've got that size', meaning, 'I will get a YTS to run up seven flights of stairs, search through the store-cupboard and run back down again with the news that we haven't'). In this case 'they' really means 'we', but carries a greater sense of objectivity and conveys the message that this is news from the frontline rather than just the work of sub-editors.

Another theory is that a secret Fifa committee handles the distribution of grand titles in return for undisclosed favours. After all, it can hardly be coincidental that nearly all the Maradonas Of hail from the old Ottoman Empire. There has never been a Maradona of the Chilterns, though West Ham's Stuart Slater for one would have fitted the role perfectly.

Match Non-Fixing Scandal

In Italy in the spring of 2006 there was consternation after an extensive police investigation revealed that 'up to several' Serie A matches in the previous three seasons were entirely honest.

Former PM Silvio Berlusconi appeared on television to break the news to the nation. 'This is a black day indeed for Italian football,' he said tearfully. 'My faith in the glorious dishonesty of the game has been totally undermined.'

Angry fans took to the streets. 'Do the presidents of these disgraceful clean clubs really think the results of a football match should be left to the ability of the players, blind luck and the roll of a leather orb?' asked one disconsolate supporter. 'Like most Italian boys I was raised on heroic tales of brown envelopes, clandestine telephone calls and the providing of prostitutes for visiting match officials,' another told reporters. 'Now it seems it was all a lie.' The Italian international squad, meanwhile, were horrified by the news. 'When you discover that you were playing in games in which the outcome depended entirely on your ability to kick the ball in the goal it inevitably leaves you feeling shell-shocked,' admitted Pippo Inzaghi before diving over a chair leg and waving an imaginary card at a passing waiter.

Match Officials and Country & Western

Country music has a long tradition of football-related songs and for complex socio-psychological reasons connected with feelings of alienation and respect for the law, these have tended to focus on the match officials rather than the players. Johnny Cash, for example, dubbed himself 'the Man in Black' in homage to his idol, referee Arthur Ellis, and recorded 'I Walk the Line', arguably still the greatest song ever written about the life of an assistant ref. Cash wrote from personal experience. At one time many US soccer pundits considered the man behind hits such as 'Rock Island Line' and 'Folsom Prison' as a future World Cup official. Unfortunately Cash's Old West attitudes to discipline inevitably led to trouble. In a Nevada State Cup match he shot a man in Reno just because he didn't retreat ten yards quickly enough, and was stripped of his flag.

Glen Campbell, meanwhile, gave us 'Wichita Linesman', the story of an official for the county FA whose weariness towards the end of a long season is palpable. Indeed the song's melancholy line, 'And I need a small vacation', was one of the first concerted appeals for a mid-season break. 'Songwriter Jimmy Webb and I both felt it was impossible for the linos to concentrate 110 per cent over a full nine-month season,' Campbell would later recall, 'especially given the pressure being applied on them by managers, players and spectators and Fifa's constant adjustments to the offside laws.'

Other country artists have also recorded songs about referees, most notably Willie Nelson whose platinum hit 'Crazy' was dedicated to Mike Riley.

Match Officials' Whistles

No one was more delighted by the Premiership's decision to start the mic-ing up of match officials in 2001 than FA stalwart Sir Bert Millichip. Sir Bert had campaigned ceaselessly for the Bastards (as many crusading modern refs have taken to calling themselves in order, in the words of Jeff Winter (Stockton-on-Tees), 'to reclaim the word and demonstrate our empowerment') to be equipped with CB radios ever since he had watched the film *Smokey and the Bandit* and begun going by the handle Greased Lightning.

In truth communication between ref and linesmen has been a besetting problem of the game ever since the 1960s. Up until then things had run smoothly thanks to the policy of only recruiting match officials from ex-forces personnel. Military training meant linesmen could use their flags to signal to referees in semaphore. Admittedly this was not without its hazards.

In a 1923 Empire Cup (African section) clash, for instance, Ethelred Proudfoot (Durban) attempted to indicate to the referee that the culprit in an off-the-ball incident was Bezuidenhout of Orange Free State and ended up in traction for eighteen months as a result.

Referees also used skills learned in the services to let assistants and players know of their decisions and intentions, blasting out well known bugle calls, or Morse code signals on their whistles. If the referee blew the retreat, for example, it informed the wall that it was not yet back the full ten yards, if he made a dash and a dot it signified a penalty, while if he made a series of quick dashes it indicated that his lunchtime beans had disagreed with him.

By the time national service was abolished, however, it was clear that things would no longer continue in this happy and well-organised manner. Modern music was largely to blame. At first football's governing bodies had hoped to use the power of pop to lure youngsters into refereeing. The original Man in Black, Johnny Cash (Memphis), for instance, was even slated to take charge of the 1962 World Cup Final before an unsavoury incident in Nevada led Fifa to strike the gravel-voiced songster from their international list. Sir Stanley Rous would later recall: 'It wasn't so much the fact that the artist behind a host of dark, country-tinged hits had shot the man in Reno, as that he did so just to watch him die that struck us as totally unacceptable. In hindsight, of course, I can see that this sort of sociopathic gunplay would actually have been just the thing to keep the Italians and Chileans under control.'

By the time the Beatles (Liverpool) came on the scene it was clear, however, that the policy had backfired badly. Firstly there was B.M. Griffiths (Newport, Mons) and his ill-fated attempt to replace the whistle with a harmonica, worn Bob Dylan-style around his neck, then during the match between Wolves and

West Brom in 1963, J.V. Sherlock (Sheffield), influenced by his idol Miles Davis's playing on *Kind of Blue,* interrupted the match with a fifteen-minute improvisation based on the modal structure of 'cornerball'.

'I been digging what Miles, 'Trane, Arthur Ellis (Halifax) and those other cats been laying down, man,' Sherlock told reporters afterwards, 'Everyone talking about 90 minutes this and 45 minutes each way that, but from now on diminution of time values is where it's at, Daddy.'

While *Melody Maker* hailed Sherlock as a genius for pushing forward the frontiers of whistling, with his revolutionary introduction of moody Ravel-like shadings, Wolves boss Stan Cullis was not impressed. 'In my experience professional footballers do not respond to dissonance,' he said. 'They need something with a beat they can tap their toes to.'

Sadly match officials ignored the Wolverhampton manager's words and since that day match officials' whistling style has become ever more wild and improvisational. A fact acknowledged by free jazz pioneer Ornette Coleman when he dedicated his 1970 album *Blow That Thang!* to Jack Taylor (Wolverhampton).

Nowadays, sadly, more and more younger referees simply cannot even be bothered to master the art of blowing up at all. A new generation of so-called 'gangsta reffas' such as Puff Cardy (Northampton) and The Notorious B.L.I.N.D. (Otley) openly confess to not knowing one end of a whistle from the other, yet both men have successfully taken charge of hundreds of Sunday matches using samples lifted from the work of seventies masters like Pat Partridge (Middlesbrough) and Clive Thomas (Treorchy). As David Elleray (Harrow) observes in his new book *The Boss!*, 'While the efforts of Puff Cardy and his ilk are perhaps not whistling as my generation would have understood it, at the behest of some of the senior members of the common room I recently went to see one Peep Blowie Blow

(Worcester) in action. Much to my surprise, I am forced to conclude that the chap is, indubitably, all that and then some.'

With Puff, Peep and their posse of followers leading the way it seems certain that in future the headset will be joined as an essential piece of the referee's match-day equipment by the dual turntable and sequencer. Everybody in the house say, 'Yo'.

Meteorologist

Midfielder who streaks around very rapidly, though nobody knows if he has any significance or not.

Hayao Miyazaki

Reports from Japan say that anime master Hayao Miyazaki's next full-length cartoon feature, *Howler's Moving Cards*, will be based on the ancient English football legend that is Graham Poll. 'Culturally the Japanese are drawn towards zany autocrats and they don't come much zanier than the Thing from Tring,' explained film critic Phil Nutmeg. Nutmeg predicts the film will feature 'a man who has been turned into a pig, for reasons that are not immediately obvious, and finds himself working in a sinister noodle factory run by creepy giant spiders and a man with a huge pumpkin-shaped head – so pretty much like the FA, really.'

'*Howler's Moving Cards* is an important step towards expanding the Premiership match official franchise in the Far East,' said Keith Hackett of the Referees' Association when asked about Miyazaki's movie. 'Already our merchandising arm has totally sold out of whistles via the Internet and the demand for fourth officials' boards has gone through the roof. From what my contacts in Tokyo are telling me, Premiership referees could be this years' pet rocks.'

Money

Financial substance that it is definitely not about. Though often what it is about (i.e. ambition, respect, feeling wanted) is expressed in purely fiscal terms. Example: 'The gaffer has proved his ambitions match my own by awarding me a 25 per cent pay rise. It's not about the money.'

Monitoring

Monitoring is what clubs do when they want to let a player know they are interested in buying him, but can't actually tell him directly because that might contravene regulations about tapping-up. And that would never do.

Motors

In November 2006 English football fans were both repelled and delighted by pictures showing the world's most tattooed centre-back Rio Speedwagon reclining semi-naked on the bonnet of his new Navaho Ninja Deathstar Fighting Dog SUV. The six-wheeled Ninja comes with a mighty 94-litre engine that generates more horsepower than Sheikh Mohammed and burns so much gas it's said that when you turn the ignition you can actually hear the gurgle of a Pacific Islander drowning.

Yet despite the fact that the Ninja has a carbon footprint the size of Stoke and is the first road vehicle to come fitted with SAS as standard (simply flick a switch and three blokes in bala-clavas pop up through the bonnet and terminate your enemies with extreme prejudice – but only if they are posing a genuine threat to human life, obviously), even this fails to impress some top footballers.

Many leading Premiership stars reject four-wheel drives in favour of the sleeker lines of the exclusive sports cars produced by the legendary Italian company Frayrari Bentos. The famous logo of the prancing pie is a guarantee of high quality because Frayrari Bentos is alone among manufacturers in still sticking to the tried and tested formula of making all its bodywork by hand out of shortcrust pastry. As a result a Frayrari never rusts, though it does go a bit soggy if you spill gravy on it.

The latest Bentos marque is the 22-cylinder Priapus, a car so overtly and unrepentantly masculine the firm even produces a circumcised version for the US market. Some have detected a Freudian undercurrent. However, when asked if he thought the car was a type of penis extension, one proud owner, Welsh midfield stalker Darren Slather, commented, 'Don't be stupid. You'd never get it down your Calvins, would you?'

The popularity of cars such as the Ninja, the Priapus and the Baby Braincell Mk6 among England's leading footballers may seem like a new phenomenon. It is not. As a brief trawl down the information superhighway on a search engine powered only by the sustainable fuel of the words 'made-up footballers and their made-up cars' confirms.

The first automotive vehicle to grab the attention of Britain's leading players was the Mountfield-Van Den Hauwe Dowager. The Dowager was the chosen mount of the Victorian era's answer to Wayne Rooney, the Hon. Vereker Fitzstanley Simpson Bart. It came fitted with a man with a red flag as standard. Although this option was later removed after Simpson had written three of them off in a single night. 'Ho ho, yes, by God,' wrote Obediah Brass in the *Daily Telegraph* of the highway exploits of this redoubtable nineteenth-century superman, 'I once saw Simpers, high as a kite on his favoured tipple of vintage hock and laudanum, swerve that Dowager of his straight into a cluster of nuns gathered round a roadside Calvary. Later he claimed he thought they were penguins attacking a tramp. Killed fourteen of them. But, you know, he did it with a bit of style, grace and charm, not like these dreadful modern fellows.' Though clearly opinions on reckless driving have changed dramatically since last month.

C. B. G. B. Frag, left-back for England and Royal Bath & Wells, holder of the world record in the standing start, All-England public school champion at gentlemen's rollover, buffet and twitch, and a man who once wrestled Lady Otteline Morrell to a standstill during the annual Garsington Manor Cornish Cross-Buttock festival, was the player who set the fashion among his contemporaries in the 1920s. Frag favoured a Fokker Dr. 1 he had captured from the aerodrome of Baron von Richthofen during a dawn raid, armed only with 'a half-finished bottle of vintage champagne and a rather charming French girl'. Soon the car parks of England's leading clubs were filled with brightly coloured triplanes, though in the interests of road safety most clubs forbade their players from firing the twin machine guns if there were horses around.

The sturdy Aubrey Norwich was the footballer's car of choice during the 1940s and 1950s. It came fitted with a number of handy dashboard attachments, including a dentures mug and a steel rupture appliance. As Scotland star Wee Jimmy Linament commented, 'I don't smoke myself, but I find the electric lighter comes in very handy for cauterising the wounds inflicted on me by full-backs.' While England skipper **Vic Loaf**, his voice dubbed by an actor so that middle-class radio listeners would not be shocked and alarmed by his unruly vowels, told the BBC, 'The Norwich is a real smasher with a large rear boot that provides adequate space for two healthy boys, a fox terrier and all my plumbing tools. My spouse and I are delighted with our acquisition. God save the Queen.'

The car favoured by the stars of the swinging sixties was undoubtedly the Mateus Fondue Ghia. **Rod Rugg**, the legendary side-whiskered traction engine of the Ottersfield Rovers midfield, recalls, 'The great thing with the Fondue was that it was actually designed so that it drove better when you were drunk. And of course the wipe-clean vinyl seating was another plus, if you know what I mean. Hurgh hurgh hurgh. Did I ever tell you about the time me and Mark Dennis . . .'

But sadly it seems we have run out of space for that one. Suffice it to say that it is a raucously amusing tale involving a large quantity of Asti Spumante, a nitespot named Rockafellas and a female singer who was very big in the Bristol area.

– N –

Next Level

Football folk are addicted to computer games and so it is not surprising that phrases from the exciting world of Lara Croft and Septictankmaster IV have entered the vocabulary of the game. Taking the club to the next level is a matter of getting enough points on this level to progress. Or at least that's what you might think. However, the manager's best mate has told him there is a cheat he has read about on the Internet. If you buy a reserve team left-back from Portugal during the transfer window, your team will suddenly be armed with ultra-powerful rocket boots and will hammer everyone in their path, a bit like that time when you pressed Esc, pause and enter and were able to call in helicopter gunship support to help your Roman gladiators defeat the Huns in Age of Gore II. Like many things you read about on the Internet, it doesn't work.

Nicknames

Suppose you had a mate called Piggy. One day Piggy comes into your local, stands on a bar stool and calls for silence. He wants to make an announcement. Ever since I can remember, Piggy says, I have been known as Piggy. Well, I feel that it is a bit out of date, doesn't sit well with the image I am trying to project and is increasingly hard for today's kids to relate to. So from now on I would like you all to call me the Stallion.

How would you react to this? A guess is that you'd say something along the lines of, 'Get down and get your round in, Piggy, you daft git.' Because it is a fact of life that you don't choose your nickname, you are given it.

Unless, of course, you happen to be a football club. Football clubs are always picking their own nicknames. At Sunderland, for example, they decided that they could no longer call themselves the Rokermen because they don't play at Roker Park any more. This is absolute rubbish. Everybody knows that a change of circumstance is no excuse to alter your nickname. There are men around who are still known as Young Alfie even though they are eighty-seven, and others who are called Little Alfie even though they are six foot five and thus considerably larger than Big Alfie, who is himself younger than Young Alfie. However, to alter these things to accommodate reality would only cause the kind of mass confusion within their community usually associated with that moment during a press conference when Glenn Hoddle opens his mouth and begins to speak. And so things stay as they are.

Not so in football. Sunderland ditched their old handle and opted for the Black Cats instead. They join a growing band of footballing deed-poll botherers. When Malcolm Allison took over at Crystal Palace, the Selhurst Park club stopped being the Glaziers and became the Eagles and Jimmy Hill's days at Highfield Road saw the Bantams become the Sky Blues. At Leicester, meanwhile, there was a time when the Fossils were the team rather than just a description of Alan Birchenall's half-time jokes.

At least Mackem fans got to vote on the Black Cats. Sadly that is not always the case. Several years ago the chairman of Stockport County decided unilaterally to ditch the tag the Hatters in favour of the Cobras, to tie in with a sponsorship deal with a lager manufacturer. He was eventually persuaded not to. Presumably when the players told him that running out to chants of 'We are Cobras' was not exactly going to boost team morale.

In a similar vein Kettering Town's head honcho once tried to change the Poppies into the Lions. His reasoning was that if the club did so it would be far easier to offer related merchandise. Possibly so, though if that is the way things are going why not really push the boat out marketing-wise and re-dub your club the Pokemons? Besides which, if the Rockingham Road side think they have problems, imagine how difficult it must have been for the marketing department at Middlesbrough a hundred years ago. Back then the team from Teesside was nicknamed 'the Scabs'. No wonder the shelves of the club shop were empty in those days.

Some clubs clearly feel that their nicknames are simply not groovy and with-it enough (as we young folk say) for the modern world. This is true enough in some ways. Often they tell us more about a town's industrial heritage than what it is like today. Thus Macclesfield are the Silkmen, Ashford Town the Nuts and Bolts, and Yeovil the Glovers. In Consett the blast furnaces are long gone and one of the main employers is Phileas Fogg. Yet the town's football team remain the Steelmen rather than the Gourmet Snack Boys.

Given time it could happen, of course. A number of clubs take their nicknames from local culinary delicacies. Aylesbury are the Ducks, Morecambe the Shrimps and Reading the Biscuitmen. Sadly Chelsea decided to opt for the Blues rather than the Buns, while for reasons of decency Bakewell don't have a team at all.

Some nicknames clearly could do with changing, though, if only for the morale of the team. After all, it can't do much for the self-belief of the players of African Guinea to labour under the soubriquet 'Silly Nationals'. While the consistent failure of Barcelona's 'other' club, Espanyol, surely owes less to lack of investment and bad management than it does to the long-term effects of being hailed everywhere they go as the Budgerigars. And what of Atletico Madrid? Bad enough for your confidence to have mighty Real as your neighbours without also being tagged the Mattress-makers.

And what of Middlesbrough's nickname, the Boro? How did it originate? One belief is that it was a piece of spontaneous verbal invention. When the team first ran out at Linthorpe Road in 1876, the crowd probably tried a few encouraging but unsatisfying shouts of 'Come on Bro', but realising it sounded a tad weedy took the unprecedented step of slipping in an extra vowel. The result was that ever since, the club has had a chantable nickname while 95 per cent of the population of Britain (and the spellchecker on my computer) has struggled to spell the name of the town correctly.

Noun Deficit Disorder

In March 2005 Alan Hansen went through an episode of *Match of the Day* without once using a noun. 'Appalling, inexcusable, unforgivable,' the Scot later told reporters, 'sloppy, lazy, complacent. Homeward, directly, uncontactable.'

Novelists

Describing the popular series *Footballers' Wives* the controller of ITV drama Nick Elliott said there would be as much football in the show 'as there was oil in Dallas'.

As far as can be gauged no actual football folk have so far had any input into *Footballers' Wives*. This is a pity as there has recently been a small upsurge in creative writing at grounds across the country. Former Wimbledon striker Dean Holdsworth has taken time out from appearing in gardening programmes, and blasting the ball over the bar from three yards out, to pen a children's drama, while St Andrews has its own literary circle in the shape of blockbuster novelist Karren Brady and manager Steve Bruce. The Birmingham City boss has a trio of novels about a crime-fighting coach on his CV. The titles, *Striker*, *Sweeper* and *Defender*, have led to avid speculation in some quarters on what position the former Man United stopper's next opus will be named after, one critic expressing the hope that Bruce will create an entire new genre, historic-soccer-detective fiction, with a novel set in the 1960s entitled *Sturdy Pivot*.

Despite the efforts of Bruce and Holdsworth it is fair to say that the golden age of the footballer-novelist was thirty or more years ago. In 1971 Terry Venables penned *They Used to Play on Grass*, a work of fiction filled with the future England manager's eerily prescient vision of what the game would look like in the 1980s ('Scottish football has improved by leaps and bounds since that inspirational performance in the 1978 World Cup'). The chief change envisaged by Venables is, as the title implies, the widespread adoption of AstroTurf. El Tel was positively evangelical on the subject of artificial surfaces at one time, an early manifestation of this enthusiasm being the Thingamy-Wig, a type of hairpiece he patented in the 1960s.

The same decade saw rugged Northern Ireland international Derek Dougan produce *The Footballer*, while Jimmy Greaves notched up four novels, one of which, *The Ball Game*, centres on the antics of a striker with the strangely familiar name of Jackie Groves (this honourable tradition of thinly disguised protagonists is upheld by Steve Bruce, whose main character is Leddersford Town manager Steve Barnes). *The Ball Game* begins arrestingly: 'Miss America said she preferred to be on top of me. I wasn't arguing.' But sadly goes downhill from there.

In the row between Maradona and Pelé over who was the

greatest player of all time, it was a surprise that nobody attempted to add lustre to the Brazilian's image by bringing up *The World Cup Murder*, a novel he wrote with the help of a fellow named Herbert Resnicow a couple of decades ago. The plot of *The World Cup Murder* revolves around the Brooklyn Booters' attempts to win the Mondial, an endeavour made all the more difficult by a group of evil communists who put pressure on Eastern bloc referees and assassinate Booters coach Gregor Ragusic.

Ragusic is a wily Serb with distinctly foreign habits ('His breath . . . smelled of garlic even this early in the morning'), who is given to utterances so gnomic they should come with a pointy hat and fishing rod: 'When iron is hot, you can make it how you like. When iron is cold, you can only break your teeth,' he observes at one point, a remark that suggests Pelé enlisted Claudio Ranieri as his translator.

According to the jacket blurb, Pelé depicts 'the poetry and mathematical precision of the game'. And that is no lie. 'To tackle a dribbler who was approaching your goal, driving the ball ahead of him with both feet alternately,' El Rey informs us, 'meant judging his course accurately without getting caught off balance or faked out, getting the foot against the ball to wedge it against the dribbler's foot, and then, at precisely the right instant to knock him off balance with the force of your shoulder against his chest without being called for roughness.'

Whatever the skills of the writers of *Footballers' Wives*, it is impossible to believe the drama will ever produce anything to match it.

– O –

Obesity

Obesity is a massive problem for the modern game. In Scotland a whole football culture based on little men scurrying about the field has been totally obliterated by the increased affordability of crinkle-cut pies. Were he to reach maturity today, it is probable that Wee Jimmy Johnstone would weigh a hundred kilos and be about as capable of jinking as the average bouncy castle.

The super-sizing of humanity has also affected the ancient art of goalkeeping. 'And the keeper made himself big' was once a popular phrase among pundits. This hard to master skill which, in the case of Oliver Kahn at least, involved the custodian inflating his body like a bullfrog, using a complex physiological process that converted a portion of his ego into hot air, is now no longer a necessity. Today's goalkeepers are already so big if they made themselves any bigger they'd fall through the earth's crust.

The same holds true of football supporters, of course. Arsenal's new stadium may hold over fifty thousand people now, but the way things are going in ten years' time fewer than half that will be able to squeeze into it and even that will be putting a marked strain on the steelwork.

Oop for t'Coop

A phonetic rendering of the way northerners say 'Up for the Cup' (apparently), the phrase was popularised by metropolitan journalists in the 1950s. Supporters of London clubs were never described as being 'Ap ferva Cap', because while northern accents are endearingly comical those of southerners are simply coarse.

– P –

Pacemaker

Player whose role in the team is to indicate to the referee that the defensive wall is not back the full ten yards.

Sid Paddle

Britain's leading independent supporter, Sid Paddle, has come to nationwide attention during the last few years thanks to a series of high profile campaigns designed to bring his own brand of commonsensical punctiliousness to the game.

Paddle first emerged in 2002 when he made the front pages, following an incident in which, dressed as Mr Willy Wonka, he sellotaped himself to Rodney Marsh to publicise his campaign to have the football authorities make it compulsory to append the suffixes BP (before Premiership) and AP (after Premiership) to every mention of the first, second or third division. 'It would prevent the unsightly use of terms such as "the current" and "as it then was",' Paddle opined to reporters above the din of passers-by shouting, 'There's some raving mad bloke here . . . and he's stuck to Willy Wonka,' into their mobiles. 'It would make everything so much clearer to the public and put an end to a huge amount of totally avoidable typing,' said Paddle.

Following that, Paddle wrote thousands of letters to MPs, the FA and the media in an attempt to clean up the language of football. 'Frankly it frequently disgusts me,' he told Sky News. He was referring, of course, to the almost compulsive use by football writers and commentators of the phrase 'North of Hadrian's Wall' to mean Scotland. 'Why don't they get an atlas out and take a look,' Paddle announced indignantly. 'They'll find most of Northumberland and an unfairly forgotten slice of Cumbria is north of Hadrian's Wall. If north of Hadrian's Wall meant Scotland, then Bobby and Jack Charlton would both be Scots, so would Alan Shearer, and Newcastle United would be in the SPL and Blyth Spartans, too, I shouldn't wonder. You'd think people would be more careful when there are kiddies about.'

Next he interrupted Prime Minister's Question Time to demand to know 'Why football matches are referred to as fixtures? If the same two teams played each other on the same date every year, then it would be a fixture. As it is it's more like a fitting, if you ask me.'

Since then Paddle has been lobbying successive Home Secretaries. He wants them to bring in a package of new measures that would compel anyone seeking to settle at a ground to learn something about its history before they are awarded a contract, to prove, as he says, that they are 'not just here for economic reasons, but really want to assimilate'.

Under Paddle's proposed scheme potential coaching staff and players would have to attend education courses organised by local supporters' groups and would not be allowed to live off a club until 'they had proved they could identify at least three members of the 1990 Zenith Data Systems semi-final team from the blurry photos in old sticker albums, and state – with a knowing yet affectionate grin – which wayward 1970s midfielder could always be found "showered, changed and standing at the bar with a pint in his hand" even before the fans themselves got to the pub.'

'Teaching is the best medicine we have to treat the disease of stupidity,' Paddle has often observed and who is to say that he is not correct?

Patents

Shortly after England rugby union hero Jonny Wilkinson applied to patent his pre-kick hand gesture Manchester United's Gary Neville attempted to trademark his own most characteristic feature. However, his application was rejected when the patent office ruled that if successful it would 'infringe the inalienable and historic right of British adolescent males and elderly ladies to grow wispy little moustaches'. There was better news for brother Phil, though, who succeeded in patenting a 'slack-jawed look of blank amazement such as you might expect to see on the face of someone who has opened the fridge door and found his or herself staring into the lifeless eyes of his own freshly severed head'.

Penmanship

A few years ago scientists made a discovery that sent the kind of panic through farmers the owner of a Ming vase might feel on seeing it picked up by **David James**. Simultaneously sheep from Tierra del Fuego to the North Cape had worked out that it was possible for them to cross a cattle grid by rolling over it. Since sheep do not have mobile phones or access to the Internet, the only conclusion scientists could draw was that a marked similarity in mental stimuli had allowed ovines across the planet to come up with this concept completely independently, yet at the same moment.

The world of professional football has much in common with that of sheep. One player dons a nasal strip and suddenly dressing rooms around the globe look like an Adam and the Ants fan club meeting. Another peroxides his locks and within seconds a mushroom cloud of noxious chemical fumes is hovering above training grounds everywhere as other pros rush to turn their hair the colour of a pub ceiling. It happens far too fast to be put down to copying. More likely, as with sheep, the powerful team instinct of football folk has created its own collective consciousness that allows the same new idea – about goal celebrations, Alice bands or fingerless gloves – to pop into hundreds of well-groomed heads synchronically.

The latest example of this incredible natural phenomenon has affected managers. In the past few months, without any warning, more and more Premiership coaches have taken to standing on the touchline with pens stuck in their mouths. Stranger still, they quite often interrupt their anxious gnawing in order to write things down on pads of notepaper.

Steve McClaren, the boy wonder with the ruddy cheeks and the coach driver's hairstyle, and Glenn Roeder are both members of the new breed of dug-out scribblers. John Gregory is another, though he is probably just writing down the lyrics of Bruce Springsteen songs, so he can paste them on to the inside cover of his science file later.

The behaviour has also been spotted on mainland Europe where Louis Van Gaal, among others, is an inveterate jotter of pitch-side notes. What the bosses are writing nobody knows. Though since Van Gaal gives the impression of someone who would happily walk a million miles for one of his own smiles, a fair guess in his case is probably just little messages to himself. 'And what time do you get off work, baby?' That kind of thing.

In the end what is being so frantically written is probably not so important as the actual process of writing it. The game has changed. Things have moved on. As the success of José Mourinho and Arsène Wenger has proved, football coaching these days is more and more a white-collar profession. And like all such jobs, it requires paperwork, whether it needs it or not.

Once a football manager was rarely seen with anything stuck in his mouth other than a fat cigar or the ear of somebody who had offended him. If he wanted his thoughts jotted down he paid a ghostwriter to do it.

Sir Alex Ferguson does not write anything down during a game. But then Sir Alex is from an earlier era when football management was more akin to being a military policeman than running a building society. In Ferguson's younger days the coaching staff featured the trainer, generally a battle-scarred ex-pro who came armed with a bucket and sponge. The bucket had limited medical application but it came in handy for swatting anyone who wasn't paying attention during the half-time team-talk.

The second in command was expected to do his bit, too. In his first autobiography, the memorably titled *Time on the Grass*, Sir Bobby Robson explains why he appointed Bobby Ferguson as his assistant when he first took over at Ipswich. 'Bobby was a Geordie. And I wanted someone I knew I could rely on when the fists were flying in the dressing room', the former Newcastle boss observes without further explanation, as if any senior role in a company would involve occasional brawls with the employees.

Coaches of Robson's generation did not scribble notes, because, frankly, 'Any more lip, sunshine, and I'll deck you' is a sentiment best delivered in person rather than via an internal memorandum.

Pets

Anyone who has gazed into the happy, trusting face of a footballer in a shop window will have felt the temptation to take him home without thought of the, often messy, consequences. And who among us did not as infants come across a stray winger or left-back in the street and, beguiled by his impish range of tricks, beg our parents, 'Can we keep him? Can we? Please! Please!', only to be told sternly that it was impractical to have one in the same house as a Swedish au pair girl and that he must be turned over to the police forthwith? ·

No one can deny that having a footballer around the house can be hugely rewarding. They are great characters, frisky, intelligent and full of **banter**. Kids can learn valuable lessons from having one. Looking after a player teaches a child about responsibility, reproduction and why it is not a good idea to start trying to lick your genitals when the vicar comes for tea.

Set against that it must never be forgotten that footballers are also a lot of hard work. They require regular exercise, eat a great deal of expensive food, need at least two hours' grooming a day and, particularly when they are younger, can do an awful lot of damage to the flowerbeds.

One lady who knows more than most about the joys and pitfalls of looking after footballers is **Mildred Jessup**. Mrs Jessup is an acknowledged expert in house-training players. According to the seventy-two-year-old, whose regimen of marrowfat peas and brown ale is credited by many for Bryan Robson's celebrated midfield bursts, the key to discipline is understanding the footballers' psychology. 'Your player is a pack animal,' Mrs Jessup says, 'and you've got to show him early on that you are the alpha dog. Hard words harshly spoken and always have a rolled-up newspaper in your hand to administer a rap on the nose if they get lippy. Your punishment should never actually hurt him, mind. The effect is purely psychological, much like the FA's disciplinary fines when you think about it.'

Sometimes, though, a rolled-up newspaper is not enough. 'The really top players can be a handful,' Mrs Jessup admits, 'because they have that leadership quality, that desire to be the boss. I remember when I had **Roy Keane** lodging with me, I used to have to flip him over, pin him down and bite his ears at least twice a week until I got him broken. And even after that if I turned my back on him for so much as a second, when I turned round again I'd find him snarling and crouched ready to spring. In the end I have to say Roy was one of my favourites. Though Mr Jessup has never forgiven him for chewing the leg off the piano when he was left alone in the house during a thunderstorm.

'Footballers do make a mess, there's no getting away from that. They bring in a lot of dirt, and their eating habits are not the neatest. Now, of course, I use a dry all-in-one food to feed my boys. It's got all the nutrients they need and it produces firmer you-know-whats. Which can be quite a bonus when they do their business in a neighbour's garden.'

Whatever the problems a player may bring into the home, Mrs Jessup is keen to remind anyone thinking of taking one in that they will be making a long-term commitment. 'A footballer isn't just for Christmas,' she says, 'he's for the length of his contract (or until a better offer comes his way from somewhere else).'

Football Pies

Football pies (so named because they are made out of old casies – what you think is gristle is actually the laces) are acknowledged to be one of the most lethal substances on earth. The mere stench that emerges when the reinforced crust cracks is enough to kill a canary. For years South American Indians used the gravy to coat the tips of their arrows when hunting capybaras. The pastry, meanwhile, is a virulent, dense grey mass, as resistant to cooking as asbestos, which causes the sort of indigestion that makes the scene in *Alien* when the creature bursts out through John Hurt's chest look like an advert for Rennies. At one time British secret agents had a miniature football pie concealed in a tooth when they went into enemy territory and the instructions to swallow it if they were captured. It was a fine plan, but one that foundered on the fact that even James Bond can't swallow his own teeth.

Pint

In everyday language a pint is a measure of liquid roughly the equivalent of half a litre. In football it refers exclusively to Dom Perignon champagne and is generally agreed to mean three gallons. Example: 'I had a pint and the next thing I knew the warder was shaking me awake and telling me my solicitor was waiting.'

Players Invisible

During Sir Bobby Robson's spell as manager of Newcastle United it was revealed that striker Carl Cort had become an 'invisible man' and been forced to wear a 'green jacket', presumably so staff didn't keep bumping into him. Sir Bobby blamed a mole for leaking the information to the press.

But the allegation that the mole had leaked the information with malicious intent was denied by one of his closest associates. 'The mole is a good-natured fellow fond of housework and baking,' Mr Badger told reporters by phone from his secret underground den. 'He is also extremely short-sighted. He may well have fallen into conversation with someone in a local inn and not known to whom he was speaking. I'm afraid his blindness is such he would be totally unable to distinguish between a booze-sodden weasel or a journalist.'

Mr Badger, who described himself as a lifelong Newcastle fan, having 'been born black-and-white', said that he felt the Newcastle boss was trying to deflect attention away from his own shortcomings by pointing the finger at the mole.

'His failure to take advantage of having the invisible man Cort in his squad is plainly a sign that his powers are waning,' Badger said. 'I mean, for a start he'd never be spotted in an off-side position, would he?'

The fact is, though, that utilising see-through forwards is by no means as simple as it may not appear. It is understood that Robson did experiment on the training ground but found that while the transparent Cort was very difficult for defenders to pick up, it was equally difficult for his team-mates to find him with passes.

'To get the best out of a limpid goal-machine, he and the visible players need to develop an almost psychopathic under-standing,' said one insider who asked to remain synonymous, 'and it just didn't happen.'

The fact that Robson was worried over the information about Cort's corporeal disappearance leaking out is instructive. Because the feeling locally is that the former Wimbledon frontman is not the only United player to have been affected by the mysterious condition. Fans recalled that Argentinian Christian Bassedas also became a spectral presence, while Hugo Viana demanded a return to Portugal after waking one morning to find his reputation had faded terribly.

'That some Newcastle players are becoming see-through is transparently obvious and it's been going on for years,' one local fanzine editor told his mate. 'Older Geordies recall how Wyn Davies used to "hang in the air". He didn't. He was just standing on diaphanous legs. Recently it seems to have become an absolute epidemic. I mean, what about John Karelse? We signed him donkeys ago. But nobody saw him for at least three years. Every once in a while I'd be down on the Quayside late at night and find myself stumbling about for no reason whatsoever. People concluded that it was an excess of drink but it's plain that what really happened was I'd been jostled by a pellucid Dutch goalkeeper.'

For some while now paranormalists on Tyneside have been speculating on what may be causing Newcastle players to surrender visibility. 'It's obvious that there is a perfectly irrational explanation for it all,' said one, 'probably involving ley lines, negative energy fields, alien abduction and *The X-Files*' Gillian Anderson wearing nothing but a look of amazed adoration. But I'm just thinking aloud here, obviously.'

Poetry

Aside from William McGonningoal, the Edwardian Scottish netminder who devoted his entire poetic oeuvre to chronicling the fortunes of his local team Fife Unacademicals (aka the Battling Numpties), poets have traditionally shunned football. Thankfully there have been some notable exceptions. Philip Larkin, for example, gained instant notoriety for his celebration of the 1966 World Cup Final 'This Be The Win', largely because of its opening lines, 'He fucked you up the Russian linesman/Ha ha ha, ha bloody ha'. Ted Hughes, meanwhile, took a typically robust Yorkshire approach to the game, winning a place in the hearts of Leeds fans with his stanza, 'Killer from the egg, malevolent fanged grin/ But he could play a bit, you know, Terry Yorath'. More latterly, Harold Pinter reacted angrily to then Liverpool manager Gérard Houllier's treatment of midfielder Paul Ince with this typically lacerating verse: 'Houllier/ Hooligan/ Everyone has a right to dignity/ You bloody f******/ shitbag arsehole'.

Pointilist

Player whose defensive role at set-plays is to indicate to the referee the exact spot from where the free-kick should actually be being taken. This is generally five yards further back from where it is now. His battle with the **pacemaker** is one all true fans of the game relish.

Post-Impressionist

Descriptive term sometimes applied to Peter Crouch.

Power of Football

Sepp Blatter once claimed that 'Football is the most powerful force in the world.' And according to the Fifa chief, the most important people in football are the players. Since previously the most powerful force in the world was the atomic bomb (which took over from God in 1961), clearly what Sepp was saying is that footballers are equivalent to the plutonium in a nuclear warhead. Anybody who saw John Craggs play will be well prepared to believe him.

So far the power of footballers has been harnessed largely for the good, but there is clearly a worry over what might happen if one should fall into the wrong hands. The threat that terrorists might obtain a 'dirty' footballer, possibly from the former Soviet Union, then set him off in a major city – a scenario used by Hollywood in the hit movie *End Zone*, in which, it will be recalled, Mel Gibson and Wesley Snipes successfully defuse a depleted Ukrainian wing-back who has been primed to explode at the Superbowl – is already being taken very seriously in Washington. Indeed next week it is believed that

President Bush will push the UN to draught a new Soccer Non-Proliferation Treaty in an attempt to head off such an event.

Luckily the players themselves have thus far refrained from invoking their own terrible power for destruction, even in the most trying circumstances. For example, good-natured Australian soap-opera star Harry Kewell elected to use the threat of the Bosman ruling rather than his own awesome force (believed by scientists to be the equivalent of three oil tankers packed with high explosives) to bring about a move from Leeds to Liverpool.

During his transfer to Real Madrid, David Beckham was reported to have said that he was being treated 'like a piece of meat'. (You have probably yet to see a leg of lamb dressed in an Armani suit and driving round in a Ferrari, though doubtless there are butchers who do that sort of thing in Hertfordshire.) However angry he was, though, the England captain refrained from using the ultimate deterrent – detonating himself. Today the knowledge that not every footballer is so restrained casts a dark and ominous shadow over the globe.

Pressure on Managers

One has only to study pictures of Terry Venables during his final days at Leeds United to see the terrible effects football management can have on a manager. His face is drained of all perkiness, sagging like an old balloon. This is not unexpected. The pressure on coaches is physical as well as psychological. The roller-coaster climax to the season produces incredible G-forces and it is the face that takes most of the strain. Imagine you are in a centrifuge revolving at 35,000 rpm with a fully-grown giant squid stuck to your cheeks and you are getting close to understanding the incredible strain placed on the countenances of Sam Allardyce and Co.

Scientists working in the FA's top-secret Boffin Suite at Soho Square believe that El Tel's face was crumpling at such an alarming rate that had he stayed on at Leeds by Cup Final day only his characteristic silvery crest would have been visible above the knot of his tie. 'When Ferdinand went early doors you could clearly see Terry's nose begin to seek cover by burrowing into his cheeks,' one expert said at the time. 'And then gradually his jowls began dropping ever deeper into the safety of his shirt collar.' Unconfirmed reports from Elland Road implied that during the home defeat to Middlesbrough the tip of the Leeds manager's chin was seen peeping out from under the hem of his warm-up coat.

Until news filtered through of Venables' departure, the football fraternity had been bracing itself for a repeat of the incident during the 1998 World Cup finals when Italy's boss Cesare Maldini's visage, already as heavily creased as a favourite goalkeeping glove, reacted to defeat in the penalty shoot-out against France by escaping down his trouser leg and hiding underneath a pile of tracksuit tops. Luckily Roberto Baggio succeeded in coaxing it out with an Amaretti biscuit before anyone noticed.

It was to tackle just such situations that the FA has over the years developed a medical team who are trained to deal with the ravages pressure can take on a manager's face. A previous incumbent at Leeds, David O'Leary was one boss rescued by them. 'The failure of his "babies" to qualify for the Champions League put such strain on David's twinkling mien that his nose began to drift westwards,' sources later revealed. 'At one point we seriously feared we might lose it altogether down his right ear-hole.' The situation was rapidly stabilised by a combination of stress counselling and a stonemason's mallet, and today O'Leary's nose is safely back where years of battling the likes of Mick Harford had left it.

The experience accrued during that operation was vital in

the next major crisis the team faced. During 'Keanegate' at the World Cup in 2002, the Football Association of Ireland called in the Soho Square outfit after it became clear that immediate help was needed if Republic of Ireland boss Mick McCarthy was not to end up with both his eyes on the same side of his nose. The team were immediately flown out to the Far East and quickly went into action. 'The left eye was cresting the nose when we arrived,' I was told, 'but we managed to wrestle it back down again with a block and tackle.'

'I looked in the mirror and I was terribly drawn,' McCarthy reportedly quipped when the situation was under control. 'It might have worked for Picasso, but I don't think Damien Duff would have appreciated the modernist nuances of it.'

Arsène Wenger is one manager who has always succeeded in keeping his face under control, even when emotions are reaching boiling point. The strain shows in other areas, though, and during the final days of the season the Frenchman's height has been known to fluctuate by as much as eighteen inches. 'Arsène is careful never to stand next to the same person more than once or twice at press conferences,' one Arsenal insider revealed, 'otherwise the situation would become obvious to the public. Before the Champions League Final, for example, he was nearly seven foot six.'

Private Hell

On the eve of England's ill-fated campaign in Germany Michael Owen told a tabloid newspaper about his 'Private Hell'. 'I think I'm quite down to earth,' the striker confessed, 'but the problem with public hell is that you get all these sinners coming up asking for your autograph and wanting to photograph you holding their smouldering babies and that. It's hard to get in any real quality torment on your own. That's why I've gone for a private hell and hired some personal demons – which are kind of like personal fitness trainers only with pitchforks and a whiff of sulphur. I confront them whenever I have the time.

'My private hell's on a man-made island of trauma in the gulf of turmoil,' he added. 'Becks, Rio, Gary Neville and Alan Shearer have got their own exclusive purgatories there, too, so when we've finished being scourged with red-hot iron flails we can all get together and have a beer and a round of golf.'

The Prof

Nickname given to any player who has mastered the art of drinking stout and watching a stripper at the same time.

- Q -

Quota for Transfer Speculation

In response to calls from environmentalists, the EU announced that it would be enforcing a summer transfer speculation quota with immediate effect from June 2008. 'Close-season football gossip is a finite resource,' said the European Commissioner for Hearsay and Tittle-Tattle, Giorgiou Quidnunc. 'If we go on using it at the rate we are doing at the moment then there will be no "Real Deal for Ronaldo" headlines left for future generations.'

In Britain there was widespread anger over the introduction of the new system. 'Fishing for tit-bits has kept thousands of folk on these islands in jobs for centuries,' said an NUJ spokesman. 'Yes, we need to limit the number of stories that are being dredged up each summer, but the problem is not caused by us. We take only fully grown tales, whereas the Spanish hacks are trawling with much finer nets and taking stories that are well below the currently legal two-paragraph limit.'

The transfer speculation quota was denounced as 'deliberately biased against Britain' by David Cameron after the EU announced that Italian reporters would be entitled to cast about in UK territorial waters for red herrings linking Francesco Totti with Chelsea. Meanwhile, Norwich chairman Delia Smith offers her own advice saying, 'With the more well-known transfer speculation such as "Red Devil Tevez?" in short supply, reporters need to take a look at the more unusual varieties such as "Moyes Eyes Savage", or "Trotters Deny Tongue Link", which, prepared in the right way, can be just as tasty.'

– R –

Records

Football records come in many forms, as this selection from **Victor Umbrage**'s bestselling *Umbo's Game Terrine – A Gentleman's Relish of Unsavoury Soccer Shite* (Is It Just Me or Do All Books These Days Have to Have Shit in the Title? Books, £12.99) proves:

Most utensil drawers in a luxury fitted kitchen: 352, Gary Neville (Man United)

Most hair gel used during a Premiership season: 37 litres, Ian Walker (Spurs)

Longest period spent living in a five-star hotel while looking for a house: 14 months, Ruud Gullit (Newcastle United)

Strangest clause in a multi-million-pound managerial contract: agreement to market a range of male grooming products through the club shop, Fabio Capello (AS Roma)

Largest number of celebrity ex-girlfriends during a season. 7, Fabien Barthez (Man United)

Most appearances in *Hello!* and *OK!* 'relaxing in his lovely new home': 53, David Seaman (Arsenal)

Largest number of newspaper column inches devoted to a single hairstyle: 32,347, held jointly by David Beckham's mohican and David Seaman's pony-tail

Largest number of newspaper column inches devoted to a single waistline: 5476, David Ginola (Aston Villa)

Biggest vehicle damaged during outburst of youthful high

spirits and good-natured horseplay: Team coach, Paul Gascoigne (Middlesbrough)

Longest interview without blinking once: 3 minutes 42 seconds, Dennis Wise (Chelsea)

Most uses of the word 'situation' during a live broadcast: 432, jointly held by Glenn Hoddle and Ron Atkinson

Highest total in compensation payments to bring a manager to a club and then get him to go away again shortly afterwards (career): Absolutely masses, Graeme Souness.

Most players 'enquired about' by a club in a single close season: 3457, Middlesbrough in 2000

Loudest wardrobe: John Barnes

Referees' Psychology

At the annual conference of the British Psychological Society in 2002 Dr Nick Neave of Northumbria University announced that football referees are 'an odd group of people'. Dr Neave has yet to say what his acutely trained mind will be focusing on next, but rumour has it that in 2009 he will reveal that Sir Alex Ferguson is Scottish.

According to Dr Neave's research, the men in black suffer from 'illusory superiority' and believe they are never wrong. Few would disagree, though one view is that these anti-social traits are not something with which referees are born. After all, can anyone really imagine a child acting like Clive Thomas or David Elleray? No, such urges as outlined by Dr Neave are not innate, but emerge as a result of the brutalising of referees by our society. The same applies to baseball umpires in the US, where a popular cry from the crowd runs: 'Hey, Ump, your ass just called. It wants your head out by tomorrow or it's bringing a lawsuit.'

What academics studying Premiership referees do not perhaps realise is the torment they have gone through to get there.

They have had to work their way up from Sunday football, something that, psychologically speaking, is the equivalent of ascending a rope ladder behind an elephant with irritable bowel syndrome.

Spend time at grass-roots football matches and one quickly begins to see the pivotal role the referee plays – not for the participants, but for the crowd. Let a home striker collect the ball from his own keeper and run with it at pace, slaloming through defenders and finishing with a crashing shot from thirty yards into the top corner and it will warrant only the most cursory display of emotion from the spectators. The minute a linesman fails to signal an opposition player offside, however, and the entire crowd will turn puce in the face and howl, 'AWAY, LINO, FETCH YOUR FLAG FROM UP YOUR ARSE.'

Society has moved on since the days when the mob could take the edge off their frustrations by torturing animals or mocking the mentally ill. It has created a better and more humane world, but it has placed a heavy burden on match officials.

Take, for example, the experiences of the fledgling man in black as he takes charge of his first match. His kit is pressed and his whistle polished as he surveys the scene before him. It is early morning, the rain is lashing down and from the houses that surround the pitch comes the howling of savage dogs and feral children. The playing surface is pockmarked with dark bald patches courtesy of the four-stroke fuel that leaks from the groundsman's mower. A drunkard has marked the touchlines, an Alsatian the centre spot. The twenty-two assembled players have the traces of the morning's fry-up on their chins, the stench of the night before's beer on their breath and murder in their eyes, but our ref cares not. He is young, full of hope and ideals. He runs out on that benighted field as if it were the San Siro, determined to do something, to put something back into society. He sees himself as a facilitator, an enabler, someone who can help create an environment in which football can flourish. And what happens? The first free-kick he awards, a fifty-year-old bloke standing on the touchline, an oily nicotine-tinged quiff curled upon his head like an Ottoman's turban, bellows, 'WHAT HAPPENED THERE, REFEREE, DID YOUR GLASS EYE MIST UP?'

When the next decision is to be made our neophyte, still stinging from the unjustified scorn that fell about his ears last time, hesitates momentarily. It is the cue for a white-haired old lady with a voice like Edith Piaf gargling tar to croak, 'IF YOU'RE NOT SURE, REF, ASK YOUR GUIDE DOG.'

After this things begin to slide. A throw-in sees a small boy remove a lollipop from his mouth, hawk a gobbet of sputum the size and texture of an omelette and squeak, 'WHAT WAS YOUR LAST JOB, REF, LOOK-OUT ON THE *TITANIC*?'

A free-kick for backing-in produces a chorus of 'JESUS CHRIST, IF YOU HAD ONE MORE EYE YOU'D BE A CYCLOPS!' The referee glances at his watch hoping for the relief of half-time, only to find that sanctuary is still forty-two minutes away.

And so it goes on for week after week. Is there any wonder, then, that referees are deluded and anti-social?

Relegation

In March the nights grow lighter, the days warmer and the little buds of football nerves begin to swell into great big blossoms. As Reg Presley almost said, 'I feel it in my fingers/ I feel it in my toes/ Whenever spring approaches/ Fear of relegation grows'.

This is the time of year when the football fan realises yet again that the truest words ever spoken about being a football fan were uttered by John Cleese in the film *Clockwise*: 'It's not the despair. I can live with the despair. It's the hope I can't stand.'

Yes, despair is brutal, but a supporter can survive it. And it has its compensations. Despair drives football supporters to memorable invective. The Middlesbrough centre-half Alan Kernaghan was not quick. Once during a dismal season at Ayresome, as he flapped in the wake of yet another disappearing opposition forward, a man standing next to me in the Holgate End bellowed, 'KERNAGHAN, YOU COULDN'T CATCH OUR LASS. AND SHE WAITS FOR MEN.'

You get a laugh with despair, but all you get from hope is a slap in the chops. Not that any fan can resist it. In the face of hope logic and experience are powerless. Hope is agony. It is a cocktail of idiocy and short-sightedness that can prolong our suffering for months.

And it is the smallest cuts that are the most painful. Take that moment on Radio Five Live on Saturday afternoon when Mark Pougatch says, 'And there's been a goal at Villa Park. Commentary from Pat Murphy . . .'

As any regular listeners knows, when the commentary comes on the team that is attacking is the one that will score. So when the fan hears the words 'and Barry now on the edge of the opposition penalty area', that should be it. He or she should accept instantly that you have gone a goal down. He should start coming to terms with his grief. Instead when Murphy says 'and Carew's free on the far post', hope kicks in and you presume that his next words will be 'Great headed clearance from the big number-five, and the red-shirted midfield dynamo controls it on the halfway line and, oh my word, Sorensen is a long way off his line and . . . the chip is going to go in . . . is it? Yes, it is!'

So when Murphy actually says, 'Emphatic finish from Carew!', you are doubly crushed. Hope is crap.

Hope is crap and yet in April every fan whose team is in relegation trouble will begin surveying the remaining fixtures of the season. You're thirteen points clear of safety. You should have given up by now. But hope came whispering in your ear,

'Don't give up. There're twelve games to go. Anything could happen. Why not see how many are at home? Your home form's not bad.'

So the supporter sits down and goes through the games. He multiplies home bankers by three, adds probable away draws and puts any doubtfuls in brackets. Then he works out the possible points tallies of the rest of the bottom eight. When he has finished it's obvious that his team has had it. But then hope comes back purring in your ear, 'Oh, come on now. Beaten at Old Trafford next week, is that really going to happen?' And then he looks again and thinks, Well, yes, if we could pick up a point off Fergie's mob while Fulham stumble at St Andrew's and Bolton ship five goals against a relaxed-because-they've-nothing-to-play-for Man City, then we'd move up two places and . . .

The next thing he knows his side have brushed off relegation worries and are pushing for a place in Europe after thrashing Newcastle, trouncing Chelsea and giving Arsenal such a hammering at the Emirates they are declared a write-off by their insurance company.

And seven days later when United crush his outfit like the beetles they are he goes back and starts all over again.

Renewable Energy

Scientists attempting to identify possible alternatives to fossil fuels believe that they may have found a source of energy that could keep Britain self-sufficient in electricity until the turn of the century: tens of millions of unread copies of England footballers' autobiographies. Asked if these will burn, one of the scientists, Professor Will Twist, told the BBC, 'The Native Americans used to make fires of buffalo dung and Ashley Cole's book has many of the same properties as bison crap, so I don't see why not.'

Resolution 162

In September 2005 UN Security Council Resolution 142 called for all good-natured **banter** about how the scorer of West Ham's winner in the 1980 FA Cup Final, Trevor Brooking, didn't get many goals with his head to be removed from BBC sports programmes, decommissioned and then buried in a safe place. Within two weeks, Gary Lineker announced that the corporation would comply. 'We can today say that the world is at last safe from feeble jokes about how the elegant Hammers midfielder must have got concussion from that one,' said a relieved Kofi Annan, before moving on to address Iran's attempts to refine weapons-grade repartee about Alan Hansen's unwillingness to run about during games.

Reticence

Sven-Göran Eriksson was often criticised for his reticence. Others saw it as a source of power. The England players believed their coach to be a man of extraordinary knowledge and boundless wisdom. To them he had an aura of infallibility. And the Swede clearly knew that the less he said, the more likely it was to stay that way.

Sir Alf Ramsey, the only truly successful manager of the English national side, also knew the power of silence. Ramsey's press conferences invariably consisted of him walking into a room, reading out the team, saying, 'Thank you, gentlemen', and then walking out again. He used similar tactics to terrorise his players.

After England lost to West Germany in the 1970 World Cup quarter-final, Jack Charlton decided it was time to retire from the international scene. On the plane back from Mexico he spotted Ramsey sitting alone and nerved himself up to inform the manager of his decision. In trepidation Charlton approached the England boss and launched into a speech he had been rehearsing. He thanked Ramsey for giving him the chance in the side, recalled the glory days they'd shared, but then said that despite all that he now considered that with his age and the situation it was probably time he stepped down and gave a younger man a chance. Ramsey, who had listened impassively throughout, nodded and said that, yes, he had arrived at that same conclusion himself. He said nothing more. Crushed, Big Jack shuffled back to his seat.

Contrast the success of the tight-lipped Ramsey with that of two of his successors, Graham Taylor and Kevin Keegan, men whose arrival in any town can be guaranteed to lead to a wave of redundancies in the donkey-shoeing industry, and you start to see the possible benefits of an implacable attitude towards the media.

Summing up his own approach to life, Calvin Coolidge commented, 'I have noticed that nothing I never said ever did me any harm.' It is to be hoped that one day an England coach will feel able to say the same thing, though only to himself and in a very quiet voice, of course.

Retroactive Sponsorship

With the appointment to the Manchester United board of Malcolm Glazer's three sons, Balthazar, François and Bob, the story of the World's Biggest Club in Association With Snoopies Official Non-Toxic Wax-Based Cheesy Snack of the Fifa World Cup™ took the sort of unexpected fiscal twist that even the writers of *Roy of the Venture Capitalists* would have dismissed as too far-fetched.

The Glazers were seeking radical ways to increase the club's turnover. Soon there was talk that the hard-nosed Americans had been shocked by what they regarded as the wasteful use of the club's resources. 'United only use their name for nine months of the year,' one insider explained. 'In business terms that makes no sense, which, let's face it, in football is the only sense there is. That is why I believe United will soon be leasing the name out during the fallow summer months, possibly to the Wednesday night five-a-side team of an egotistical Eastern oligarch.'

Fans of the club understandably saw this idea as the thin end of the wedge and were already predicting that it was a step towards what they fear most – Manchester United doing a sale-and-lease-back deal on its name.

'The worry then is that when the lease comes up for renewal we could be outbid by the likes of Chelsea, who are capable of buying Manchester United just as a squad name to use in Carling Cup ties etc.,' said Trevor Grubb of UFACA (United Fans Against Crap Acronyms). 'Ultimately you could end up with Manchester United forced to name-share with Oldham Athletic or Bury.'

Some hard-hearted business types have, of course, already suggested that it is ludicrous in this day for two teams in the same conurbation, such as Manchester United and Manchester City, still to have separate names at all. 'Name-sharing makes clear economic sense,' said financial analyst Damien Trough. 'Clearly if clubs, such as for example Liverpool and Everton, pooled their resources, they would be able not only to save a huge amount of money on stationery, personalised crockery and so forth, but also to employ the best marketing and advertising people to come up with a brand new state-of-the-art name more fitting to a twenty-first-century globalised Western capitalist society – Merseyside Sexy Jet-Powered Cash-Cow, or something along those lines.'

Offering retroactive, or historical, sponsorship rights was another course of action the Floridian business titan explored in his characteristically charismatic trousers-hitched-up-to-his-armpits fashion. Soon there was talk of a deal that could yet see the Busby Babes become the Busby Babes in Association with Budweiser. 'Budweiser is a brand that resonates throughout the chronological time-sweep of humankind's epic story all the way from caveman to Letterman,' a spokesman for the US brewing giant said in an unfeasibly deep voice, 'and we would be delighted to find that ours was the official fizzy alcoholic non-vinous beverage of Matt Busby's talented and ultimately tragic young squad.'

However, Budweiser found themselves locked in a silent bidding war to sponsor the Babes with a number of other companies who also saw 'time independent' sponsorship as a better long-term investment than sticking their name on a club shirt. Snickers, Citibank and Fosters Lager (already sponsoring the London Blitz and reportedly now looking to expand into D-Day, the German Economic Miracle and Britain's postwar austerity years) also expressed an interest.

'With history you always know what you are getting,' said PR guru Trevor Grumpy of top London advertising agency Fire, Plague, Pestilence and Grumpy. 'If you were to retrospectively sponsor Stan Matthews in the 1950s, for example, you'd know your product is bound to be associated with winning the FA Cup – could Wayne Rooney guarantee you that? And with modern CGI technology there's no reason why Matthews, Tommy Lawton and so on shouldn't have a sponsor's name added to all footage and photographic images. It's the way forward. Certainly, if I was a dead footballer I'd be looking to sign with an agent as fast as I could and tie up my image rights before it's too late.'

Road to Wembley

It takes a minimum of seven and a half hours of football for a team to get from the third round to the final. Coincidentally, this is the same length of time it takes to get from central London to Wembley by car.

The Robbo

The most important yet undervalued job in England's World Cup build-up is that of the Key Player Whose Fitness Everyone Is Very Concerned About Because Let's Face It We're Stuffed Without Him – or The Robbo as the role is generally known.

Like the scapegoat in ancient Israel, The Robbo's task is one of self-sacrifice. The scapegoat carried the sins of the tribe into the wilderness. The Robbo must draw in all the nation's hopes and become the focal point for every dream of triumph, so that his eleventh-hour relapse will plunge England into not so much a Slough of Despond as an entire Urban Berkshire of Suicidal Despair.

With him we might have paraded the Jules Rimet Trophy; without him to reach the quarter-finals will represent a moral victory. Thus does The Robbo lift the weight of expectation from the shoulders of his team-mates and carry it bravely with him into the desert, or at least up into a position in the stands where the cameras can pick him out looking pensive, allowing John Motson to intone wistfully, 'And you have to wonder what thoughts are running through his mind, with England just three minutes away from exiting the World Cup . . .'

As its colloquial name implies, perhaps the ultimate Robbo was Bryan Robson. Robson was a sporting hero, but like all heroes he had an Achilles heel. Unfortunately Robson's Achilles heel was his entire body. Before every major tournament throughout the 1980s some pundit would voice the opinion that England would like 'to wrap Bryan Robson in cotton wool until kick-off'. This was probably true, though a feeling persists that if he had been protected in this manner

Robson would have suffered an allergic reaction to the lint, sneezed and slipped a disc.

It was Bryan Robson's frailty allied with his playing ability – an injury to Paul Mariner would hardly have had the same gravitas – that so perfectly suited him to the role of Robbo. In 1986 he made his debut in the new position in Mexico with a dislocated shoulder and England were happy to reach the quarter-finals. Despite this promising beginning, the England manager Bobby Robson decided foolhardily to dispense with The Robbo for the 1988 European Championships. Bryan Robson went into the tournament in one piece and England, crushed by national expectation, lost every match.

Before Italia 1990 Bobby Robson remarked, 'I need Bryan Robson to be Bryan Robson because that's the only Bryan Robson I want.' Thankfully Captain Marvel was only too happy to oblige. Back in his more customary role as Robbo he played a pre-tournament blinder, involving daily medical bulletins, a mysterious toe injury and a trip to a German faith healer. Buoyed up by this spirited display, England reached the last four.

While he undoubtedly carved the job of Robbo into the shape we all know and recognise today, Bryan Robson was not its originator. Nor, for that matter, was England the only nation to have employed such a figure. In 1982, for example, West Germany had an excellent traditional Robbo in Karl-Heinz Rummenigge, while in 1994 Diego Maradona brought his own audacious Latin American twist to the job. Perhaps the cleverest continental Robbo, however, was Johan Cruyff who, in 1978, managed one of the greatest-ever performances in the position despite never leaving home or even bothering to get injured.

The prototype Robbo was Gordon Banks in 1970. Like Bryan Robson, the brilliant goalkeeper left his run till late, but it was perfectly timed and there is no doubt that his act of self-sacrifice with the bottle of beer before England's quarter-final with West Germany left enough room for what-might-have-beens to make the resulting defeat seem almost a triumph.

Ron Greenwood for one recognised the value of Banks's performance and in 1982 experimented with what we would now recognise as a twin Robbo spearhead of Trevor Brooking and Kevin Keegan, both of whom missed practically the entire tournament with niggling injuries, leaving the nation convinced the eventual outcome would have been very different, if only they had been fit.

Since Bryan Robson retired, England have been lucky to discover a number of fine replacements. Firstly Paul Gascoigne filled the role with aplomb in 1998 – failing to make the squad thanks to a brilliant display of reckless drinking. In 2000 the nation's spirits were lifted as they watched David Beckham being stretchered off in La Coruña just weeks before the World Cup began, while radio and television commentators asked, 'And what effect might this have on England's chances in Korea/Japan this summer?' in the doom-laden yet concerned tones of Michael Buerk introducing a news item about an oil slick menacing a cocker spaniel sanctuary. And now we have Wayne Rooney, a man who seems destined to fill the Robbo role for decades to come, just so long as he doesn't do something totally stupid. Stay match fit, for example.

Sir Bobby Robson

In 2001 Alan Shearer informed us that Sir Bobby Robson 'is only six months older than he was last season'. The previous season had ended three months before. What Shearer appeared to be saying was that Robson is ageing twice as quickly as an ordinary human being. The Newcastle centre forward advanced no explanation for this bizarre phenomenon. Though scientists later concluded that it might be connected to the same rapid metabolism that allowed the then Magpies boss to speak at double the speed of sound.

Shearer did not say if one 'Bob year' had always been the equivalent of two human years. Assuming that it has, then Sir Bobby is not really seventy-five at all, but either a hundred and fifty or thirty-seven and a half, depending on how you figure things. Most experts favour the former explanation because otherwise it means Robson was appointed manager of Ipswich before he was born – an event too weird even for the world of football.

Role Models

In 2005 it was revealed that on the weekend after pictures of Robbie Fowler in a nightclub drinking beer and smoking a 'hand-rolled cigarette' were published tens of thousands of British youngsters, inspired by the former England striker, went out and did exactly the same thing. 'I would never have thought of this, if it hadn't been for role models such as Robbie,' one eighteen-year-old told reporters, adding, 'Next could you print some photos of top Premiership stars having sex outside a stable and loving relationship as I am quite keen to give that a go at some point.'

If nothing else the furore surrounding the nose-plastered billionaire forward at least exposed once again one of the great fallacies of our era, that children imitate professional sportsmen. That this is true is taken for granted by the vast majority. It is a belief held by more intelligent people, however, that instead of asking whether sportsmen are good role models for our kids, society should be asking whether our kids are good role models for our sportsmen. Certainly all the evidence points in that direction.

We know, for example, that the stars of the 1950s were

gentlemen to a man. They played fair, spoke only when asked a direct question, shrugged off defeat and reacted to victory with no more than a shy smile and a muttered, 'Golly, what a stroke of luck!'

As to the children of the same era, well, we have only to consult the collected works of the great Nigel Molesworth to see that they were, if anything, even more unruly, insubordinate and violent than the present generation. They were, as the author of *Down With Skool!* so memorably sums up his contemporaries, 'oiks, tuoughs, weeds, wets, bulies, snekes, cads, dolts and knaves'.

Since footballers' conduct has got worse over the past four decades and that of youngsters remained at much the same execrable level, it is surely worth considering the proposition that, far from children's behaviour deteriorating as a result of copying sports people, it is athletes' behaviour that has gone downhill as a consequence of imitating children.

Faking injury to get others into trouble, falling over at the slightest push, throwing tantrums when denied victory, random or retaliatory violence and the constant questioning of every statement or decision made by anybody in authority (for parents substitute referees), all these things have gradually crept from the playground into the stadium.

The timing of the collapse in player morality adds weight to the argument. In the era of Wright and Finney blokes left home early in the morning, returning only after their offspring were safely locked away in the nursery. On Sundays while the children ran loose, the sporting father hid himself away in a convenient shed with a copy of *Health & Efficiency* and a pipe. Then a social revolution occurred. As a result since the mid-1960s sportsmen have been exposed to the pernicious influence of youngsters almost daily. The effect has not been edifying.

Go into any child-friendly café on a Sunday lunchtime and you will witness quite horrific scenes: gangs of children, some of them mere babies, running about the place, yelling, throwing food, exposing their bottoms to total strangers and demanding that respectable women expose their breasts for their benefit and enjoyment. Youthful exuberance some might say. But you must ask what the effects such a spectacle would have on a group of impressionable young footballers. Would they not be tempted to imitate such appalling behaviour? It is all very well to fulminate against the exploits of Craig Bellamy and Kieron Dyer, reprehensible as they have been, but you have to ask what kind of example they are being set by the nation's under-sevens.

Of course, we all know that being a child is a short career that can be ended any moment by a brutal collision with puberty, but things have changed. The authorities have acted to outlaw common practices of the past such as the whack from behind, leaving the old-fashioned, uncompromising enforcers of yesteryear such as Mr 'Bites Yer Legs' Chips chuckling rue-fully about how if they were still involved in the game Esther Rantzen would have had them jailed by now. And childhood is no longer an amateur pastime, to be enjoyed only when the serious business of cleaning chimneys, polishing shoes or picking pockets is done. Nowadays it is fully professional and the financial rewards for the youngster are greater than ever before. Surely with that comes some form of responsibility?

For that reason and for the sake of Robbie Fowler and all football stars, many will feel it is time the Government threw the book at misbehaving infants. And the board rubber and the chalk, too, if necessary.

Ronaldos

Cristiano Ronaldo is, according to Eusébio, 'waiting to become an icon'. Given footballers' passion for mobile phones, he is actually probably waiting to become an emoticon ;-). But it is easy to see what the Benfica legend is getting at. After all, it is as tough to stand out in football when your name is Ronaldo as it is to gain a reputation as a drug-fuelled crazy in the world of rock 'n' roll. Or professional cycling.

In Portugal at the last count there were at least another three Ronaldos, plus a Ronaldinho. In Brazil in the mid-nineties, meanwhile, there was a goalkeeper called Ronaldo, a centre-half named Ronaldão (Big Ronaldo) and a pair of Ronaldinhos or little Ronaldos. The younger of these eventually grew so large he became Ronaldo again and, judging from photos of AC Milan's recent outings, at the rate he is going he will be Ronaldão before the year is out.

Some will feel that Sir Alex Ferguson was simply lovelorn when he signed the Portuguese teenager – jilted by the notoriously flirtatious Ronaldinho, he picked up another Ronaldo on the rebound. In fact it has lately been revealed he had intended to buy them both (though contrary to rumour Ferguson was never interested in Borussia Dortmund's Brazilian midfielder Leonardo Dedê, despite the opportunity it offered to form a line-up of Dedê, Ron, Ron).

Fergie believed that the Two Ronnies would set the Premiership alight with their dazzling skills, intricate double entendres and memorable catchphrase 'It's good night from me . . . And it's not good night from him because he intends to spend the next thirty-six hours chasing lap dancers round a luxury hotel suite.' Alas, it is not to be and he had to make do with one Ron.

As it turned out that was quite enough because it rapidly became plain that there was more to the young fellow than flair, panache and an irritating lack of spots for a lad of his age. Apparently the step-over prodigy was named in honour of Ronald Reagan – Ronaldo's father being a passionate advocate of all things American, but sensibly deciding to stop short of calling his son Momsapplepieo.

Some will wonder at the wisdom of naming a child after a man who gave the impression he wouldn't be able to find the ground if you pushed him out of a tree, but at least Reagan had a sports background, of sorts. He spent most of his high school years driving his classmates and teachers insane by constantly imitating radio sports commentators. Later he landed a job as one himself.

When Arnold Schwarzenegger became Governor of California much was made of the implausibility of an actor becoming Prime Minister of Great Britain, but it is surely more likely than the chances of John Motson striding into the Houses of Parliament with a mandate from the electorate. Though obviously Motty would be a lot more precise with his facts than some of the people who hang around 10 Downing Street.

Had United's boy-wonder been five years older, his dad would presumably have named him after Reagan's predecessor in the White House and Cristiano would have spent his life labouring under the moniker of Jimmyo.

Cristiano Ronaldo is not the only player to have been named after a politician, of course. Brazil once fielded a player named Bismarck and a midfielder with the single name of Kenedy played for Estrela da Amadora in the Portuguese top flight at a time when the Superliga also boasted a Brazilian named Wellington.

And while it is a fair bet that the trio of Titos who play in the Iberian Peninsula were not named after the leader of Yugoslavia, or that the Nixon Dias who once turned out for Sparta Rotterdam didn't owe his Christian name to a parental fondness for Tricky Dicky, the same cannot be said of a Venezuelan who plied his trade in the Belgian league with Standard Liège, Stalin Rivas.

Given Fergie's hardline attitude and tendency towards historical revisionism, a Stalin might have suited his squad well. All in all, though, it was probably for the best that United's

Ronaldo's father wasn't an Anglophile. Otherwise the famously left-wing Sir Alex would have found himself lavishing praise on young Cristiano Ironladio.

Rotation

At Anfield in September 2006 Liverpool's victory over Aston Villa was acclaimed as ultimate vindication of Rafa Benítez's squad rotation system by his replacement in the dug-out, Big Karen from catering. 'It's all right these old pros banging on about the 1970s when Bertha McConnell's squad served chip butties every Saturday for fifteen seasons without a change of personnel, or indeed cooking fat,' Big Karen told reporters, 'but with the pace of point of sales purchases these days you cannot expect anybody to stand behind the tea bar staring blankly at customers for thirty or forty games a season.' Visiting manager Martin O'Neill was generous in his assessment of Big Karen's tactics. 'She wrong-footed us, no doubt about that,' said the Irishman. 'Having Steven Gerrard working a turnstile, Rafa himself heavily involved with the raffle tickets and chief executive Rick Parry playing at left-back confused us totally, and to be honest we never got to grips with the groundsman's mower in the centre of the park.'

Rod Rugg

Legendary 1970s midfield death-star, wit, raconteur and inventor of the radio telescope, Rugg's infamous autobiography *Tackles, Shoots and Heaves*, written when he was finished in football and earning a precarious living on the pro-celebrity panel-beating circuit, remains to this day the only volume ever to be withdrawn from sale because booksellers quite literally refused to touch it. The behaviour of the player whose trail of mayhem left the East Midlands' soccer scene sprinkled with broken promises and broken teeth led that doyenne of 1960s football writers, Godfrey Cheese, to describe him as 'lurking dumb, malevolent and uncaring like a hardened artery in the heart of the English game'.

Rumours

The world of football is perpetually abuzz with rumour. This is nowhere truer than in the North-East. In this far corner of England the departure of any player or manager creates a tidal wave of scurrility. For at least a fortnight after Kevin Keegan quit St James's Park, for example, a person could barely step out of his front door without some complete stranger grabbing his coat and saying, 'Well, what I heard was . . .'

Many heard their first incontrovertible and totally false reason why Keegan had walked away practically before he had slammed his sponsored Mercedes' door in the club car park.

Then there was the time a big-name striker suddenly left one of the region's clubs. The first whisper about that came from the social club. The social club is the fount of all football information in the North-East. In fact many wonder why journalists bother hanging round the training ground and the manager's office, when they could get all the stories they need just by sitting drinking Federation bitter and listening to the blokes playing dominoes at the next table.

The word coming out of the social club on that occasion was not impressive, however. Nor was the whisper emanating from the newsagent's. Admittedly the newsagent had an impeccable source – a bloke he met while out walking his dog had a brother whose son-in-law was Bobby Moncur's milkman – but his rumour was exactly the same as the one the manager of a London club once called a press conference specifically to deny even though most people had never heard it. It therefore had to be discounted on the grounds of unoriginality.

Thankfully the insurance man was soon on the scene. The insurance man is one of those people with the genius for turning even the most banal and believable tale into such a baroque fantasy it might have been dreamed up by J. R. R. Tolkien after a feast of magic mushrooms.

As the insurance man weaved his gossamer web of footie falsehoods the region sat back and admired a true artist at work. Every element of the great football rumour was in place. First there was the labyrinthine trek from the source to the teller ('Now, my wife's cousin by marriage was bridesmaid at the wedding of Barry Venison's nephew's window-cleaner's uncle and what Barry told his nephew was . . .'). Second there was the substantiating non-sequitur ('And he just happens to be on first name terms with the Bishop of Armagh') and the subtle yet glittering detail ('But when he came back into the bathroom the soap and the chihuahua had disappeared').

The insurance man has moved with the times, too. He no longer bothers with drink and gambling stories any more. In the past all football rumours centred on drinking and gambling. Whenever a player left a club people would say it was because he had run up huge debts with a dodgy local bookmaker and had had to flee the city. Nowadays, though, you need something more hip and contemporary. You need cocaine, preferably in a lap dancer's cleavage.

Outsiders might think that with the increasing slickness of the Premiership PR machines these rumours would now have been spun or massaged out of existence. In fact the opposite seems to be the case. Many clubs now operate as plcs and the business world has never been averse to destabilising share prices with a few well-aimed gobbets of scandalous gossip about senior figures within a company. They don't rely on newsagents and insurance men to circulate their carefully contrived tales, of course. They use the Internet – the disinformation superhighway. Nowadays we are all living in a global social club.

Russian Pun Crisis

In 2004 the news that oil billionaire Ralif Safin was considering taking the plunge and alighting on the verge of launching discussions about a possible takeover of Manchester United led a number of pundits to warn that the influx of businessmen from the former Soviet Union could be about to push the English game into crisis. 'With Safin's Red Army at Old Trafford and Roman Abramovich's Chelski at Stamford Bridge, we are already running desperately short of stereotypical Russian puns,' said one senior tabloid sportswriter. 'To prevent future problems we would like to see the FA make it illegal for Russians to buy any more English clubs. Unless they happen to be on Teesside or in South Wales, in which case we can do Middlesboris or Vodkardiff.'

– S –

Sacrosanct

What goes on in the dressing room is sacrosanct and no player or manager will ever discuss it in public. The only time the silence is broken is when the manager loses the dressing room. Inevitably when this happens the dressing room tends to be discovered by outsiders who are alerted to its presence beneath a hedge or in some nettles behind a shed by the sound of the players whingeing that the coach is a total loser and they are going to try and get a move to Spurs.

Saipan Martyr

The Pacific island of Saipan was the site of **Roy Keane**'s brave and lonely campaign to have Gary Breen and his Irish teammates upgraded to business class from economy. Who can forget the Irishman's impassioned chant, 'What do we want? Free refreshing lemon-scented cleansing wipes! When do we want them? Now.'

Satanic Sponsorship

The possibility that from the start of the 2010–11 season the FA Cup could be sponsored by Satan was greeted with predictable howls of indignation from moral arbiters. Some have put the prospect of allowing princeofdarkness.com to stamp its famous forked red tail logo on the enchanted silver pot in the same bracket as the ill-fated Napalm-B52 Formula One team of the late 1960s. Others have compared it to the time in the 1970s when the Symbionese Liberation Army almost donated a young player of the year trophy to the Mid-Cumberland Under-Tens League.

Those on the outer fringes of the debate have even gone so far as to describe the putative deal as the most controversial act in British sport since 1937. Then, as readers will not need reminding, the Football Association forced England players to act as judges in a show trial before a game against a Workers XI in Moscow, so as not to offend their host Joseph Stalin. 'Sending recidivists and counter-revolutionaries to the Gulags wasn't really our sort of thing at all, but Sir Frederick Wall said that it was only good manners and we must crack down on class traitors like we jolly well meant it, or we would all be made to walk home,' recalled **Vic Loaf**, who made his England debut that day as a running dog of capitalist imperialism.

Others looked to 2006 when the FA was called on to act over rumours that the Four Horsemen of the Apocalypse were about to buy a stake in a Premiership club. According to supporters groups, the quartet (War, Plague, Pestilence and some Russian bloke) ought to have been disbarred from ownership under the 'fit and proper person' rule. However, a lawyer acting for the Four Horsemen – who apparently fell in love with the English game while watching a match at the Reebok Stadium – was quick to address this accusation. 'They say my clients are not fit to run a football club,' she said. 'But I put it to you that that is exactly what they are fit for.' And looking at the smouldering and skeletal foursome's impressive record of woe, misery and destruction, many found that a hard argument to counter.

Still, as numerous ex-players who had not paid to get into a game for thirty years were quick to point out, the fans do not care where the money comes from, just so long as at least £8 million of it is invested in a peevish-looking thirtysomething from the former Eastern bloc who stooges about in midfield for eight months with an expression on his face that suggests he has just sat in something warm and squishy until they let him go to some Greek side on a free.

The Football Association is of course fully aware of the moral issues of sponsorship. 'At the moment we are looking at a straight choice between the Devil and McDonald's,' said a spokesman a few days after Beelzebub's offer had been revealed. 'Some will say that an organisation with notoriously hellish working conditions and which spreads disease and filth across the globe should not have its name associated with the FA Cup. And if it wasn't for the libel laws I'd conclude this joke with the punchline most of you saw coming ten seconds ago.'

As for the Great Beast himself, he was said to be very upset about the way he was portrayed in the British sports media and totally refused to speak to the BBC over remarks made by Alan Green, in which, he alleges, the outspoken commentator compared him to Malcolm Glazer (a charge Green denies).

Speaking on behalf of Mr Beelzebub, a press relations expert who definitely wasn't Max Clifford said, 'Lucifer is no angel, well, not any more anyway. He has done a number of things of which he is not proud, i.e. Tempting Christ, the Black Death and *Big Break* with Jim Davidson, but he has got all that behind him now. To say he shouldn't be allowed to sponsor the world's oldest cup competition just because of his reputation for malevolence is, I'm afraid, just another example of political correctness gone mad.'

The only relief for the FA came when it was announced that another prospective sponsor, the H5N1 strain of bird flu, had dropped its interest in the Cup. 'Having been named by Fifa as official health scare of the 2010 World Cup, H5N1 felt that it could not do justice to both events. It is hoping to be as successful in South Africa as herpes was in Spain in 1982 and will be concentrating all its efforts on that,' said a spokesman for the deadly virus, which many feel has already had more publicity than most of us can stand.

Jochen Schlumpf

Renowned Zurich-born **banter** coach who became a national hero in his homeland, where he is known to this day as 'the man who made Young Boys laugh', after his work in Berne with the football club of that name. Schlumpf came to international attention when he was appointed as banter coach to the Swiss national team in the late 1990s by Roy Hodgson. While Hodgson took his share of the plaudits, many Swiss believe that Schlumpf was the catalyst behind the national team's decision to abandon its long-standing policy of 'booted neutrality' in favour of giving the opposition the occasional hiding. According to insiders, the turning point came when Schlumpf altered the clock in Hodgson's office so that every hour a little bird popped out and said 'Poo-Poo' instead of the usual 'Cuckoo'. 'When his team saw the results of his handiwork,' Swiss journalist Beat Mutter recorded in his biography of Schlumpf *Always Jochen*, 'they shed their famous icy Alpine reserve and abandoned themselves to a spontaneous yet well organised orgy of uninhibited laughter that reverberated for fully five totally liberating seconds. In that moment of puerile ribaldry a new, modern football team was forged.' Later Schlumpf worked with Christian Gross at White Hart Lane where he is remembered best for trying to fuse the technical French style of dressing-room ribaldry, based on the work of Jacques Tati, with the traditionally more earthy false breasts of the British professional.

Sex in the Seventies

Much fuss is made about the behaviour of modern footballers, but hasn't the game always had its fair share of bad boys? Were the crazy Brylcreem-and-Brut-soaked escapades of yesteryear so very different from what Premiership stars get up to today?

Yes, was the firm answer given by seventies soccer legend **Rod Rugg**, who alongside team-mates Mick McMugg and Trevor Thugg formed the notorious 'Lichfield Three', a trio who once terrorised large parts of North Staffs with their boozing, bruising and extravagantly horrible dentures.

'Sex?' Rugg growled when a visiting journalist raised the topic. 'No, as far as Muggy, Thuggy and me-gy were concerned, shagging was for girls. Don't get me wrong, it wasn't for lack of opportunity.' He indicated a picture on the wall behind him. It showed a young Rugg sitting in a circular bath with celebrated British actress Lulu Twickenham, star of soft-core comedy classics *Ooh La La There Go My Trousers* and *Ooh La La There Go My Trousers (Swedish Style)*.

'She said, may I join you in that jacuzzi?' Rugg cackled. 'I said, it's not a jacuzzi, love, I've just had a curry. Cor, we had a laugh. But there was nothing soppy went on, mark my words.

'See, the three of us were real men. Fighting, vomiting in cupboards and driving a stolen British Rail loco the wrong way down the dual carriageway, plastered and with our bare backsides stuck out of the windows, was how we got our kicks. But doing anything illegal, that wasn't our style.

'Mind you, I'd have to say it's not football that's responsible. The whole of society has gone down the pan, hasn't it? There's no respect, there's no discipline, there's no celebrity five-a-sides with Ed "Stewpot" Stewart and that bloke off *Robin's Nest*. You know who I blame for it, don't you?' he said, thrusting a

sovereign-encrusted finger in the direction of the window.
'Everybody else, that's who. They've ruined this country, they
have.'

Sexy Football

Julie Burchill once noted that any pop song with the word 'sex'
in the title is guaranteed to carry all the erotic charge of a bag
of frozen mince. A similar situation is to be found in football.
When a team's playing style is promised to be 'sexy', you can
stick your mortgage on them shrivelling up at the first
encounter with a chill breeze.

When did sexiness, in this sense, enter our game? Some will
blame the Brazilians for it. They will point to the coach João
Saldanha and his instruction that his players 'make love to the
ball'. This is usually interpreted as a metaphor, though given
that – according to biographer Ruy Castro – one of Brazil's
greatest talents, Garrincha, lost his virginity with a goat,
Saldanha may well have been speaking literally, if only to head
off trouble with local farmers.

Whatever, as far as most right-thinking people are concerned, it was Ruud Gullit who started the sexy thing. The fact
that a goofy Dutchman with a history of silly moustaches introduced Britain to the concept of seductive sport should surely
have been a warning sign. Gullit made a habit of odd pronouncements ('We had 99 per cent of the game and they had
only the other 3 per cent', 'It is like a time bomb that can
explode in a good or a bad way', 'She is the perfect woman: the
body of a twenty-one-year-old and the mind of a twenty-eight-
year-old', and so on) and he arrived at St James's Park in 1998
promising to bring 'sexy football' to Tyneside. Newcastle
promptly lost their first home game under him 4–0 to
Liverpool leading practically every national newspaper to run

the match report under the headline 'Ruud Awakening'. In the end the way the Magpies played under Gullit was not so much sexy as sordid, involving much scuffling about at the foot of the table while Alan Shearer watched from the bench.

Shirt Numbers

The owner of Manchester United Malcolm Glazer is as shrewd as only a man with a cunningly concealed ginger beard can be. He has his own ideas on how to maximise the potential of Old Trafford. One area he might be considering is the trading of shirt numbers within the squad. This has long been the norm among US sportsmen. When he arrived at the Cleveland Browns, for instance, Kellen Winslow's first act was to purchase the number eighty from team-mate Aaron Shea in return for a package of designer clothing, free dinners and a holiday said to be worth in the region of $30,000.

For some sports stars the trading of numbers is as regular a source of additional income as playing the stock markets is to Magnier and McManus. Jeff Feagles of the New York Giants, for example, swapped his number ten shirt with new quarterback Eli Manning for a week's holiday in Florida and took the number seventeen instead. Six months later Feagles handed over this shirt to wide receiver Plaxico Burress in exchange for a luxury outdoor kitchen.

The question Glazer and others must ask is, how come these highly paid players are making money out of something that by rights belongs to their employers? And if they are going to resell their shirt numbers, isn't it about time they started paying for them in the first place?

Outside the USA the potential of shirt numbers has never really been fully exploited. There have been only brief flurries of interest. Johan Cruyff, a player always ahead of his time, insisted on wearing number fourteen (the age at which he had won his first trophy with Ajax), even though the 1974 Dutch squad was allocated numbers alphabetically and he should by rights have worn number one. Cruyff also took umbrage at the three Adidas stripes on the Dutch kit and had one of them removed. This decision, however, had less to do with the ancient art of numerology than it did with his lucrative boot sponsorship with Puma.

When David Beckham joined Real Madrid there was speculation concerning a potential squabble over the number-seven shirt between himself and the incumbent, Ronaldo. Beckham sidestepped the conflict by opting to take the Meringues' number-twenty-three jersey instead. As mathematician Marcus du Sautoy pointed out in a fascinating article in *Plus*, 'the magazine of living maths', by choosing twenty-three Beckham had opted for the smallest prime number with consecutive digits, one that represented the number of human chromosomes, the number of times Julius Caesar was stabbed, the prison cell in which Princess Leia was kept in *Star Wars* and the favourite prime number of maths genius John Forbes Nash. Of more interest to Beckham, though, was surely the fact that it was also the number worn by Michael Jordan, demigod of basketball and product merchandising. As with Cruyff, it was not so much the number as the figures Beckham was interested in.

And this, of course, is where Glazer comes in. If instead of simply being handed their numbers the players had to buy them, then a whole new income stream would open up for clubs. Imagine if at the start of every season, for example, Beckham and Ronaldo were forced to go after that number seven at auction, *mano a mano* (or, more accurately, money a money). The potential is enormous, and it doesn't end there.

Les Ferdinand was rumoured to have asked to be given the shirt number ninety-nine after Alan Shearer usurped the Newcastle number-nine shirt from him. Sadly Sir Les didn't pursue it and so a lucrative sponsorship tie-in with ice cream vans across the nation was missed. Glazer will not make the same mistake as the St James's Park board. Next year Gabriel Heinze will be wearing fifty-seven, just you wait.

Short Shorts

For the middle-aged football fan there is nothing worse than showing some young shaver an old David Coleman football annual only to have him point at the pictures of Kevin Keegan and Stanley Bowles and snigger, 'Hey, look at those shorts! They're *sooooo* . . . tiny.'

Yes, for years now the children of the sixties have had to endure one of the cruellest pranks that wicked joker-in-the-pack Old Father Time has ever played – making the sort of baggy breeks that gave the baby boomer generation such a gusset-busting fit of the giggles whenever we caught sight of a snap of Alex James (whose nether garments looked like they had been made by stitching together a couple of downed Zeppelins) into the style garments of choice for the younger generation.

In some ways the turnaround is hardly surprising. After all, while the groin-gripping style may have flattered svelte Spaniards and suave Italians, it hardly did much for the rumbling jugger-nauts who were such a feature of British football during that glorious era. Sandro Mazzola and Luis Suárez may well have looked cool in the sporting equivalent of hot pants, but they didn't do much for a burly beast such as Dave Mackay, except possibly save him the bother of buying a rupture appliance.

Short shorts became the vogue on the Continent way back in the fifties. When England played Hungary in that famous game at Wembley in 1953, Puskas and his mates were horrified by how old-fashioned their opponents looked, and no wonder. While the Magnificent Magyars were rigged out in the latest lightweight, streamlined style, English players still persisted in the belief that it was possible to run about effectively in garments that flapped like a topgallant. English players also wore outmoded heavy boots, and just as well. If they hadn't many of them would simply have blown away in the first high wind and never been seen again.

The advent of European club competitions saw English sides finally cottoning on to the new wave of stylish accoutrements. They were quickly embraced by English clubs eager to get away from the distinctly retro image projected by an older generation of players whose knees, like vampires, hid from the daylight and whose prematch preparation invariably meant handing their valuable false teeth over to the trainer for safe-keeping with the words, 'And if anything happens to me out there give them to our Denise so she'll have something to remember me by.'

Despite the efforts of such trendsetters as Frank Worthington, it wasn't until the 1980s, however, that the English really caught up with Continental skimpiness (and even then we still lagged way behind those masters of the tight troose, Argentina, whose 1978 World Cup-winning team wore such savagely tight trunks they looked like they might have come from a do-it-yourself vasectomy kit). By that time shirts had started to shrink, too, and clung to the wearer like a wet T-shirt. Liverpool's mid-eighties kit, for example, looked as if it had been designed to fit a set of garden canes. This was unfortunate as the squad at Anfield contained some of the heftiest men ever to trundle on to a football field. The new form-hugging jerseys clung to every luxuriant ripple of Jan Molby, John Barnes and Steve Nicol's bulging torsos and suggested a profitable new market for manufacturers of sports bras. The shorts, naturally, were minute silky items of a type nowadays seen only on Moroccan middle-distance runners and showed more thigh than an ostrich during carnival.

Clearly such good times could not last. By the 1990s French sides such as Bordeaux had begun to pioneer a return to the baggy look. Short shorts were consigned to soccer's style purgatory.

Siege Mentality

At the Riverside Stadium in 2005 it appeared that one or two players may have taken manager Steve McClaren's call for his team to adopt a 'siege mentality' a bit too literally when Chris Riggott and Stuart Parnaby were sent off for pouring a cauldron of boiling pitch over Arjen Robben, and Emmanuel Pogatetz was cautioned for flinging a dead cow into Chelsea's dug-out.

Silent Tribute

Ignoring claims from some hard-hearted individuals (i.e. Alastair Campbell) that there are now far too many commemorations in football, in 2005 Fifa announced that from 2010 all club and international shirts will come with an integral black armband and every game will be preceded by a minute's silence 'so nobody gets left out'. 'This is a sad day for football,' said Sepp Blatter. 'As indeed is every day.'

A Slump Arrested

The February of 2007 saw Premiership strugglers West Ham finally arrest their slump. However, legal experts forecasted that the slump could be released on bail before the next match against Charlton despite widespread fears among Hammers fans that it might offend again. 'I don't care what a load of leftie do-gooders say,' commented one Upton Park diehard, Keith Slap, 'that slump is a threat to the lives of all our kiddies. They ought to string it up.' West Ham boss Alan Curbishley also spoke out on the issue: 'I'm not a legal person, but it seems to me that when you've got something like this slump that is running around threatening the livelihoods of ordinary people such as Lucas Neill and Nigel Reo-Coker then the authorities really have got to be looking at locking it up and throwing away the key. I mean, they tell me that under British law a slump has the same rights as the crest of a wave or a lucky streak – where's the sense in that? It's political correctness gone mad.'

Spitting

For far too long our nation's leaders gave the sticky topic of players' sputum a wide berth. Down the years only the occasional demented maverick has been prepared to wade in and voice mounting public fears about what jinking right-winger Enoch Powell so memorably characterised as 'the River Tiber flowing with much gob'. Then at the dawning of the new millennium the courageous sports minister Kate Hoey broke ranks and did what none of her predecessors dared: put her foot down firmly on the expectorating issue, calling for it to be banned.

The resulting squelch produced an all too predictable outcry from the Professional Footballers' Association's chief executive Gordon Taylor. Down the years the PFA has fought tooth and nail for its members' rights to behave in as uncouth a manner as possible. The campaign began at the turn of the century when Billy Meredith led a go-slow against the compulsory use of brilliantine and reached its apotheosis in 1963 when Jimmy Hill threatened to lead a players' strike unless the tucking of the vest into the underpants on match days was made optional. It is only the vast amount of money on offer from the likes of Adidas and Nike over the past two decades which has prevented the two teams taking the field in greasy T-shirts covered with egg yolk and ketchup stains *à la* Homer Simpson.

Little wonder, then, that instead of welcoming Hoey's call for greater public decency, Taylor poo-pooed the suggestion of a cessation of expectoration, claiming that if players didn't spit they might fatally choke. How the world has changed! In the days before our national game entered the permissive age, players never spat. Indeed, faced with the choice offered by Gordon Taylor, one suspects the dignified idols of yesteryear such as Tom Finney or **Vic Loaf** would cheerfully have embraced the Grim Reaper. One has only to recall the case of the honourable Colonel Du Canne of the Royal Engineers, who in the 1879 FA Cup semi-final shot himself with his service revolver rather than suffer the 'fate worse than death' of having to blow his nose in front of several thousand paying spectators, many of whom were representatives of 'the other ranks'.

While some may quite rightly argue that the lack of spitting in the 1950s owed less to good manners and self-discipline than to the fact that saliva was severely rationed as part of the postwar austerity package, it remains true that up until the sixties players' bodily fluids, along with their personal appearance, were strictly controlled by the Football Association. In 1938, for example, the great Alex James of Arsenal was found to have ungentlemanly dark rings in the underarm area of his shirt during a half-time referee's spot-check at Highbury and immediately banned for six months for 'perspiring without due care and attention'.

While no one in their right mind would call for a return of the draconian 'parting fines', under which an instant financial penalty was imposed on those whose hair wasn't neatly divided by a line of scalp so broad and straight a half-inch ball bearing could be rolled down it without let or hindrance, it has to be said that the old laws kept players' spittle where it belongs, in their throats. Liberalisation is generally to be applauded, but it must be admitted that the relaxation of the rules governing footballers' phlegm has placed the game on a slippery slope.

This is not simply a knee-jerk reaction. There are health issues involved. **Sid Paddle** has long campaigned for recognition of the dangers of passive spitting, namely: disease, hazardous slipping and being cemented to the turf by the tacky gunk expelled by some midfield dynamo with heavy catarrh. Before rejecting Kate Hoey's suggestion, Gordon Taylor might like to consider the effects on the groundstaff of his members' intemperate expulsion of slime. Taking a flymo to the grass after a Premiership game must be the equivalent of being a member of the Clash *circa* 1976.

And what of poor Didier Drogba? As anyone who has studied him will be aware, Chelsea's strapping striker clearly has a playing contract which demands he spends at least five minutes each half lying flat on his face clutching the back of his head. As he falls cheek down upon the turf one can only imagine what horrific pillow the assembled olfactory systems of John Terry, Claude Makélélé and Michael Essien have prepared for him. That he goes down at all in such circumstances is proof of the Francophone star's professionalism, that he can prise his skin free from the ground at the end of his sojourn a glowing testimony to the power of his neck muscles.

In calling for an all-out ban many believed Kate Hoey was going too far too fast. Like many pernicious habits, spitting is a hard thing to kick. Better by far to have begun gradually by first introducing clearly marked non-spitting areas to the playing area, so that those players who choose not to spit can at least benefit from their wise and healthy decision. If she had adopted this more gentle approach then her campaign might just have succeeded.

Frank Stella

American artist whose concept of minimalism was grounded in a conviction that Malcolm Allison wasn't really as large as everybody said he was.

Street Football

Throughout the first half of the twentieth century, British footballers honed their skills as youngsters by playing in the street. This produced a generation of players with great ball skills, but left tremendous psychological scars. Men who had learned their craft in an environment of rugged, house-proud old ladies waving rolling pins and tubby firm-but-fair coppers who sent errant lads home with a clip round the lughole inevitably developed patterns of behaviour they found hard to break in later life. For example, it was common right up until the mid-1960s to see a British defender slice a clearance into the crowd, yell 'Window, window!', and run off and hide behind the nearest outhouse. Often he was followed by both sets of players.

This trait did not go unnoticed by the more cunning of England's continental foes. In Budapest in 1954 the Hungarians exploited the English team's deep-rooted fear of a good hiding from old Mrs Garbutt from number fifteen by mounting a small brick shed on the back of an army flatbed truck. The first time the white-shirted players made their traditional scarper for cover the lorry drove slowly away. Billy Wright and Ivor Broadis were halfway to Vienna by the time the Magnificent Magyars knocked in the final goal of a 7–1 triumph. By the late-fifties the placing of a greenhouse behind the home goal was common practice among European clubs looking to unsettle British forwards.

Stupid Injury Syndrome

The former Manchester United goalkeeper Alex Stepney once dislocated his jaw by shouting at central defender Martin Buchan; David Seaman confessed that the shoulder damage which kept him out of the game for half a season was sustained while wrestling with a large fish; and Barnsley's Darren Barnard slipped on some puppy urine on his kitchen floor, the resultant knee ligament damage keeping him out for five months. These are just three examples of Stupid Injury Syndrome, a disorder that affects hundreds of footballers around the world every year. Goalkeepers dropping aftershave bottles on their feet, full-backs crashing golf-carts, Mexican strikers colliding with cacti may all seem a bit of harmless fun but sometimes things go terribly wrong. In 2005, for example, the England team's injury crisis deepened after a relaxing pre-match game of Ker-Plunk went tragically awry leaving seventeen members of the squad with a variety of marble-and-pointy-plastic-stick-related injuries. 'I think perhaps it is good we did not play Twister,' commented the imperturbable Sven-Göran Eriksson. In order to ensure the World Cup qualifier was played the next day Liechtenstein lent England two players, on the condition that they played out of position, kicked with the wrong feet and didn't have to kiss Phil Neville if they scored.

Suits for the FA Cup Final

Bespoke jackets and trousers specially made so the finalists can get a feel of the Wembley turf without dirtying their kit. Sometimes teams that are winning in a semi-final are already being measured for them, making it all too easy for the opposition to equalise.

Super Fan

In recent years the broadcast media has become obsessed with super fans, people whose devotion to their club is so psychotic they are like Charles Manson in bobble hats. The super fan's idea of a top meal out is to sit in the rain eating pickled onion crisps and a Wagon Wheel. He refuses to take the kids to see *The Lion King* because he hates Millwall. He watches matches on Ceefax. He tapes James Alexander Gordon reading the scores on Radio Five Live and has made a CD compilation of his favourite ones which he listens to when he's depressed. He was gutted when he discovered that Forrest Gump wasn't a biopic of Frank Clark.

He picks up a copy of the *Playfair Football Annual 1988* to read over breakfast and the next thing he knows it is dark, the cat is crying for her dinner and the enzymes in the yoghurt in his fridge have evolved to the point where they bark and hunt in packs. When he wakes up on mornings in July he cannot think of a single reason to get out of bed.

He deliberately pours salt on his cornflakes on Saturday morning because once when he did that they got a point at Old Trafford. He genuinely believes that he can conjure a goal by going to the toilet midway through the second half and has been arrested for loitering on several occasions as a result. He can name the price of a cheap day return train ticket to Carlisle. And Wigan. And Northampton. And Torquay.

Sometimes when there is a live match on TV he puts the set on the lawn and watches the game from the greenhouse pretending he is in an executive box. On days when there isn't a game he drops a ping-pong ball into the aquarium and encourages the goldfish to play three-and-in. He has mentioned several times that when his family's car was burned out by joyriders it sparked a ten-match unbeaten run and when relegation threatened was twice caught in the garage with a burning rag.

Sometimes he spends all evening working out what the League tables would have looked like in a selected year if the verdicts of the pools panels had stood as real results. Or if there had been three points for a win in those days. Or if goal difference rather than goal average had been the criteria. And vice versa.

He once replayed all the seasons lost to the First and Second World War, using statistical analysis and dice rolls to represent 'the random element'. As a result he believes that Hitler may have invaded Poland just to prevent Oldham Athletic from becoming a real power in the game.

In a tragic incident last winter the hot water pipes burst in the spare room, spilling gallons of hot water over his coveted collection of match-day programmes. In the resulting landslide the dog was buried alive. Still at least his family have a papier-mâché cast of her. And if you look closely at her tail you can make out a picture of the Bury team of 1973.

His in-laws refuse to speak to him after he chanted, 'Going down, going down, going down', at what they considered an inappropriate moment. Though he maintains that his mother-in-law, whose funeral it was, would have appreciated the gesture.

Sweatshops

In June 2006 a number of leading sportswear manufacturers announced that they would investigate Oxfam's claims about the sweatshops of South-East Asia. 'These reports are extremely alarming,' said a spokesman for Puma. 'We were totally unaware that there was even a market for sweat in the Far East. But with all those people out there it is clearly a huge retail opportunity.' Umbro, meanwhile, took immediate steps to deal with the demand, launching its new range of Premiership secretions that 'accurately recreate the odours of the post-match dressing room of your favourite club'. Nike's spray-on 'sweat with the swoosh' followed shortly afterwards, promising 'a little more perspiration from a lot less action', and offering the 'authentic glistening sheen of Roberto Carlos's thighs' in an aerosol can. 'Rest assured the sweatshops of the world will never run short of stock while we are around,' said the crazed ex-hippy responsible.

Tags

A few years ago then West Bromwich Albion striker Kevin Campbell spoke of his hope that the Baggies would one day 'shake off the yo-yo club tag'. Wise words indeed, but then the big centre forward had been around long enough to know that in football if you don't shake off a tag it can quickly become a millstone round your neck.

While West Brom might want to shake off the yo-yo club tag their Midlands neighbours Wolves still aspire to wearing it. They have spent years trying to shake off the far more onerous sleeping giant tag. In football giants are generally slumberous. Occasionally you come across a true giant of the game, but that generally means he has just died. This is much like sleeping, but with the added bonus that the kids won't wake you up by jumping up and down on your chest and demanding to know why you didn't buy any Coco Pops. Sometimes, of course, a wakeful giant is slain, generally by an underdog, or a minnow, who bring him down to earth with a bump using a banana skin, but that is a different matter altogether.

If Wolves could shake off the sleeping giant tag, Leeds would surely be delighted to pounce on it in the hope of shaking off the crisis club tag. Sadly this seems unlikely as Elland Road's downward spiral has become a vicious circle, which makes it almost impossible for them to turn the corner without the wheels coming off.

Gary Megson and Bryan Robson must take a lot of the

credit for putting Albion into a position from which they could even begin to talk of shaking off tags. When the job at the Hawthorns came up many felt Robson wasn't in with a shout of getting the nod to be in the frame because of the baggage he was carrying. He had picked up the baggage while riding on an emotional roller-coaster at Middlesbrough (who themselves only recently shook off the yo-yo club tag by ending a hoodoo and establishing themselves as a fixture). As Robson would be the first to admit, his time at the Riverside was a steep learning curve that eventually went pear-shaped.

In many ways baggage is even worse than a tag. Though, of course, sometimes baggage comes with a tag. And more often than not, if you open the baggage you will find it contains a bit of previous and some old doubts that will probably resurface if he doesn't keep his head on straight. Unlike a tag, you can't shake baggage off. In the case of some players this is not totally a bad thing, because if you took away his baggage you would be taking away 75 per cent of his game. In this instance what the manager has to do is retain the baggage, but get the player to put it in a place where the referee won't keep tripping over it.

Football management is about dealing with those kind of conflicting demands. In football you must be solid and fluid. You must be consistent but not predictable. You must keep your shape but not be rigid. This defies all the laws of logic, physics and human nature, which makes coaching a team more or less impossible unless you are a total one-off, a genuine character, or were a great thinker about the game even when you were a player.

If a manager can do that then he will silence the knockers, who otherwise might jump on the bandwagon. However, he must be careful when silencing the knockers that he does not quiet the crowd. This is vital, because the team needs a full house to become a twelfth man by really getting behind them.

The players can play with freedom with the crowd behind them. Because when the crowd is behind them they know it will not get on their backs.

A team with a crowd on their backs is even more handicapped than those that are carrying baggage, or trying to shake off a tag. And the crowd only gets on the players' back after something has silenced them. In many ways the crowd at a football match is like a World War Two doodlebug – it's when it stops making a noise that those on the ground should panic.

The manager should also never forget that football fans have short memories. They are also always harking back to the glory days. Because of their short memories, this is often as long as seven days ago. That is why in football you are only as good as your last result.

If West Brom ever do shake off the yo-yo club tag they will need to move up to the **next level**. For inspiration they can look to Fulham. Fulham have been a yo-yo club and a crisis club and probably would have been sleeping giants, too, if they'd come from a hotbed of soccer. Nowadays, though, the Cottagers are a beacon that other teams can use as a template. Bolton Wanderers might have been a template, too, but when they made Big Sam Allardyce they threw away the mould.

Teacups

When a British manager is angry he throws teacups in the **dressing room** at half-time. It is always the teacups the boss hurls rather than the more sturdy and dangerous mug. The fact that the players have cups and saucers at all suggests a world that is not quite as rugged as we are led to believe, one in which a hostess trolley is wheeled in at the interval and there are gasps of astonishment from all sides if whoever was responsible for arranging the French fancies, eclairs and the macaroons has put them on a kitchen plate rather than the usual silver cake stand.

Throttle-merchant

Title given to a player who specialises in diplomatically restraining an opponent during a fracas by grabbing him round the throat and shaking him until he sees the error of his ways or goes limp.

Total Chaos Theory

In 2005 scientists revealed that they had a new unifying theory of the football universe. 'We have dubbed it total chaos theory,' said Professor Andrew Nuttall of the University of Hard Knocks (formerly Mortal Coil Polytechnic). 'The idea is that if a diminutive England striker flutters his eyelids on the shores of the Mediterranean, then forty-eight hours later on the edge of the Irish Sea a fan sticks his head in his hands and groans, "Jesus Christ, we've bought Brett Emerton."'

Tournament Mascots

Since England started the ball rolling with World Cup Willy in 1966, mascots have become an integral and increasingly irritating part of any major football competition. At first they were relatively inoffensive things such as Juanito, the urchin in the sombrero, from Mexico 1970. Since then, however, the quest for originality has seen the designs become ever more desperate. We have had Naranjito the football-playing orange, Pique the football-playing chilli and Ciao the football-playing green-red-and-white Lego-man. And the odder the mascots have become, the more Fifa has felt compelled to embellish them, adding ever-stranger back stories and cod folkloric explanations to justify their selection.

For Korea/Japan 2002 millions of workers stamped the images of World Cup mascots Ato, Nik and Kaz on everything from T-shirts to chopsticks. According to Fifa's marketing arm ISL, Ato, Nik and Kaz represented 'energy particles in the atmosphere'. Regrettably they were not quite so small. Speaking of the brightly coloured trio who apparently hailed from 'the Kingdom of Atomzone', a land located in the earth's stratosphere, Choi Chang-Shin, secretary-general of South Korea's World Cup organising committee, said, 'They have mysterious powers to fan enthusiasm among the audience at football matches.' To which the only sane response was, 'Quick, somebody take that cutlery off him.'

Tracking

Tracking is basically a type of proactive **monitoring**. There is a fine line between tracking and stalking and most clubs tend to stand on the edge of it bouncing up and down on the balls of their feet and just waiting for the chance to spring. One man who does a lot of tracking is that wiliest of football's wild frontiersmen, Harry Redknapp. The Pompey boss is always tracking someone. Just how he does his tracking has never been revealed. Some believe he attaches one of those bugging devices to his target's underside while the big fella (or wee Serbian winger) is distracted by a chorus of cuckoo clocks or some such, and then simply sits back in his office at Fratton Park and follows the player's movements via the winking lights on a massive wall-map of the world.

Others, however, feel that Harry is too old-fashioned a

player-hunter for anything so hi-tech as that. They believe he tracks players using the skills he learned as a youngster at Upton Park under the tutelage of Ron 'Hawkeye' Greenwood.

Greenwood was very much the Daniel Boone of football tracking. So finely tuned were his observational faculties it was said he could tell if a player was suffering from a hamstring injury or a dodgy groin just by studying his stud prints in the turf. The West Ham boss, so legend tells, could follow the traces of an out-of-contract striker with vision and a decent touch across Alaska at night in a snowstorm (which, in fact, was how he eventually got Bryan 'Pop' Robson, the balding Geordie maestro eventually cornered and forced to sign on the dotted line on the upper slopes of Mount McKinley after a three-week pursuit across the icy tundra). Harry Redknapp was Greenwood's most promising pupil.

Like all great trackers, Harry makes a detailed study of the habits of his prey. Then he follows them across golf courses and through the VIP lounges of West End clubs, checking the ground for the tell-tale signs that an experienced Premiership professional has passed by (broken twigs, flip-flop prints in the mud, copious amounts of gob and discarded Harvey Nichols bags).

Once on the trail Redknapp is as unshakeable from it as John Motson is from the belief that all Italians work in the catering industry. He will follow the transfer target o'er hill and dale, through streams and shopping malls and slightly-too-showy nightclubs, until he chances across some droppings early one morning and upon touching them murmurs, 'Mmm, it's still warm. He must be close by.' Then Harry's sinews stiffen and his nostrils quiver as he prepares to make a shock swoop.

Transfers and How They Work

Two seasons ago Big Sam Allardyce came desperately close to pulling off the transfer coup of the century at Bolton as he almost signed one of the planet's most recognised and charismatic stars for nothing from a 'foreign-looking bloke' he met at a car boot fair. But how did the deal to bring the celebrated Leaning Tower of Pisa to the Reebok come about and what finally scuppered the chances of Wanderers' fans watching the 654-year-old galactico playing up front with Kevin Davies? Here for the first time is the true story.

London-based super-agent **Pini Colada** approaches the Leaning Tower of Pisa claiming that he has just received an enquiry from a 'leading Premiership club', who are looking for 'a Renaissance campanile of historic quirkiness' as a replacement for the ageing Ivan Campo.

At the same time the Israeli talks to a friendly journalist at the *Daily Mirror* about the Tower's predicament. The following day the *Mirror* runs the story under the headline, 'Pisa-ed Off: "End My Tuscan Hell" Want Away Unesco World Heritage Site's Heartfelt Plea'.

The paper alleges that the Leaning Tower desperately wants a 'fresh challenge'. According to 'a friend', 'Leano feels he is getting stale. He doesn't get the same buzz from being photographed by InterRailers pretending they are propping him up as he used to. He dreams of England. When he was a foundation he had a picture of Stonehenge on his wall.'

The following day the mayor of Pisa denies that his star is unsettled and assures fans at the city's famous Field of Miracles that 'the Leaning Tower of Pisa is going nowhere'.

Colada phones the mayor to say that the Eiffel Tower is unsettled in Paris and might be interested in a move to another city 'whose ambitions match his own'.

Bolton deny that they have made an approach for the

Leaning Tower: 'As far as we are aware the Leaning Tower is under contract to Pisa and any attempt to contact him would therefore be in contravention of Fifa rules.' The club does acknowledge that they are always interested in improving the squad, 'whether that means bringing in the Leaning Tower, Rivaldo, the Great Wall of China, or whoever'.

Wanderers fans, however, are already excited about the move. 'It's just brilliant that we're being linked with one of the great ones. I mean, the Leaning Tower of Pisa is right up there with the Hanging Gardens of Babylon and Frank Worthington. It's a legend,' says one old bloke with nothing better to do than hang around outside the main entrance all afternoon in the hope some pressman will ask him a question.

Spanish sports daily *La Marca* mocks Bolton's comments about the Great Wall of China as 'silly and laughable'. It claims that Real Madrid have already got a pre-contract agreement with the Great Wall, which the club sees not only as the ideal way of breaking into the lucrative Far Eastern market but also of solving recent defensive problems. Real president Florentino Pérez denies the story saying, 'The Great Wall will never play for Madrid. That is final. I have spoken. Put that in your pipe and smoke it. Non, no, nien, niet. Finish. Kaput. Definitely. Maybe. Possibly. Get his people on the phone and let's talk image rights.'

Meanwhile, the Leaning Tower denies that it is unhappy in Italy. 'Pisa has been good to me,' it tells *Gazzetta dello Sport*. 'But at the end of the day being a leading tourist attraction is a short career that could be ended at any moment. When you have had as much surgery as I have just to stop you from falling over then that really brings it home. I love Pisa but I have to think of my family's future.'

'China is my middle name, but when Madrid come calling you owe it to yourself to listen,' the Great Wall confesses to Singapore television.

In Paris news that the Eiffel Tower may be leaving the country gets a mixed reaction. A survey carried out by *Liberation* asks French citizens if they would be prepared to see the 350-foot steel structure leave the country. Just 2 per cent answer 'Oui', 5 per cent say 'Non', 13 per cent say 'Pfuph', and 80 per cent shrug their shoulders in a way that conveys resignation, indifference and contempt simultaneously.

With Chelsea said to be on the verge of a £20 million move for the Palazzo dei Cavalieri and Barcelona offering Samuel Eto'o plus cash for the Piazza del Duomo, angry Pisan supporters take to the streets in protest. As tensions mount, Italy's President Berlusconi secretly agrees to intervene to prevent any transfers.

Seven days after the whole thing started, the Leaning Tower agrees to stay in Pisa with an improved contract and a six-figure loyalty bonus. Pini Colada trousers 10 per cent. The next day he phones Hadrian's Wall with news that China may be looking for an ancient fortified linear structure.

Tribute Teams

In Norway English football is so popular it has created a burgeoning market for tribute teams. Like tribute bands such as Björn Again and the Bootleg Beatles, the tribute teams seek to recreate the look, style and onfield nuances of some favourite squad from football's past. The Norsemen's popular Chris Waddle double of the 1990s, Peter Rudi, for example, had begun his career as one of the stars of Geordie Vision FC, an Arthur Cox-era Newcastle United play-alike outfit who were good enough three years ago to win the Norwegian tribute teams' equivalent of the Premiership, the Binaryship.

This, it should be said, was no mean feat. Geordie Vision had to beat off stiff competition from the likes of Revie Revisited, a troupe who promise to 'recreate Leeds United *circa*

1970, down to the very last kick (or spit, or punch)', Wasgood, who offer to do the same for the Chelsea team of that period, only with longer sideburns, Back to the Futchers (Luton Town, mid-seventies), Nishtalgia (Derby County, 1974), and Young Trafford, a unique cross-generational tribute team made up entirely of people who look and perform like those Manchester United players who have over the decades been hailed as 'the new George Best'. According to reports, the Ralph Milne is so spot on it's scary.

Trivia Accumulation

A few years ago in Spain the Celta Vigo player Borja Aguirrechu tested positive for nandrolone. It turned out to have come from the pills he was taking to prevent baldness. This is the kind of useless piece of information football fans pick up over the years.

He or she is never sure when, where or how he found out that hirsute PSV Eindhoven wing-back of the 1980s Eric Gerets has the unlikely middle name of Maria, but he knows that when this thought pops into his head it will shortly be followed by the fact that Bob Wilson's middle name is Primrose and that the Paraguayan manager Cateyano Re responded to being ordered from the touchline during the 1986 World Cup by saying, 'Fifa would have treated me with more respect had my surname been longer.' The supporter cannot recall reading or hearing these pieces of trivial nonsense. They have simply appeared in his head as if by some form of mental osmosis.

Collecting useless facts is largely a male trait. It stems from man's earliest role as the hunter-gatherer. In prehistoric times a bloke would have returned to the cave carrying a dead stag and a basket of blackberries and his family group would have celebrated by dancing round a roaring fire and singing praise songs in his honour. These days he comes back with the news that British Sugar Fonnereau Athletic of the Suffolk and Ipswich League began life as Silent Youth FC and that the Broadmoor Staff XI play in the Chiltonian League (and as the pundits say, 'Nobody relishes a trip to Broadmoor in February'), and his family group celebrates by raising their eyebrows in unison, sighing and muttering, 'God, what a saddo.'

Once a fan knows that a team named Thornaby Utopians played in the FA Cup, he just has to tell someone. Facts are like coins – you can be fined for taking them out of circulation. Besides, bottling things up can be dangerous. Imagine if you or I discovered that Lewes FC played at the Dripping Pan, or that the father of ex-Republic of Ireland manager Mick McCarthy founded England's first Gaelic football team (who did they play, by the way?) and didn't tell anyone? We'd have a hernia.

At some point even the storage space used by a football fan for squirrelling away pieces of arcane info such as the fact that RWD Molenbeek of the Belgian League once had a forward named Lambic Wawa or that Espanyol are nicknamed 'the Budgerigars' (RWD, by the way, stands for Racing White Daring) must reach capacity. The human mind is like a library with facts instead of books: there is only room and budget for a finite number. There must come a time when the shelves are full to overflowing and the fan realises he is going to have to make some tough decisions – his car registration number or the news that former Middlesbrough and Republic of Ireland centre-half Alan Kernaghan's uncle was the little bald bloke on *The Benny Hill Show*; his blood group or the fact that in the film *This is Spinal Tap* bass player Derek Smalls is seen wearing a 1970s Shrewsbury Town shirt; his address or the information that Ronnie Corbett played for Hearts' youth team.

Just as a person goes down to his local library with the express intention of getting something intellectually challenging and stimulating, such as Gabriel García Márquez's latest, and ends up instead with the large-print edition of Kevin Beattie's autobiography (the brilliantly titled *On the Beat*, incidentally), so it is with his mind. He enters searching for something genuinely important, such as his PIN number or the birth date of his eldest child, and returns brandishing the news that Young Boys of Berne play in the Wankdorf Stadium and were once managed by a man named Grip.

Can't remember his wedding anniversary? Don't worry, the knowledge that Dion Dublin's dad was a session musician with Showaddywaddy, whose drummer Romeo Challenger (father of British high jump champion Ben) was on Leicester City's books, will do instead. No, let's face it, this is not going to save his marriage, is it?

The Tunnel

Football fans rarely get a look inside the tunnel on match days. Our only chance to glimpse this legendary alleyway is during those fleeting post-match interviews in which a man with earphones twice the size of his head (in days of yore, the splendid Gary Newbon) attempts to get more than four syllables out of a sweat-soaked striker who is plainly distracted by something going on off camera. 'Yeah, well, y'know, as I say,' the footballer mumbles while all the time nervously sliding his eyes this way and that, like a naughty puppy who's not sure from which direction the next slap is coming.

It has to be said that in this case the player's fear of incipient fisticuffs is well founded. The tunnel may look innocuous, but, like the sea or Ashley Cole's love life, you disrespect it at your peril. Much has gone on here down the years: mice have run out of it (at Old Trafford), players have thrown up in it (most recently at Upton Park, where three Spurs players divested themselves of some beef stroganoff) and words have been scrawled on it (by Vinnie Jones, who took a magic marker to Liverpool's famous 'This is Anfield' sign and wrote, 'We don't care' underneath), but most of all footballers have scuffled in it. Because the tunnel is the game's most volatile zone, its Middle East; a place linked in tabloid sports headlines with the word 'incident' even more frequently than 'nightclub'.

A classic such outburst of tunnel-related shoving and shouting occurred in February 2000 at Stamford Bridge when Chelsea players clashed with those of Wimbledon following an exchange of words between Dennis Wise and Kenny Cunningham. 'Definitely something happened. But I think that for the sake of everybody it is better to keep it quiet,' said Blues boss Gianluca Vialli, honouring the tradition of tunnel omerta. His assistant Gwyn Williams sidestepped questions by taking a leaf from the Metropolitan Police excuses manual. 'Someone fell down the stairs,' he offered as his explanation of the twenty-two-player flare-up.

January 2006's Carling Cup semi-final offered a nice two-way spat between Rio Ferdinand and Robbie Savage. 'It was just handbags,' the Manchester United centre-half volunteered afterwards, a remark that suggested that his 'clipping' (as Mark Hughes described it) of the Blackburn midfielder in the Old Trafford tunnel was the result of the Welshman making snide remarks about his ponyskin Fendi baguette.

It should be said that football folk are not alone in suffering from furious tunnel syndrome. Years ago in the USA the grid-iron tunnel tiffs became such a hazard that nowadays the players are not allowed to leave the pitch simultaneously. And in Ireland the Gaelic Athletic Association has handed out six-month bans after a series of tunnel-inspired assaults involving Gaelic footballers.

Nor are things any different in Europe. It was in the tunnel at the Camp Nou that Chelsea goalkeeping coach Sylvinho

Lauro got involved in a tussle with Barcelona assistant Henk Ten Cate, the incident apparently provoked by the sight of Barca boss Frank Rijkaard chatting amiably with creosote-tanned match official Anders Frisk. 'All I said was "Hello, pleased to see you",' the Dutchman reported afterwards, but in the explosive atmosphere of the tunnel even that sort of insignificant politeness can spark a riot.

The covered lane that joins the dressing rooms with the pitch generally consists of nothing more than a pair of white-painted breezeblock walls and a concrete floor that is generally covered with AstroTurf, as if the players, like young cattle, need to be lured out of their cosy bedding by the prospect of fresh grass. Yet something about this bland alley drives sane men mad.

Some judge that this is because the trip down it reminds the players and coaching staff of the trauma of their birth. Linking the inviolable, womb-like safety of the **dressing room** (which as we know is '**sacrosanct**') with the public arena of the pitch, it is indeed tempting to see the players' emergence through the tunnel as football's equivalent of that first great journey – a conclusion that is only added to by the PA announcers recently acquired habit of declaiming, 'The players are in the tunnel!', in the excited manner of a father-to-be crying, 'I can see the top of the head!' This is a terrible mistake, though. Because however bloody and painful delivery may be, it is unlikely that any child coming down the birth canal will pause to bellow, 'Do you want some?', and then throw pizza. Nor is it likely to be accompanied by the playing of 'We Will Rock You'.

The tunnel is the wild frontier of football; a lawless zone between field and changing area, its close confines and harsh echoes awakening the sociopathic tendencies of even the most mild-mannered of men. The effect of the tunnel on Arsène Wenger, for example, is similar to the full moon on a werewolf, or the sound of Alan Green's voice on anyone except possibly Alan Green. 'He came sprinting toward me with his hands raised, saying, "What are you going to do about it?",' a shocked Sir Alex Ferguson noted after one tunnel-crazed Wenger attack in Manchester.

At Sunderland on the opening day of the 2001–02 season, meanwhile, the Arsenal boss, driven barmy by the Stadium of Light tunnel, allegedly threatened fourth official Paul Taylor with physical assault. Even the cosy familiarity of the Highbury tunnel was capable of turning the ordinarily studious Alsatian into a foaming-mouthed hellhound apparently capable of confronting Edgar 'Pit Bull' Davids and poking him repeatedly in the chest with a rigid index finger while yelling about cheating. Whether the Emirates Stadium tunnel is any more soothing remains to be seen. If not then some sort of tunnel anger management course is surely called for.

Tyson's First Law of Sport

Tyson's First Law of Sport states, 'Tattoos expand as performance dwindles.' This immutable rule is, of course, named after Mike Tyson. The New Yorker was once the most terrifying boxer on the planet, but that was long ago. And the more his fighting skills have eroded, the more elaborate his tattoos have become. Nowadays he's just a Celtic 'winking eye' belly-button design away from an invitation to step through the ropes with Audley Harrison. In football Tyson's First Law has been brilliantly illustrated by David Beckham and Christian Vieri, quite possibly literally. After all, no one would rule out either of them having it scrawled across a vacant buttock. Assuming there is one.

– U –

Victor Umbrage

Recently retired from hosting Nemesis FM's award-winning The Four Immortals phone-in with East Midlands soccer myths **Rod Rugg**, Trevor Thugg and Mick McMugg, Victor 'Umbo' Umbrage was the doyen of football radio commentary. For many fans his evocative off-the-cuff wordscapes remain the definitive sound of the British game. As John Major noted when Victor finally stepped away from the microphone to spend more time with himself: 'Listening to Umbrage made you feel as if you were standing on a freezing cold terrace on a dark afternoon with rain dripping down your neck, the scent of last night's brown ale in your nostrils and a tattooed psychopath urinating in your pocket.'

To many fans Umbo's verbal portraits of the greatest players of the postwar era are far more memorable than the players themselves:

'Bobby Charlton uses his feet like Dr Crippen used arsenic – to lethal effect.'

'Klinsmann is having a quiet game. But then Klinsmann is a bit like a limpet mine: you don't notice he's there until he explodes.'

'I may not have come across a banana until I was twenty-two thanks to Mr A. Hitler Esquire, but I know a banana kick when I see one, and Garrincha has produced one there from right out of the top drawer and stuck it straight in the fruit bowl next to the satsumas!'

And few could forget Umbrage's famous description of the final moments of the 1966 World Cup Final: 'Hurst . . . Hurst! . . . Huuuuuuuuurst! Unbelievable!' Or Ricky Villa's wonder goal in the FA Cup Final of 1981: 'Villa . . . Villa! . . . Villllllllla! Unbelievable!' Or his final-whistle summary of Manchester United's extraordinary comeback in Barcelona: 'United . . . United! . . . Uniiiiiiiiiiiited! Unbelievable!' These truly are the words which for many millions of supporters, young and old, rich and poor, fat and spotty, ugly and ill-dressed, will always be synonymous with this great old game men call association football.

Unbelievable

The notion that because somebody does something constantly they will inevitably become good at it does not impress football folk such as Alan Hansen. To them every act of skill is a miracle; an accurate cross-field ball a mystery on a par with that of the Holy Trinity. That is why 'unbelievable' is the most common adjective applied to things. On any Saturday night Alan Hansen, who like his fellow countryman Andy Gray is a devout non-believer in the evidence of his own eyes, will spend practically the whole of *Match of the Day* in a state of advanced incredulity. 'Unbelievable pass,' he says. 'Unbelievable save. Unbelievable atmosphere. Unbelievable that the world's most expensive defender should stand there waving forlornly in the breeze like an abandoned carrier bag while a bloke from the lower divisions sneaks in behind him and scores.' (Actually one of those is made up.)

Is it the wide-eyed wonder of an innocent child that renders the great man so incapable of acknowledging the reality of the slow-motion replay? Or is it that he always remains fully conscious of the myriad threads of chance and blind luck that have guided us to this happy state we call top-class football? Most thinkers believe it is the latter. Because when you consider how different things might have been here on Earth if there had been slightly more hydrogen in the atmosphere, the dinosaurs hadn't been rendered extinct by a meteor strike, kangaroos had developed opposable thumbs, Martin Luther had been struck by that lightning and Ryan Giggs was English, then frankly it does stretch credulity that Wayne Rooney can some-times almost kick a ball into a goal from twenty-five yards. After all, had things worked out even slightly differently, the England captain might have been a two-foot-tall, cold-blooded, twenty-two-limbed invertebrate speaking Latin. Or John Prescott.

Undynamic Duos

There was a time when football clubs felt that foreign players, like guinea pigs, should be bought and kept in pairs. Frans Thijssen and Arnold Mühren at Ipswich, Ricardo Villa and Ossie Ardiles at Spurs and Joe Baker and Denis Law at Torino are the obvious examples. In each of those cases both players gave full value (though with Law and Baker it was only to the Italian gossip columns, obviously).

This is not always so, of course. In 1996, for example, the German club Bochum forked out for the Bulgarian inter-national forward Giorgi Donkov and also brought in his compatriot, the splendidly named Engibar Engibarov. Engibarov spent a year at the Bundesliga club and played not a single game, but at least for twelve months Donkov had some-one with whom he could share ironic banter about 1980s Bulgarian TV soap operas.

When Sunderland signed Jim Baxter from Rangers they also bought his cousin George Kinnell to stop the Slim One getting homesick. Baxter was sick on many occasions, but generally it wasn't home that caused it. He and Kinnell did everything together, including getting arrested during a club tour of Canada for attempting to buy liquor with counterfeit dollars. Eventually Sunderland sold Baxter to Nottingham Forest, while Kinnell was offloaded to Middlesbrough for £40,000. He was not a success. In his first game for Boro the Holgate began to chant, 'We paid £40,000 for Kinnell/ We paid £40,000 for Kinnell/ We paid £40,000 fuckin' hell'. It has been reported since by those who saw him that George (or Foo as he was nick-named) Kinnell was actually quite a tidy player, but the Ayresome Park crowd knew well enough that you should never let the facts get in the way of a good gag.

Meanwhile the French have a tradition of amicable team selection. In the build-up to France 1998 many French journalists claimed that Christophe Dugarry's place in the squad was down to the influence of Zinedine Zidane. 'Dugarry is Zidane's chouchou,' they would assure listeners with a knowing look. Most English journalists were a bit unsure of what being a chouchou actually involved, though based on the evidence of Dugarry's contribution, running hopelessly about the place bleeding from the nose would seem to have been a big part of it.

The Universe

In 2005 a New York-based mathematician, Jeff Watts, spent his days using a Wilkinson microwave anisotropy probe in an attempt to discover the shape of the universe. By so doing he proved, he said, that it was a solid composed of twelve pentagons, or a dodecahedron. In other words, the universe is football shaped.

How it got to be that way Watts does not speculate, but it is possible it was stitched together by an underfed South-East Asian child – the blind sweatshop worker theory.

If the US scientist is correct it seems entirely possible that our universe is not only shaped like a football but actually is a football, in all probability being kicked about by giants who are themselves living in a football-shaped universe being kicked about by giants who are themselves . . . And so on and so forth into infinity (a distance in time and space most scientists now consider to be located a few moments before Garth Crooks finally gets to the end of his question). Whether the game is a top of the table tussle or simply a playtime round of three-and-in we will never know. Perhaps our universe is goal-bound, or has just ricocheted down off the bar. Maybe it is at the midway point of a long, high punt out of defence, or possibly a fat bloke in a Burberry baseball cap is refusing to throw it back to an opposition player because his team are 1–0 up in a crucial rele-gation six-pointer with the clock ticking down and he is hoping to waste a bit of time.

And of course, if our universe is a football it must also hold true that our footballs are universes, each filled with a network of galaxies and solar systems, stars and planets populated by people with hopes, fears and dreams much like our own. Now if this is what is going through Rio Ferdinand's mind, is there any wonder he sometimes forgets who he is marking?

- V -

Velvet Bag

The vessel from which Ted Croker and Bert Millichip would traditionally make the FA Cup draw. Particularly effective on radio, which gave full play to the rattle of the box-wood balls and the whispering rasp of the cloth, it never quite had the same magic on TV and has since been retired.

Vermin

In recent years the pest that has posed the greatest threat to the delicate ecosystem of our island home has been the League referee.

A cursory glance at the back pages after any weekend of action provides ample proof that when it comes to doing lasting damage to our environment, the haughty and mendacious match official makes the muntjac look like, well, a pedal-bin-sized oriental ruminant with what appears to be two bottle-openers sticking out of its skull.

Every Saturday evening horrified managers such as Steve Bruce reveal how referees have ruined the afternoon for 20,000 fans by making it easier for their team to win by sending off an opponent for no good reason other than that he has stamped on somebody's head. Others will rage indignantly at the arrogant refusal of the man in black to help their side stave off relegation. While one or two will go so far as to accuse the match official of ruining the playing surface before kick-off by 'rooting about in the turf with his whistle looking for juicy bulbs and tubers'.

Add to such accusations those that linesmen at football grounds have taken to nibbling all the paint from the base of the goalposts causing them to rot; the claim by spectators that match assessors' droppings sometimes turn up in **football pies**; and complaints from local residents that fourth officials roosting in the eaves of the City of Manchester Stadium keep them awake at night by flashing their electric boards at one another in some primitive territorial ritual, and a very disturbing picture begins to emerge.

Thanks to recent mild winters and a proliferation of the televised football on which they feed, League referees are now more prevalent than ever. 'They say that nowadays you are never more than two yards from a ref,' Alan Curbishley once admitted, adding, 'Just thinking about that is enough to send a shiver down the spine of any team, which knowing my luck will result in Nigel Reo-Coker slipping a disc.'

'Make no mistake what we are facing today is the greatest threat to these shores since Eric the Red Card first came ashore in AD 956 and subjected the citizens of Wessex to a series of inconsistent and arbitrary decisions that totally lacked any common sense,' observed phlegmatic Bolton boss Sam Allardyce reflectively chewing on his afternoon thistle in 2002. 'The big trouble is that from prolonged exposure to managerial wrath this new breed of what naturalists and pest controllers have dubbed the "super-ref" has become totally immune to even the most poisonous remark. Sometimes when I recall that it's hard for me to keep smiling.'

'What we are looking at here is a terrible plague. I call it the Man-in-Black Death,' commented a typically calm Graeme Souness handing his jacket to a friend and rolling up his sleeves in 2003. 'People who do not live and work in football will probably think of the ref as a cute little creature who turns up occasionally on *Superstars*. That's the Disney image. But believe me if they could see the horrible carnage just one referee can wreak on a dressing room full of footballers nobody would think they are cuddly.'

After hearing what Souness had to say Chelsea boss Claudio Ranieri joined in the chorus of disapproval: 'The referees. What can I say? I am the tinkerman. The tinkerman. Yes, that is me, the tinkerman. Hahahahahaha.'

After seeking the advice of Martin Jol, who recently found a nest of referee's assistants in the mop cupboard at White Hart Lane, mayor of London Ken Livingstone has recently made it illegal for Londoners to feed referees. In the long run even that may not be enough. Experts believe a more radical solution is needed. They say that if we do not start to follow the old country ways and start eating the likes of Mark Clattenburg and Rob Styles, then endearing native species such as Paul Jewell and Harry Redknapp may well go the way of Glenn Hoddle and disappear from our lives for ever.

Vest Decorating

In Newcastle at weekends you can hardly move these days for young blokes wearing T-shirts emblazoned with their nicknames – 'Cidergut', 'Sumo', 'Nobby' – and an announcement of whose stag night they're on. It's as if they need a constant reminder of who they are and the mayhem they are bent on. Without the shirt, you suspect, they would totally lose focus and start calling each other Orlando, sipping mint tea and discussing French symbolist poetry.

A visceral need to celebrate and affirm through the ancient medium of screen-printing afflicts footballers, too. Spurs striker Jermain Defoe's decision to send a congratulatory message –

'Happy Birthday baby' – to his girlfriend during a game with Middlesbrough was one glaring example. The goal celebration that ended with the England international stripping his shirt off has been described as premeditated. So it was, but the hasty look of the scribbles on Defoe's vest suggests that it wasn't that premeditated. In fact, as anniversary slogan T-shirts go it was the equivalent of a box of Ferrero Rocher and a copy of *Bella* from the filling station mini-mart.

It was evangelical Christians in South America during the early 1990s who really popularised the football message T-shirt. At the behest of the organisation Athletes for Christ, devout Brazilian goalscorers began broadcasting the good news by pulling off their shirts to reveal snippets of useful advice from the Bible (Love thy neighbour, don't eat cormorants, that kind of thing).

The first real insight fans in Britain got of the possibilities was in 1995 at the end of the Auto Windscreens Final when Birmingham City's Paul Tate unveiled a T-shirt bearing the slogan 'City Shit on the Villa'. As far as anyone was aware this was not taken from the Bible (though admittedly most people haven't read all of St Paul's Letter to the Corinthians).

A couple of years later Robbie Fowler was fined 2000 Swiss francs for celebrating his second goal against Brann Bergen in a Cup Winners' Cup tie by revealing a 'Support the 500 Sacked Dockers' T-shirt. And then along came Ian Wright with a run of self-trumpeting vests commemorating his approach to, equalling and then beating of Cliff Bastin's Arsenal goalscoring record – a sequence which it seems to many fans, though memory may be playing tricks, lasted for well over a decade.

At the time Wright's vests appeared deeply annoying. His subsequent TV performances, however, have proved that in fact the slogan-daubed T-shirt is by far the best way for him to communicate to the public. During Euro 2004 many viewers would have been delighted if at half- or full-time Wright had simply pulled apart his jacket to reveal a magic marker-ed 'I'm gutted, Al', 'Wha'did I tellya?' or a simple 'Woargh!', rather than actually attempting to say anything.

Since Wright's efforts there have been an endless flow of messages delivered via 100 per cent cotton. Some have been written with a biro, others bear the dead hand of the Nike marketing department. There have been pictures of newborn babies, or in the case of Greece's Andreas Charisteas, a young nephew, declarations of love and affirmations of undying loyalty ('Once a blue always a blue' Wayne Rooney's T-shirt said, though the Manchester United forward was speaking spiritually rather than physically, obviously). And since the T-shirts tend only to get revealed after goals or victory, it is scary to think how many more have passed unread by the masses and into the clothes recycling bin outside the local Morrisons.

While some T-shirt slogans such as Thierry Henry's 'For the new born Kyd' have a clear purpose – celebrating the arrival of Sharleen Spiteri's daughter Misty Kyd while simultaneously informing the world that the Arsenal striker is a good mate of the Texas singer, a life-enhancing piece of news that might otherwise have remained private – the reasoning behind others is arcane. Rumour has it that the Arsenal players were wearing T-shirts bearing the slogan '50 Not Out' under their kit at Old Trafford to celebrate a fifty-match undefeated run. As it turned out they didn't get to show them off, but if they had for whose benefit would it have been?

Defoe was fined by his club after receiving a yellow card for his T-shirt-revealing antics, but it is unlikely to stop others following in his footsteps. Many would like to see players branch out and express more of their hopes and fears on their T-shirts. 'Help! I've Got a Coke Habit', 'Keep Dreaming I'm a Woman', or simply a childlike drawing of a shark eating a man's genitals would surely engage the sympathy of the paying public. And while never taking our eyes off the positive, let's not lose sight of the negative either. Graeme 'Foxy' Fowler was once castigated for faxing his wife the news that he was leaving her. It's surely time a Premiership player conveyed the same message by the popular vest method. At some point in the next few seasons we will no doubt see a goalscorer lifting his shirt to reveal a muscle top embossed with the sequins that spell out the words 'Lawyer up, slapper. I'm shagging someone off *Emmerdale*'.

Vintage Football Phone-In Caller

The magazine for those people who like to call up radio stations and give their verdicts on matches they haven't actually attended. 'We're aimed very squarely at the Everton fan from Devon who likes to tell the world that "I wasn't at the game today but from what I could tell from listening to your most excellent commentary, Alan, the linesman was having a laugh",' says editor Jim Sloth, adding, 'We like to think we offer our readers commonsense and consistency without taking the fun out of it because at the end of the day that's what this game's all about, isn't it? Great to talk to you. How's your good self? Love the show.'

Vulture

A popular question on the terraces in the early 1990s was: would the inclusion of vultures in Premiership squads be a good thing? Clearly having one on the pitch from the outset would be of limited use – they can't tackle and, as they themselves would be the first to admit, their distribution is woefully predictable – but when a team is winning by a single goal, the opposition dominant and there are just a few minutes left on the clock, a vulture could be brought on as sub. At the first opportunity the ball is chipped on to his back and he climbs rapidly into the sky and begins to circle on the hot air rising from the dug-outs, mindful all the time of the need to remain within the markings of the pitch. The ball is still live, but the opposition cannot get at it. As a method of time-wasting it is at once as legitimate as a player running the ball into the corner and then standing over it with his legs apart and his bum sticking out, and at the same time more graceful and aesthetically pleasing.

The tactic is not foolproof however. If, to bring things up to date, Arsène Wenger adopted it with his team 2–1 up against Bolton at the Reebok Stadium, would Sammy Lee not immediately fish in his kit bag for a piece of rotting road kill, toss it on to the pitch and instruct Ivan Campo to loiter close by until the vulture was tempted down to eat?

It might work, too. Though, of course, the canny Wenger, fully aware that vultures only feed on a carcass when other animals higher up the food chain have finished with it, would probably have a hyena warming up on the touchline just in case.

- W -

Andy Warhol

The US pop artist and self-styled Frank Worthington of the Way Out, Andy Warhol was an unlikely soccer fan. Indeed his immersion in the seamy subculture of football was only finally revealed in Tamiana Sonic's seminal 1998 biography *Andy Warhol – A Life In Specs*.

'Names were very important to Andy Warhol. He often said that they were like a linguistic badge that told people what you were called. From his teenage years when the world knew him as Andrew Bovril of Styrofoamcup, Michigan, he was seeking a new sobriquet. He found it during a visit to Newcastle, a tough northern suburb of London, England. Here an unintelligible phrase yelled repeatedly by the fans of the local soccer team resonated with his bruised and alienated soul. When he returned, he told Factory habitué Daniel Crimplene, 'I am not Andrew Bovril any more. From now on I am Andy Worholteamsshiteman.' Later Andy dropped the teamsshiteman part when he discovered it was taking him longer to sign his work than it was to make it.

After the success of his screen-prints *Mao*, *Marilyn*, *Mancini* and *Marsh* and his nine-hour film of the outside of Elland Road ('So much more stimulating than the inside,' Andy drawled laconically), the Velvet Underground rock band became his passion. The band had already recorded some of the most significant football songs of all times, including 'Sister Ray', a blistering, discordant attack on Wrexham stalwart Ray

Mielczarek, viewed as 'a bit of a Jessie' by Cale, and 'Venus in Furs', a thinly-veiled critique Bond's spell in charge of Manchester City. Andy soon brought the German chanteuse Nic (inevitably dubbed 'Nico' by the Factory squad) into the line-up on a free transfer and began planning the vast multi-media soccer happening he had been turning over in his mind for years: The Exploding Plastic Inevitable – the only major artistic event in history to be named after a Frido football.

The Exploding Plastic Inevitable was to be a ferocious cultural melange of film, music, poetry, five-a-side and inflatable bananas. The centre piece would be a celebrity three-and-in competition featuring Factory personnel such as Edie Sedgwick and acquaintances from the New York demi-monde like tough-tackling talk show guests Truman Capote, Gore Vidal and Princess Margaret.

Kenneth Anger, delighting in the delicious S&M overtones of his all-black uniform, was an impressively authoritarian referee, while between the sticks Liz Taylor showed a remarkable ability to make the goal seem very, very small indeed. The game was played out to a searing Velvets soundtrack, with Warhol himself as head coach ('And you can make of that what you will, baby,' he quipped to Jackie O on opening night) projecting ironic phrases – 'Channel him!' 'Grab his bollocks, Nobby!' – on to a massive white screen.

Inevitably after such a period of heady success the Factory squad began to break up. Andy resigned his position in the dug-out, Capote was suspended by Fifa for making a bitchy remark about João Havelange and Sedgwick was lent to Brighton and Hove Albion for a year. The latter event led Factory supporter **Bob Dylan** to pen one of his most vitriolic lyrics: 'How does it feel?/ To be out on loan/ Never playing at home/ At the old Goldstone'.

Warhol's mercurial spell in football was over. The man in the white wig was never again to apply his genius to the business of running a football club. Though he was tempted by the Aston Villa job on a few occasions, obviously.

Watchman

A player whose role in the side is to approach the referee tapping his wrist throughout the last five minutes plus injury time of any game in which his team are leading by a single goal.

Wealth Redistribution

Following the Premiership's refusal to distribute 5 per cent of its yearly income to lower division clubs, the All Party Football Committee proposed a new measure to try to rectify the imbalance between the game's rich and poor. 'We often hear of how a new manager at a club has "inherited a great squad" from his predecessor,' said Labour MP Alan Keen, 'but such inheritance clearly helps perpetuate the imbalance in our footballing society. Under our proposal a modified form of death duty would see 25 per cent of the playing staff immediately paid to the inland revenue whenever a manager left a club. The Chancellor would then be in a position to redistribute these footballers to the people who really need them. If this law were in force now, for instance, we might next season be watching James Beattie banging in the goals at Brunton Park, Nicolas Anelka terrorising defences at Southend and Wes Brown standing scratching his head and looking bewildered at the Reynolds Arena.'

Wedding Day

Every year since 1871 at least one lifelong fan has found his or herself getting married on the afternoon of their team's first appearance in the Cup Final for ninety-two years. This is bad news for him/her but good news for the local paper, which runs a humorous item under the headline, 'Romance of the Cup!'

Wenger Magic Eye Books

Using the latest scientific and ophthalmic research, these beautifully-produced books offer a completely fresh range of optical illusions. Look at the picture. At first it appears to show a simian-faced man jumping about like a deranged baboon, but study it more closely and the ugly figure disappears to be replaced by a tranquil lake, flying swans and the sun setting majestically behind the mountains. 'It's amazing,' explained one satisfied customer from north London. 'One minute you are looking at someone jumping up and down on another man's head, the next at the fountains and roses of the Alhambra Palace.'

Rachel Whiteread

Contemporary British artist. Whiteread proposed celebrating the 1996 European Championships with a football version of her most famous work, *House.* Unfortunately Scotland boss Craig Brown refused to let her fill Andy Goram with concrete. However, circumstantial evidence suggests that he was too late to prevent her carrying out a practice run on Richard Gough.

Woolifan

Following the success of the *Hoolifan* TV series on the history of soccer violence came *Woolifan*, a beautiful coffee-table book devoted to the glory years of knitted football favours, an epoch that stretched from the Great War until the moment in 2004 when the European Courts declared all football-related scarves, bobble hats and mittens illegal unless they were woven by the club chairman himself. In *Woolifan* the reader learns about legendary figures such as eighty-year-old Betty Barmcake, whose acrylic blue-and-yellow poncho once generated enough static to power the floodlights at her beloved Boundary Park, West Ham's notorious ICF (Into Crochet Firm) and the infamous 'Chelsea Mad Man', who attempted to weave a financial rescue package for Leeds United using yarn spun from his own beard.

World Class

What exactly the phrase 'world class' means in football terms is very hard to define. Some people think it means that if Fifa selected a World XI to take on Mars then these are the players who would be included in the sixteen. There is no evidence to support that theory. In fact there is no evidence to support any theory whatsoever. That is because the whole nature of being 'world class' is so complicated that only one person can fully grasp it – Alan Hansen. And if he explained it to us our brains would get so overloaded with pure facts we'd end up running round with our pants on our heads making clucking noises. So instead he just tells us who is world class and we believe him. Hansen by contrast does not believe anything (see **unbelievable**).

World Cup Film

The official World Cup film began life in Sweden in 1958. **Ingmar Bergman** was the director and the result, *Gloomy Samba*, was a predictable mix of metaphysics, pessimism and Nacka Skoglund, in which the great auteur chose, as his visual motif, a sinister shrouded figure who forever lurked on the periphery of the action. Critics have traditionally suggested that this represented Death, though closer inspection shows that it is actually a young João Havelange lobbying the Concacaf delegation.

Since then World Cup films have ranged from the dire (Wes Craven's stalk 'n' slash *And Then There Were Two* made for USA '94) to Luis Buñuel's 1978 masterpiece *The Discreet Charm of Willy Van Der Kerkhof*. When Buñuel was initially selected to direct the film of the Argentinian World Cup some argued that his mix of surrealist subversion and absurdist dislocation was not suited for a major football tournament. But they reckoned without Scotland. In France in 1998 Éric Rohmer was in the director's chair. The result, *Ronaldo's Knee*, is so subtle and understated that as yet nobody has managed to watch it without falling asleep.

World Cup Phoney War

As with a war, a World Cup is preceded by a lull during which fans sit listening to the slow ticking of the clock, waiting for the inevitable moment when the balloons go up (usually accompanied by fireworks and a bombastic anthem) – in short, a phoney tournament.

The phoney tournament is a period of terrible calm in which nothing much happens and is then analysed in minute detail. There are endless discussions of players' hairstyles. Men of a certain age pass long hours trying to recall the exact composition of the 1970 Esso World Cup Coin Collection and every house in Britain contains enough free souvenir wallcharts to paper the sitting room and take care of the lifetime bedding requirements of several gerbils.

The hiatus cranks up the tension until even the nerves of the battle-hardened sports fan are twanging like banjo strings. But at least the veterans among them know what to expect.

There will always, for example, be some peculiar transport-related dispute involving one of the sides. In 1998 it was the Brazilians fighting over who got to sit nearest the front of the plane (a situation which has also vexed the normally tranquil **Roy Keane** on international trips). In 2002 it was the Russians who were angry because their flight out to the Far East had been scheduled to include a stopover at Khabarovsk. 'The team is used to flying non-stop,' a spokesman commented, 'and the players are both very superstitious and sensitive.'

The new scientifically designed World Cup ball will be introduced and immediately damned by the players. Proving that, though it was their first appearance in the finals, they were well aware of the traditions, Slovenia got the grumbling off to a start in Korea/Japan when attacking midfielder Zlatko Zahovic complained that the Adidas Fevernova was 'the worst ball I have ever played with'. According to the Slovenian number ten, it was 'like a balloon'.

There will be several front-page stories involving the England squad and drink. Bryan Robson will appear on TV to tell us that there have always been footballers who liked 'a **pint**'.

At least four teams will declare themselves the world's unluckiest when it comes to injury. In 2002 England and Germany were joined by Belgium, whose coach Robert Waseige declared, 'A spell has been put on our dressing room.'

The country will suffer a fearful World Cup trivia

bombardment that will see the public's minds stuffed with details of how Cameroon's shirt has transparent sleeves, what the nickname of El Hadji Diouf of Senegal is (the Serial Killer) and the significance of Saudi Arabia's Nawaf Al-Temyat being dubbed 'the new Saeed Owairan'. Eventually there will be no space left in our brains for data such as pin numbers, passwords or how to put socks on.

One of the African countries will sack their manager and arrive at the tournament with a coach most of the players have never met. A team will threaten to quit unless they are paid the money they are owed by their national FA. A retired national manager will launch savage attacks on the present incumbent for playing a style of football that 'betrays our heritage'. Philippe Troussier, formerly of Japan and Cameroon, will become involved in a controversy. An entire team will dye their hair aubergine.

And so the phoney war will roll remorselessly on until even those who regard football with bitter loathing will be begging for the World Cup to start and so put an end to the barrage of guff, blather and baloney.

– XYZ –

X-Treme Groundhopping

Finding that visiting as many football grounds as possible just didn't offer a sufficient challenge even if you only counted them when you had licked each corner flag while play was in progress, Hitchin-based groundhopper Bob Brown invented the hobby of X-treme groundhopping. Turning the trusty Ford Orion over to the tender care of the memsahib, Bob paraglided into his first game at the Dripping Pan back in 1999. Since then the hobby has taken off in a major way with more and more highly motivated anorak-clad hoppers power-kiting and bungee-jumping into the likes of the Ray Hurd Pavilion, Narborough (near the M1 bridge), each week. Served by the magazine *Outlaw Groundhopper*. The latest issue looks at the attempt by a team of French free-jumpers to visit five grounds hosting Kent Plaaya Senior Trophy matches in a single afternoon without once touching the ground (or 'terra firma' as Bob prefers to term it).

Zenith Readymix Biscam

Recently announced as the Official Grouting Material of Fifa World Cup 2010.